THE CAPITALIST AND THE CRITIC

# THE CAPITALIST AND THE CRITIC

*J. P. Morgan, Roger Fry,*
*and the Metropolitan Museum of Art*

CHARLES MOLESWORTH

University of Texas Press
*Austin*

Requests for permission to reproduce material from this work should be sent to:
Permissions
University of Texas Press
P.O. Box 7819
Austin, TX 78713-7819
utpress.utexas.edu/rp-form

♾ The paper used in this book meets the minimum requirements of
ANSI/NISO Z39.48-1992 (R1997) (Permanence of Paper).

LIBRARY OF CONGRESS CATALOGING-IN-PUBLICATION DATA

Molesworth, Charles, 1941– author.
The capitalist and the critic : J. P. Morgan, Roger Fry, and the Metropolitan
Museum of Art / Charles Molesworth. — First edition.
pages  cm
Includes bibliographical references and index.
ISBN 978-1-4773-2706-7 (pb : alk. paper)
ISBN 978-1-4773-0841-7 (library e-book)
ISBN 978-1-4773-0842-4 (non-library e-book)
1. Morgan, J. Pierpont (John Pierpont), 1837–1913.   2. Fry, Roger, 1866–
1934.   3. Capitalists and financiers—United States.   4. Art patrons—United
States.   5. Art—Collectors and collecting.   6. Art critics—England.
7. Metropolitan Museum of Art (New York, N.Y.)   I. Title.
HG2463.M6M65   2016
708.147′1—dc23
2015016164

doi:10.7560/308400

*This book is dedicated to C. H. M.*

*Love is dead in us
if we forget
the virtues of an amulet
and quick surprise.*

——ROBERT CREELEY

# CONTENTS

# ACKNOWLEDGMENTS

THOUGH I HAVE WRITTEN THREE PREVIOUS books that relied on the kindness of archivists, I remain thoroughly grateful for their skill and generosity. Several curators, archivists, and institutions were of persisting help in my writing this book.

James Moske, managing archivist at the Metropolitan Museum of Art, assisted me with the correspondence by and about Roger Fry's period of employment at the museum. He also went the extra mile in helping me obtain photographs and images related to that period. The curatorial staff at the Morgan Library and Museum made items available with a sense of welcome ease.

Robbi Siegel of Art Resources displayed equal parts helpfulness and patience in regard to my search for images. Photographs and material related to Roger Fry were graciously sent to me by Patricia McGuire, archivist at King's College, Cambridge. Both Chris Sutherns, at Tate Images, and Alice Purkiss, Tate's Library Executive, helped in selecting the photograph of Fry and his wife, Helen. Jennifer Bahus, of the North Carolina Museum, located the photograph of William Valentiner, taken by Ben Williams in 1956. Susan K. Anderson, the Martha Hamilton Morris Archivist at the Philadelphia Museum of Art, made the pen-and-ink portrait of John G. Johnson available for my use.

The staff of the Thomas J. Watson Library at the Metropolitan Museum Library made their holdings, along with their sophisticated equipment, readily usable. Lyndsi Barnes and Joshua McKeon of the

Berg Collection at the New York Public Library were helpful and cordial, allowing me to study Clive Bell's rare memoir.

The *Apollo* article on Horne and Fry was expeditiously sent to me by Imelda Barnard. Martha Hackley, of the Frick Collection, generously sent me a copy of Colin Bailey's article on Fry, Frick, and the *Polish Rider.*

The stanza from Robert Creeley is an excerpt from "The Warning" from *The Collected Poems of Robert Creeley: 1945–1975.* Copyright © 1962 by Robert Creeley. Reprinted with the permission of The Permissions Company, Inc., on behalf of the Estate of Robert Creeley.

Susan Dackerman shared with me a book on Bernard Berenson just as I needed it, and her discussion with me about the concept and practice of connoisseurship proved clarifying.

Fred Kaplan stood out as the most reliable person to read early drafts and to reiterate a trust in the project not always fully available to the author.

Norman MacAfee's keen-eyed copyediting prevented dozens of infelicities from persisting, though all that remain are due to me alone.

Sarah Rosen, editorial assistant at University of Texas Press, remained steadfastly corrective as I dallied over and confused the acquisition and arrangements of the images in this book; her help is greatly appreciated.

My editor at the press, Robert Devens, never allowed my anxiety and doubt to reduce his commitment to moving forward. And so we did.

THE CAPITALIST AND THE CRITIC

# INTRODUCTION

## *Two Differing Portraits*

ONE WAY TO ENGAGE WITH J. PIERPONT MOR-
gan and Roger Fry is to examine their respective portraits. The most
famous one of Morgan, the photograph by Edward Steichen, continues to circulate widely. Much of what we know of the man in the
portrait rests on rumor and is concretized by myth. The story goes
that Steichen was able to capture Morgan's fabled sternness—manifest in the glare of his dark eyes, once compared to the force of an
oncoming locomotive—by a simple device. Steichen, after Morgan
had laid aside his cigar and taken his seat, asked him to adjust his
pose. The imperious sitter swiftly conveyed the resulting annoyance.
"His expression had sharpened and his body posture became tense,"
Steichen later recalled. "I saw that a dynamic self-assertion had taken
place." Steichen quickly took a second picture, and this is the one
most often seen and discussed. The resulting grimace of disapproval
summarized Morgan's attitudes toward most things, and most people. Indeed massive disapproval must have been hidden behind that
glaring figure; it was generally assumed that he felt time was being
wasted on photography, time better spent on calculating the value of
investments or interest rates or buying works of art.

The predatory nature of finance capitalism radiates from the reflection of the left-hand armrest of Morgan's chair. Many have de-
lighted to see in it a metaphoric knife blade; once offered, the association is hard to dispel. Again, how much of Steichen's final image
arose from luck and spontaneity and how much from pure artistic insight, we can never certainly know. The year of the photograph was

*Edward Steichen,* J. P. Morgan, Esq., *1903: Morgan (1837–1913)
was described as having eyes like an oncoming train. His public image
was defined for many people by Steichen's modernist portrait.*

1903; Morgan's Library was under construction, about to become one
of the most famous private residences in the country (and eventually
one of its finest cultural institutions). Morgan looks placed, situated.
But at the same time the slight tilt to the right of his upper torso suggests a readiness to rise up and strike. The dominant sense intimates

someone being intruded upon, even as he realizes he must pause and pose, if only for a brief menacing moment. We can be forgiven if the image of the dragon-like guardian of wealth comes unshakably to mind. About the wealth itself, there is no room allowed for fancy. Its extent was quite real, amounting a decade later to about $60 million when Morgan finally forever left his position as the wealthiest collector of art in America, and its most transformative banker. The myths appear plausible, as myths must.

For picturing Fry we might best turn to Fry, for he was a seriously committed painter, whose self-portrait reveals a good deal of self-scrutiny. Painted in 1930, it now resides in the National Portrait Gallery in London. At that time Fry's encounter with Morgan was more than two decades in his past. But Fry's version of himself shows the seriousness he had already absorbed when, in January 1905, he first met Morgan. Fry was in many things, especially the visual arts, a thoroughgoing critic, a person with strong opinions and ready judgments, who operated with the felt necessity of clear, scrupulous, and engaged knowledge. A slight wariness guides his glance, turned not to us but to the mirror (presumably) in which he watches himself, musing on what to think even as he thinks it. Perhaps a hint of quite dry humor, almost certainly of the ironic sort, slips out, as if the prospect of an absorbing narcissism—necessary in this enterprise— can be the butt of its own gentle mockery. Seeing him dressed in coat and tie, we recall that less than a hundred years ago the studio of a painter still involved some formality, even if the other aspects of Fry's life were decidedly bohemian. The upper portion of his palette suggests the top edge of a shield. We know from several accounts that he was a guarded man, though not one to avoid a struggle when occasions arose.

The half-darkened left side of his face adds to the sense of wariness or skepticism. Along the right edge of the canvas another right edge is depicted, as Fry lets us see the thin and nailed-down edge of the stretched canvas. This reminds us that here he engages in facture, putting together and putting into place a representation. In a busy life, he spent considerable time and energy founding a cooperative enterprise, the Omega Workshop, influenced by the Arts and Crafts movement, which was in turn inspired by John Ruskin and led by

*Roger Fry*, Self-Portrait, *1928: Fry (1866–1934) labored at his painting with determination, often doing his best work with portraits. Courtesy of National Portrait Gallery, London.*

William Morris. For Fry, like John Dewey, the highest form of artistic work existed in a continuum with the everyday objects and skills that introduce grace and beauty into human society at all levels. Fry committed himself to various collectives and institutions during his extended career as a painter, art historian, and critic, but an aspect of his temperament was always connected to socialist causes and values. The furrowed forehead and slightly lifted eyebrow display a serious, judgmental mien. Many of the Americans he was to meet during his singular sojourn in the New World found him priggish, and his views on art elitist to a fault.

This book seeks to explore the connections—and oppositions—between commerce and art, or what we might call more narrowly finance capitalism and formalist art. It further seeks to do this by using these two extraordinary individuals—J. Pierpont Morgan and Roger Fry—and their respective (and contested) relationships with each other, and to the Metropolitan Museum of Art.

The theater, so to speak, in which Morgan and Fry acted out their encounter was the Metropolitan Museum of Art. Founded in 1870, during a period when many cultural institutions enjoyed generous inaugural gifts by a number of wealthy benefactors, the museum eventually was housed in a building on Fifth Avenue, along the eastern edge of Central Park. When the New York State Legislature incorporated the museum in April 1870, it owned no paintings or any other works of art. The legislators were undeterred and composed for the museum a high-minded charter. It stated that its mission was to set about "encouraging and developing the study of the fine arts, and the application of arts to manufacture," but then added a more inclusive set of social goals, with the hope "of advancing the general knowledge of kindred subjects, and, to that end, of furnishing popular instruction and recreation." Eventually, after decades of growth that seems at times exponential, the museum would refer to itself as encyclopedic.

Morgan, who became a trustee of the Met in 1888 and stayed on as president of the board of trustees until his death in 1913, enjoyed a connection with it that went back to his father's early involvement. Junius Morgan had contributed a large amount to pay for a collection of Cypriot antiquities, discovered by General Luigi Palma di Cesnola, the museum's first director.[1] (In 1904, Sir Caspar Purdon Clarke, a personal choice of Morgan, would replace Cesnola, who retired after twenty-five years of service.) The general was of doubtful expertise when it came to the science of archeology and even more so the growing science of museology, but by the end of the nineteenth century the Metropolitan had begun to upgrade its staff's professional qualifications. As Morgan's involvement grew, the museum itself reflected larger historical forces, such as cultural nationalism and the democratization of education in the fine arts.

These forces, the product of both social and economic willfulness, had shaped the country for several decades, and now it seemed that art and culture should be the target of the fearsome energies of those people whose destiny it was to manage them. Here is how one recent historian of the museum framed the shaping context: "Today the innovations that progressive connoisseurs made in museum policies of access, education and display hardly seem radical, but they nevertheless represented a significant rejection of many of the ideals upon which art museums had been founded in the nineteenth century." Those ideals, of course, arose from the society that contained them. "The museum had always been a product of industrial capitalism, from the origin of endowment funds to the bequest of collections, and ideas about the civilizing influence of cultural institutions informed the founding of many museums in the 1870s, alongside parks, libraries and theaters."[2] These large changes and developments, embodied in and projected through "the civilizing influence of cultural institutions," affected large portions of the populations, so we can at least subjunctively assert, as the historian goes on to say, that "Most nineteenth-century Americans would have understood that the golden age of museum building had been a reaction to industrial modernization." Of course, it is exactly that set of massive and still emerging forces called "industrial modernization" that Morgan, himself an avid collector of many kinds of art, all of them of considerable artistic value, did much to advance and build into the fabric of society. Looking at this possible contradiction, between commerce and art at their highest levels, one can resort to either the ironizing lens of history or a Hegelian synthesis to harmonize the disparate phenomena.

The historian quoted above reviewed the other similar cultural institutions founded in the last third of the nineteenth century and concluded that "the Metropolitan Museum most personified the social anxieties that accompanied industrialization, and the supposed balms a museum could provide." Why the Metropolitan Museum of Art? Mainly because of its location in the most dynamic and wealthy city in America, and because its supporters and benefactors had more than enough money to make it happen. A portrait of the Met could take many forms, and be illumined by many different points of view. More than a reaction to—or expression of—industrial modernization is at stake in the museum. Since large public museums have a history that extends at least as far back as the founding of the Louvre in 1793, more than twentieth-century forces and values must have shaped them.

Two values can be seen as preeminent. The first is the cultural activity of collecting; the second is the belief, even the trust, in our ability to draw up a history of esthetic accomplishments.

Collecting in its most fundamental aspect involves a recurrent psychology that seems to explain, even naturalize, a propensity that is, finally, not that widespread or always edifying. Here is a modern, twenty-first-century look at it, led on by disenchanting skepticism:

> I don't understand why collectors get the kind of praise and attention they do, unless it's because of universal sycophantism. Collecting is just shopping, and when you have close to infinite wealth, and the money to pay for the best advice, nothing could be easier. Any decent curator with a few billion dollars in her pocket could build a collection like this [Leonard A. Lauder's collection of Cubist masters] with her eyes closed. (Or maybe I should say without breaking a sweat.) And of course it's worth remembering that Lauder only has his pockets so full because the thousands of people who work for him don't; give those workers a bigger slice of the American dream, such as they used to have, and Lauder starts hogging less of it—to spend on things like fabulous Cubist art.[3]

Morgan did have something like infinite wealth, and some wags even said his collection occurred while his eyes were closed. But whatever collecting involved—as psychology, as social phenomenon, as personal temperament—Morgan clearly stands as an exemplar of one way to do it.

As for Fry, he could never afford to collect, with anything like Morgan's rapacity, the kind of art he championed, and his championing of it only raised its prices still further. But he trusted in the museum, in its ability to salvage the threatened esthetics of modernity, and so preserve the beauty of the past and make that of the future imaginable. His approach can be called, roughly, formalist. This posits that in art it is the forms, and the sense of formal energies, that provide the esthetic experience with its emotional force. Some thought this meant Fry's formalism was an elitist opting out of history, since form is often described as atemporal, unaffected by time and change. By a paradoxical stance, however, Fry affirmed the atemporal, suprahistorical nature of artistic forms while recognizing how they constitute (or can be shaped into) a narrative of historical dimensionality and depth. Here, again with a twentieth-first-century voice, is the way one commentator sees it by glossing a passage from one of Fry's lectures: "Some of Fry's other verdicts, concerning previously unexplored areas such as the Baroque, also sank as quickly as they had surfaced. Sample a statement such as 'It must not be thought that the Baroque in giving up tactile experience and confining itself to [the] visual, lost thereby the sense of plastic relief; by a strange paradox it actually heightened the pictorial expression of mass and volume.'" Fry's lecturing style—and its sometime exuberant drawing of historical schema—is being implicitly critiqued (for using paradox to float an outsized stylistic claim), but this only makes the turn (to an extended historical framework spanning three centuries) that much more surprising. The commentator concludes: "[Fry] goes on, for the remainder of an interminable paragraph, explaining this 'strange paradox,' succeeding only in muddying the waters still further. And yet, on the very next page, a flash of genius: 'I think we may give to Caravaggio the honour of having been the first purely popular artist, the real founder of the Royal Academy, the Salon and almost the whole art of the cinema.'"[4]

The "flash of genius" and the leaps in logic in that final sentence represent one way to play the game of cultural commentary (some might even call it analysis). But Fry's passage clearly combines (or attempts to) the synchronic forms that make painting different from "unconstructed reality," so we might grasp the historical threading together of the moments of esthetic triumph that a focused experience of form makes possible. Such a line of descent, from the fraught dynamics of Caravaggio to the flickering light of the movies, is the sort of connection that makes some art historians smile and others groan. Of course, we know that Fry disliked the rigidities of the Royal Academy and the French Salon. So reading and pondering Fry means constantly shaping and reshaping one's opinion and taste, bringing together single artists and large historical and stylistic constructions. In this particular case Fry dissents from the popular reputation of Caravaggio, which has only gained adherents since his death.

Morgan as collector could be no more than an avatar of cupidity, and Fry as a critic of art could be a resolute mystifier. But they can each be seen as more than that, because in many ways they catch up and clarify forces that are larger than they are. The points of comparison between them can begin to tell us what those larger, containing forces are. Morgan, for example, can be seen as a financier—not a banker or capitalist, merely, but a man who sought to trade and deal in finance itself, and in the forces that finance makes available. Having perceived early on that money is not a thing or a force even, but a medium of exchange, he realized that one could control—that is, buy and sell—the medium itself. Money could be commodified while remaining a force—part object, part energy—that is bought and sold, made available or made scarce, have an asking and a selling price. Then, when amassed and controlled, and another kind of market came into view, it could be traded for beautiful, otherwise "priceless" things. Fry, both a maker and a historian of art, saw painting as an activity whereby made objects, artisanal wares, could contain forms of beauty so brightly inexplicable as to tell us our highest truths. These truths could be contained in beautiful and beautifully made objects, and so passed down, conquering time and decay to form a cultural bulwark, a historical record that reveals a truth.

Both men wanted to get at the heart of things, being ambitious, shaped by powerful fathers, desiring pre-eminence in their fields, and having plans to further their beliefs and values. What they discovered, each in his own terms, was an area of human endeavor that in many ways could render justice to the complexity of their experiences. They grew up as their chosen arenas of experience were changing quickly and thoroughly, but this only made it more imperative that they choose the right contested space. For Morgan it was commerce; for Fry it was art.

As a pair of men of singular qualities and accomplishments, Morgan and Fry offer both useful comparisons and contrasts. Both men, for example, can be seen as re-circulators—Morgan by bringing European art to an American citizenry, and Fry by bringing high standards of art history from the world of connoisseurs to a general public. Both men also transformed their chosen fields. When they met near the start of a new century these transforming activities were overlapping. Morgan possessed great amounts of art that were like extensions, even demonstrations, of his wealth. Fry needed money, needed simply to make a living, and, relying on cultural habits and taste, earned it by helping set prices on works of art. But their core commitment meant that Morgan stood for finance capitalism and Fry stood for formalist esthetic values. To understand where their stories connect is to see how economics and esthetics can come together. The terms of their conjunction may only be fitfully and uneasily translated, but they do affect one another.

In this book, I do not lay out an overall explanatory scheme, preferring instead to look closely at a singular test case that involves two individuals. I try to bring Morgan and Fry together, under the aegis of the Metropolitan Museum, to see how they illumine one another even as they pursue different objectives and enact different narratives. I have resorted to using selective biographical studies of both men, along with an extended analysis of Fry's esthetic ideas. The mass of biographical material on Morgan is intimidatingly huge, and the commentary on Fry as an esthetician is also formidable. The book begins with Morgan's life and ends with Fry's theories; in between I try to sketch out relations, some straightforward, others more nuanced. Since the time both men flourished much has changed in the field of art history, and in finance as well. The era of modernism has not relented in its hunger for change, even if a more recent era—called post-modernist by some—has often revalued not only the worth of new things but the notion that change can be usefully measured, narrated, or understood. But the traceries of Morgan and Fry, these two agents of change, might still offer some instructive patterns.

# CHAPTER I

# THE BIRTH OF
# DYNASTIC FINANCE

## *J. Pierpont Morgan*

JOHN PIERPONT MORGAN WAS BORN IN HART-
ford, Connecticut, on April 17, 1837, the greatly privileged son of an
extremely wealthy banker. From the early years of his maturation,
he followed his father into the world of finance, extending the family
fortune to immense heights. His life as a famous collector of art began flourishing in 1890, the year his father died. Morgan's two lives,
his two identities—finance capitalist and art collector—were not entirely separate by any means. The wealth of the former made the latter possible, and the depth of the latter redefined the former. As for
the extent of his art, he left behind a collection valued at $60 mil-
lion.[1] The collection itself comprised many thousands of objets d'art,
such as Chinese porcelain and portrait miniatures, rare manuscripts
and first editions, as well as a considerable number of European oil
paintings, all of which Morgan bought with a willfulness that astonished everyone. Almost everyone agreed that the scale of his success
as both a banker and a collector made him the epitome of the acquisitive capitalist.

Morgan's early life bore all the markings of his parents, both of
whom were descended from well-established families who were settled in America before the Revolutionary War.[2] His mother, Juliet, included among her forebears James Pierpont, a well-known
preacher whose daughter married Jonathan Edwards, the legendary formulator of Protestant doctrine in the American grain. Morgan throughout his life devotedly attended Protestant services, and
was deeply attached to the hymnal, often animatedly joining the

*J. P. Morgan at eighteen: He was born to wealth, and his place in the family dynasty was to become dominant. His father, Junius, raised him with the role of banker in mind. Courtesy of Morgan Library and Museum.*

choir in song. Morgan's paternal grandfather, Joseph, founded the Aetna Fire Insurance Company, and his father, Junius Spencer Morgan, first prospered as a dry goods merchant in Hartford and Boston, dealing mainly with the export of cotton. Family cohesion and family wealth were harmonized among the Pierponts and Morgans, and it was especially Junius Spencer Morgan who passed on to his son not only a large fortune but also a sense of character marked by discipline and eventually more than a little self-righteousness. The family would become known as the House of Morgan, a tribute to the strongly bonded sense of loyalty that underpinned their dynastic wealth and pride.

J. P. Morgan's schooling began in Hartford at a public high school and continued in Boston, at the English High School, situated next to Boston Latin. Boston English stressed preparation for business and commercial occupations, whereas Boston Latin focused on more of a classical, pre-college curriculum. Early legends formed around Morgan's ability to do sums accurately, without the need of pencil and paper; it was said later that he could calculate cube roots in his head. At the same time he had chronic health problems, and he was sent at the age of fifteen on a long trip by himself to the Azores as a way to strengthen his recovery from a bout of rheumatic fever. This would be the first of many sea voyages for Morgan, whose frequent and extensive travels, transoceanic and transcontinental, came to symbolize not only the age of the steamship but that of the railroad as well. The boy demonstrated his ability with, and fondness for, details, as he kept meticulous records on the weather, the barometric pressure, the ocean currents, and other natural phenomena during his voyage of recovery.[3] Then in 1854, the year he graduated from high school, his father, for business reasons, moved the whole family to England.

First Morgan had to continue his early schooling with some time at a Swiss boarding school, and then a year at Göttingen University, where he became fluent in German, and added proficiency in French as well. Morgan was wild and undisciplined as a young boy, but while he continued his school-based learning, his father made sure that his skills in the matters of economics and finance were of a high order. The elder Morgan developed plans for his son by encouraging the habits of thrift and trustworthiness, impressing on the twenty-year-old that bankers thrived only when and if their reputations were beyond reproach. This sense of probity and trustworthiness, self-measured to be sure, remained for the Morgans—especially J. Pierpont—an essential element of the banker's morality. Junius set himself up in London, where he had obtained a partnership in George Peabody & Co., a merchant banking firm, later renamed Peabody, Morgan & Co. As he had no children, Peabody was in search of a partner to whom he might leave the firm when he died. Achieving his financial success by selling bonds and raising money from English investors for American firms, he attained a position as one of the world's most influential investment bankers. The prominence of England's role in international finance made this success possible: "At the turn of the century, London had many more banks than any other city, and 45 percent of the global stock of multinational investment in 1914 originated in the U.K."[4] Morgan, in part through his association with Peabody, would become instrumental in the eventual—and momentous—passing of this leadership from the United Kingdom to the United States. It became common practice for an investment firm like Peabody, Morgan & Co. to supply even the US government with loans, which they did for other nation-states as well. As the borrowers grew in size and power, so did the firm.

Guiding the immense flow of capital from the British to the US economy, Peabody engaged in a large-scale process that would eventually be mastered by Junius. Peabody put into place a forward-looking sense of finance—for example, using the Crystal Palace Exhibition of 1851 as a showcase of US products and inventions, such as the McCormick reaper. Much of the capital controlled by Peabody flowed into the rapid expansion of the railroads in America, and was also swollen by the discovery of gold in the American West. The benefits and prestige of the partnership with Peabody, something Junius was eager and willing to share with his male heir, signaled the start of a series of father-and-son relationships with financial institutions. Fortunes as large as Peabody's and Morgan's almost demanded that passing on wealth to male heirs become a central activity.

As he set out on his way to adulthood, J. P. Morgan crossed the Atlantic a number of times, sharing in the work of Peabody, Morgan & Co. and learning about American opportunities. He returned to America in 1857, where his undergraduate studies at Harvard exposed him to the lectures of such influential teachers as Henry Ward Beecher and Oliver Wendell Holmes. He began his employment as an unsalaried clerk at the New York office of his father's firm. There, he soon experienced the vicissitudes of high finance, as demonstrated in the Panic of 1857, when grain sales slumped, causing a loss of fees for the railroads that shipped the grain. In turn, loans had to be called in, and it soon became apparent that the international network of bonds, loans, and investment schemes had grown overly complex and sensitive to international events. Finally the Bank of England had to offer a huge loan to Peabody, Morgan & Co. in order to stabilize the firm. Morgan thus had his first taste of the economic activity that would shape his fortune—and whose fortune would shape other such events—as the surging flow of capital in the nineteenth century continued its cyclical rise and fall.[5] Perhaps his most valuable lesson took the form of his knowing that the very scale at which he operated made him fearless.

Two years after the Panic, Morgan tried out his skills in a transaction that brought him considerable, and largely unwelcome, attention. He was working for the investment firm of Duncan, Sherman at the time, just beyond his twenty-second birthday. Despite the depression and joblessness brought on by the downturn of 1857, Morgan decided to put his mercantile interests to the test. On a visit to New Orleans, he heard about a boat loaded with coffee that was marooned in the port because its owners could not find a buyer for the large shipment. Sensing that quick decision making would be the crucial element, Morgan took funds from the firm and bought the entire shipment at a below-market price. Almost immediately he was able to sell the coffee at double the price he had paid for it, completing the prototypical transaction in merchant banking. However, the managers of Duncan, Sherman were highly disapproving and refused to bestow a partnership on Morgan, a judgment with which Junius agreed.[6] Biographers point to this as an example of either Morgan's agitated impulsiveness or his ability to proceed with calm calculations. Such a contradiction in the differing estimations of his skills nevertheless granted Morgan a leeway of acceptance, if only because the scale of his transactions would increasingly impress everyone concerned. In addition to continuing as the American agent for Peabody, Morgan & Co., he shook off his bosses' disapproval, formed his own self-named firm, and rented offices at 54 Exchange Place in the financial district. It was here that he would become a fixture in the country's economy.

His return to New York had also brought Morgan into a social world where he would appear not only ambitious but accomplished. Then his fortunes altered dramatically, and with an unknown element of dark fate. He met a young woman, two years his senior, Amelia Sturges, nicknamed "Memie." Her family life differed distinctly from Morgan's, as she was familiar with artists such as Frederic Church and Asher Durand, both of whom would make landscape the predominant genre of nineteenth-century American painting. They were among the many artists and intellectuals entertained in her father's house. What she lacked in the experience of world travel, such as Morgan had already absorbed, she made up for with charm and beauty. Morgan fell in love with her very quickly. Junius, acting as paterfamilias, arranged for her to come to Europe, where she would follow an itinerary devised by a doting Morgan. When she returned from this trip, in 1860, he proposed marriage, and she accepted.

Rather like Morgan, however, Amelia seldom enjoyed robust health, but she was even more delicate. Many suspected she had contracted tuberculosis, since she was often unable to stand for any lengthy period. She asked to postpone the nuptials until her health improved. Despite this plea, Morgan insisted they not delay and offered a Mediterranean honeymoon as a curative, perhaps remembering his own healing trip to the Azores. She relented and they were married on October 7, 1861, setting off for the Mediterranean shortly afterward. Morgan was looking past the fact that he had had to carry her downstairs and hold her up at the wedding ceremony. But the hoped-for cure failed, and Amelia weakened even more—a definite diagnosis of tuberculosis confronted her in Paris, on the way to the Mediterranean—and she died in Nice four months later. Many of Morgan's biographers would later trace both his willfulness and his piety to his love for and loss of Amelia. (Some even trace his life-long disposition to depression to this chapter in his life.) It is true that he often found himself drawn to Madonnas among the many dozens of oil paintings he would purchase later in life. Also, it is hard to resist a comparison with Henry James's love for his cousin Minny Temple, whom he reshaped into a number of his heroines, preserving their beauty and innocence in the wake of their ill fortunes and untimely deaths. A half century after Memie's death she was memorialized by Morgan when, with a bequest of $100,000, he dedicated a lying-in hospital in New York City named in her honor.

Externally Morgan was able to set aside mythology and any sense of an *anima* figure, as he began to devote countless hours to his work in the world of banking and finance. He joined with a cousin, James Goodwin, in 1862 to form the first of many companies that would manage and increase his own wealth by overseeing that of other people. Around this time he engaged in a transaction that some felt tarnished his reputation, and many entered it on the negative side of the ledger as far as his moral probity was concerned. This involved the purchase of army rifles, re-boring their barrels, and then reselling them to the government, but with a very high markup in price, for use by the Union soldiers in the Civil War. That Morgan made such profits during a war that he had avoided fighting in, paying $300 to free himself of an obligation to comply with the military draft, hardly added to his moral capital.[7]

This transaction with Union rifles appeared to many observers merely a typical form of war profiteering, refracted through the framework of mercantile capitalism—following its cardinal principle of buying low and selling high. But Morgan chose not to remain in the world of mercantilism, as his father had done years earlier. Instead he made the transition from mercantilist to financier. Rather than using his money to buy and sell merchandise, Morgan moved into the practice of making capital itself available as something that could be bought and sold and managed as to its price; he would always remain cognizant of its available supply and a concomitant increase or decrease in its value. The uneven progress of the Civil War shook the financial markets, which were constantly rising and falling. British investors withheld their support when it looked as if the South—and its chief crop, cotton—would succumb to Northern strength. The uncertainty caused the price of gold to fluctuate, and Morgan's continued speculation in the market for the precious metal caused Junius great distress. But capital itself could be treated as a commodity, with all the attendant fluctuations in supply and price. Here lay the object of Morgan's lifelong attention.

At this time Morgan became a founding partner of the firm Dabney, Morgan & Co. In fact, Junius, who used funds from his English firm to start up Dabney, Morgan, masterminded this institution. Some saw his effort, which entailed Dabney being the senior partner, as a way Junius had to make his son pursue sounder fiscal practices, and to direct his son's attention away from his personal grief to his work ethic.[8] But as the Civil War ended, Morgan fortunately found an immediate relief for his sorrow in the form of Frances Louisa Tracy, the daughter of a prominent lawyer. They were married in the summer of 1865, and spent their honeymoon traveling through Europe. The marriage would become a most unhappy one, but because Morgan's sense of propriety rendered divorce unthinkable, the two stayed together—though spending long and frequent periods apart—for the next fifty years. Over the course of the first few years Frances—"Fanny"—bore four children, three daughters, Luisa, Juliet, and Anne, and a son, John Pierpont Morgan, Jr., known as Jack, Jr. This son would extend the family tradition and financial strength well beyond his father's lifespan, and do so with rather more self-discipline than his father exhibited. The House of Morgan was amply prepared for the next generation.

Building his family as he did, shortly after his marriage, Morgan began to develop the habits and practices that would solidify his personal character and reputation. This meant periods each year of a frenetic, disciplined work routine followed by lengthy vacations—typically three months long, with some lasting a year or more—and travel to distant places. One of the first long trips covered over 6,000 miles to and throughout the American West, as if to test the efficiency of the railroad lines Morgan worked diligently to capitalize. The journey was occasioned by the completion of the transcontinental railroad in May 1869, and fully demonstrated that Morgan and his railroads were becoming a symbol of the transformation of space and time in the second half of the nineteenth century. The railroad, for example, could cut from three months to three days the time it took freight to come from Chicago to New York and the eastern states. Competition among various railroad companies, bitter fights over transport fees, and moves toward monopolized arrangements and interlocking directorships became the dramatic elements in a fractious industry.

The history of rail travel and commerce in America could never be complete without an account of Morgan's part in what was such a momentous undertaking as to resemble a social revolution. The most fabled story, perhaps, concerns how he managed, just returned from his transcontinental trip, to outmaneuver the crooked methods of financiers Jay Gould and Jim Fisk in obtaining control over the Albany and Susquehanna Railroad in 1869. He then added to his triumph by appointing himself director of the line and connecting it with other routes so as to maximize its place in the market. A central part of Morgan's values, and his image of his own higher purposes, involved a strong desire to harmonize and unify the rail system throughout the country, something he regarded as a public service of a high order. Where some saw greed and monopolies, he saw efficiency and order.

Beginning with the railroads, Morgan involved himself in the crucial industries and markets that were flourishing after the disruption left by the tragic Civil War. This meant in the long run that Morgan was transformed into a titan in areas such as steel and oil, the crucial elements in the rapidly developing social and commercial arrangements of a soon-to-be thoroughly industrialized, mass urban society. The year 1890 in America has been earmarked as the moment when the total of industrialized goods outstripped that of agricultural production for the first time. The transformed country would need to complete several subsidiary transformations in the wake of this fundamental change in its social arrangements. Morgan never approached this necessity in a shy manner.

Questions of scale and coordination lay behind much of what Morgan managed throughout the last third of the nineteenth century. Most immediately perhaps, this involved the railroads. Requiring as they did immense quantities of steel and fuel, railroads were an industry that utterly outstripped, in scale and planning, anything like an artisanal or mercantile basis, thus transforming the lineaments of society itself. What supported such large-scale industrial undertaking was an almost measureless need for capital. So one large-scale process begat another. Investment bankers like Peabody were able to respond to such a need for capital, but at the same time they were planning and building a framework in which they played a crucial role. In America there existed at the time no central bank, no structure that would serve as the later Federal Reserve Bank served, a resource that could support and stabilize other banks. This lack of a central bank meant a form of banking that operated without strong regulations, utilizing an unstructured assembly of institutions that made competition fierce and frequently led to fraud and abuse.

Morgan excelled at the new model of banking. This involved a new set of ethical values and business standards that extended the system of capitalism in ways that were seldom foreseen and which appeared unlimited. Ron Chernow coined the phrase the "Baronial

Puck *magazine cartoon, Morgan and his banks: Morgan not only acquired single banks but amassed enough of them to control the financial sector. He was early and often the subject of editorial cartoons.*

Age," meant to convey the way in which bankers like Morgan answered to virtually no one.[9] Because they needed access to the supply of credit, industrialists, entrepreneurs, inventors, and all kinds of developers had to approach the banker in order to tap into the lifeblood of the capitalist system. The typical large-scale banker, meanwhile, did not need to solicit clients, let alone advertise, nor did he need to fear government agencies, since the use of regulatory oversight was still in the future. This system has been much described and analyzed, but what marks it out most distinctively is how removed it was from the vast majority of the citizens whose lives it shaped. Ordinary people had access to wealth, currency, or material only in minute portions when compared to what Morgan shifted every business day. At a minimum this system created a closed circle of individuals whose skill and willfulness were beyond the comprehension of ordinary people.

Though obscure in its workings from a layperson's point of view, the new model of banking lay exposed each time there was a financial panic. Morgan's great skill was that he not only knew what stood behind the circumstances leading to a full-blown panic that threatened the efficient operation of the system, he knew how to stabilize the forces that had apparently run beyond anyone's control. After the Panic of 1857, the US system had other panics, in 1873, 1893, and 1907, all marked by a run on the banks, or the threat of a run, and the consequent freezing up of the flow of credit. The most significant panic—from the vantage point of Morgan's ability to restore order and further enhance his reputation—was the Panic of 1907.

It was perhaps coincidentally in 1907 that Morgan was enjoying his position as a cultural baron, having become three years earlier the chair of the board of trustees of the Metropolitan Museum of Art. This position brought him considerable public notice, and large amounts of strife and cooperation among the other trustees, while increasing his sway over many different activities. But he always operated among like-minded, and like-situated, leaders of society; he was also on the board at the American Museum of Natural History, the Wadsworth Atheneum in Hartford, Connecticut, the American Academy in Rome, and other such institutions. While he continued with his tireless work schedule, it nevertheless looked as if he was shifting his focus more to art than to commerce. However, his success at managing to restore order in the Panic of 1907 would become like a template for his actions and reactions in the social and cultural realm.

When Morgan stocked the board of trustees at the Metropolitan Museum of Art with bankers and plutocrats such as himself, and when he called these men into his private residence to "solve" the fiscal crisis of 1907, he operated beyond public control and scrutiny. Any report—through a newspaper column or raw gossip—that apparently told the story of what "really" happened was engaging in wholesale illusionism. This high-level secrecy contributed to the making of various myths and fabulous accounts. One of the most often circulated told of how Morgan sequestered all the participating bankers into one room of his Library and locked the door, while in his private office he busied himself with an extended game of solitaire, his favorite pastime. By the sunrise of the second day, the bankers had reached their compromise and Morgan proclaimed success. All the allegorical elements, each adding to the Morgan legend, were present in this narrative: the group of minions controlled by the magus, the lonely mastermind in control of the contingent events, ending with the triumphal fulfillment of the natural sense of justice. Whether seen as supporting the ship of state or manning the engines of financial markets, finally the machinery of capitalism again ran smoothly.[10]

These bankers have to a large extent been characterized with such terms as "robber barons." It is clearer, however, to think of them as finance capitalists, since the main feature that separated them from other capitalists is the extent to which they controlled all the major functions of banking, or what came to be known as the financial industry. Such men had power because they owned enormous amounts of wealth—in various forms such as currency, real estate, monopolized industries, and so forth. But what Morgan and some others represented, as they passed beyond the imaginable bounds of mere accumulated wealth or ownership, was the control of the financial system itself.

Like electricity, capitalism is less a thing than a way of explaining what happens; as such, capital must keep moving, as electricity must, or else, when nothing moves, nothing happens, and the system ceases to function. If all businesses were to become monopolies, if all transactions had to be built without recourse to credit, if competition no longer sparked growth and profitability, the resulting stagnation would be the death of finance. The finance capitalists—with Morgan as the virtual prototype—had to maintain and control the flows within the capitalist system. Such flows were often increased when money was borrowed, and as long as the increase of debt did not result in unsustainable losses or reckless inflation—the so-called bubble—increased force was applied chiefly by how the financiers decided to leverage their power. The word "leverage" came to be a perfect euphemism for indebtedness, since the system worked only as someone was pushing forward, while another was maximizing the pushing force because he had control of the fulcrum points, where pressure was strongest.[11]

Morgan's success and the respect he won among his fellow bankers derived in many ways from his life experience in England and European countries. With fluency in languages and an appreciation of European culture, he thrived in the growing internationalism of the financial industry. The laying of the transatlantic cable in 1866, after four unsuccessful attempts, made timely communication exponentially swifter, and spurred the internationalism that was being aided by the flows of capital. But there was also the central fact of Morgan's American identity, and the fact that he was living during a period of phenomenal industrial expansion and with an inchoate banking system that had yet to devise meaningful, let alone strict, regulations. Morgan saw his role as bringing trust and fidelity to banking, but one lesson to be derived from his actions in the Panic of 1907 was that his power was so singular and unbounded that he himself served something like the function of a central bank. One study of his banking practices contrasts his model with that of the Bank of England. The latter was often pilloried in contrast to the American banks, which were often hailed as providing for the best of all possible worlds. The two countries have often been characterized as having a "special relationship" in matters of culture and foreign relations. But in terms of how they conducted the banking systems that shaped their respective national wealth at the beginning of the twentieth century, the contrasts outreached the comparisons.

Leslie Hannah, an economic historian, summarizes the standard version of how the two systems were evaluated: "Before 1914, London had a stock exchange that was larger and qualitatively more developed than New York's. Yet the London Stock Exchange has received a bad press from historians, while the New York Exchange has achieved star billing."[12] But the victors, as usual, write this history, and it is possible that a nonstandard version might be more illuminating. As an exponent of the nonstandard history, Hannah argues that New York's stock market grew rapidly not because of its better methods or sager management but because it took advantage of less scrupulous methods and a greater expansion of America's industrial base: "Morgan's higher profits in New York derived partly from insider deals and partly from monopolistic exactions that U.S. protection-ism facilitated but that proved more problematic in the U.K.'s open, competitive markets. Morgan's contributions to the impressive catch-up process by the New York Exchange are more plausibly viewed as successful emulation of European securities-market precedents on routine matters than of the allegedly path-breaking 'information sig-naling' innovations of more Panglossian accounts." The term "in-formation signaling" usually refers to a company's actions—such as the issuance of special bonds—that serve to forewarn well-informed investors what the company's future plans and strategies are. Han-nah here suggests that US markets did not act in a progressive way to make information more available to investors, or at least did no more than was standard practice in other stock markets. Meanwhile Mor-gan profited from activities that would eventually come under regu-lation, through the creation of the Federal Reserve and the Securi-ties and Exchange Commission. Prior to such regulation he relied on his power to control the flow of information about his activities and those of others, largely through an oligarchic structure in which lim-ited partnerships, along with a guild mentality, led bankers to trust one another and avoid any sort of cutthroat competition that would endanger the smooth functioning of the flow of capital. There had to be honor among bankers, and Morgan saw to it that there was.

For Morgan, success bred success. What most commentators had in mind when they talked of his financial wizardry was his ability to bring together otherwise disparate or competitive companies into a larger, integrated whole. His success here was so remarkable that the process came to be called Morganization. For Morgan himself, Morganization was on display and most historically forceful with his shaping of a conglomerated single entity that became the General Electric Company in 1892. He then topped this feat in 1901 by merg-ing several companies and arranging the financial instruments that brought forth the United States Steel Corporation, the first industrial company to be valued at a billion dollars.

Morgan's banking practices were different from those of the typ-ical US corporation, which was then in the early stages of develop-ment. Rather than relying on the sale of large volumes of common stock to investors with modest means, Morgan ran his business more like that of a family, a financial "house" (in fact Morgan continually referred to his offices as "counting houses"). Assembling a collection of wealthy financiers like himself who lent their own considerable sums of money, when needed, and relying on the fees they charged for arranging financial instruments and services that others used to supply capital for their business ventures, the resulting partnership required an extraordinary level of mutual trust and constant consultation. Morgan's enterprises needed a sense of cooperation with other bankers, even as the restrictive, closed circles of those with sufficient capital controlled the flow of wealth, and its terms and conditions of availability and use. "Morgan therefore began the 1890s with as large a position in London as he held in New York (at 23 Wall Street), and many of his U.S. clients were 'inheritances' from the British partnership. Pierpont, in the 1890s, decisively shifted the balance to New York, seeing himself as the bearer of the sound London practices of an ethical conservative banker to a new venue where they were badly needed. He persisted in referring to his New York firm as 'merchant bankers' in the English fashion," as Hannah concluded.

Morgan's view of himself as ethical and conservative (even as he was self-serving and willing to remold traditional practices) mimicked a classic form of self-mythologizing, and it gained plausibility because Morgan often set the rules. In the United States, corporations in the crucial industries—steel, railroad, mining, and so forth—were controlled by the major stockholders, men who had acquired such a large portion of a company's financial power that they could easily dictate all the important decisions that were to be made. The rule of the markets was in the sway of oligarchs, and the more democratic model of the small investor was thoroughly overshadowed. Morgan's business style represented this system with near perfection, and he often expressed his faith in his own rectitude, believing that only through the trustworthiness of like-minded individuals could the system be stabilized and allowed to flourish. The style combined a controlled English gentlemanly reserve with a rapacious American optimistic growth, the combination both expressing and profiting from the energy of the era.

Morgan enjoyed his role as one of the chief shapers of the new banking system, if not the most forceful of all. He drew on English models and his experience with his father as far back as the Peabody days, but he also played a crucial role in helping the United States become the main source of capital for the future. The parallel with his life as an art collector suggests itself. The tide of history would not yield to any individual, but it at times seemed to answer to Morgan as he set out to redirect the attention of the world to the realm of American art and culture as he had done for banking and finance.

With Morgan the individual, as distinct from his identity as a member of a class or a type, in his later years the main course of his life outside banking was taken up with his role as a collector. He displayed marked shifts from financial involvement to collecting at two points: when his father died in 1890, and after the Panic of 1907. The passing of Junius Spencer Morgan allowed his son to assume the leadership of the family business and to have an immense fortune to spend on himself and his family. He had organized his holdings into a single banking institution, J.P. Morgan & Co., in 1895. By the turn of the century, Morgan was placing more and more of the family business into the hands of Jack, Jr., who would earn his father's trust as surely as Pierpont had earned that of Junius. Jack, Jr. also watched over the business transactions while Pierpont went on his three-month vacations, much of which time was spent buying artworks and sending them back to his house at Prince's Gate in London. Eventually the collection filled the residence, and so Morgan bought the house next door. There—at 13-14 Prince's Gate—notable visitors came to admire and be impressed.[13]

At Prince's Gate Morgan eagerly displayed his wealth, and also his taste in the visual arts. No photographs of the interior of the Prince's Gate houses survive, so we cannot know exactly how Morgan hung the paintings for which he had paid handsomely. But in 1895 he purchased a number of important masterpieces, often by English artists—his Anglophilia was always a considerable factor in his taste—and having as their subject full-length portraits of beautiful ladies. This group included notable works by Thomas Lawrence, Joshua

Reynolds, Thomas Gainsborough, and George Romney. He also coveted various examples of landscape, and bought one of John Constable's greatest paintings, *The White Horse* (1819), which was originally titled *A Scene on the River Stour*. Taking just these works into account, a visitor might well have thought the residence was that of English royalty, or at least a peer of the realm. In 1901 Morgan opened the collection to carefully selected viewers. The elitist atmosphere was heightened by the tours of the art being conducted by the Duveen brothers, Joseph and Joel, the dealers who had advised Morgan on his purchases. The approximately sixteen hundred objects Morgan had put on extended loan to London's South Kensington Museum (renamed the Victoria and Albert Museum in 1899) supplemented the riches of the Prince's Gate locale. All in all, before he became the president of the board of trustees at the Metropolitan Museum in 1904 (after previously being a trustee for several years), Morgan might possibly have appeared more of a cultural presence in English than in American life. At the least, his taste was imbued with the Anglophilia of his friends and associates in the world of American high finance.

Freed from total involvement in, and concentration on, the banking business, Morgan immersed himself in collecting art on an ever grander scale. One major obstacle confronted this strong urge and the satisfaction it should have provided: Morgan's art was not readily available to him in America. Because of the 1897 US Government Revenue Act a prohibitively high tariff of twenty percent of the assessed value had been placed on the importation of artworks. Consequently most of what Morgan had collected remained outside America, stored in his English residences or on extended loan to the South Kensington Museum. He chafed greatly under this imposition, as did all of his fellow wealthy collectors. Some of them resorted to various ingenious deceptions, becoming in effect self-serving smugglers, in order to pass through customs on their return to America without paying what would often have been very high tariffs. Books and manuscripts were exempt from the tariff, so Morgan was able to import many of the bibliophilic treasures he had amassed, but the oil paintings remained in London as symbols of elegance. In the meantime, however, Morgan waited and lobbied the politicians who were all too willing to move slowly in eliminating an accustomed source of revenue. He presumably saw no reason why the manner in which he transferred capital from England to America through innovative banking practices could not be applied as easily in the realm of culture.

Since his art possessions had grown so greatly in number that he could no longer store them at his residences in England and New York City, he decided to build a library. The obvious location was next to the family's brownstone, on the corner of Madison Avenue and 36th Street. He commissioned Charles McKim, of the renowned architectural firm McKim, Mead & White, to undertake the design. Building began in 1902 and was finished three years later. Designed with Morgan's collection in mind, the books and manuscripts—there were something like ten thousand altogether—went into the East Room, and Morgan's office occupied the West Room. Morgan oversaw the details with his stern eye, and spared little expense. "I want a gem," he told the architect.[14] He allowed Charles McKim to use an ancient method, adapted from the Acropolis, of joining the marble blocks of the outer structure without mortar—held in place only by small metal pins—at an added cost of $50,000. Though his final will and testament would speak of a desire to make his collection available to the American public, the Library—later the Library & Museum—had its origins in the dramatic display of personal wealth. Some critics have called McKim's work his masterpiece, and certainly in the eyes of many it outshone those comparable mansions—such as Isabella Stewart Gardner's in Boston and Henry Clay Frick's on New York's Upper East Side—designed specifically as personal showcases of cultivated taste.

These multimillionaire collectors competed with each other in acquiring the masterpieces of European art, and so it was only expected that their display cases would be equally models of elaborate attainment. Still, as the highly restricted class of plutocrats and the barons of wealth formed itself around certain standards, it called forth an answering class, made up of men who could not merely appreciate the art but validate it. Each of these two classes—a symmetrical formation and counterformation—resulted from a welter of forces, perhaps chiefly the twinned factors of ever increasing wealth and a

*McKim rendering of Morgan Library: This neoclassical building was the most public display of Morgan's wealth. Morgan's residence was on the same block, but the Library was the cynosure. Courtesy of Morgan Library and Museum.*

limited supply of the most desirable objects. Critics and historians of culture have adduced a panoply of other factors, including America's supposed inferiority complex when faced with older, more seasoned values frequently handled more deftly. Where Morgan stands singled out in this historical confluence, however, is his apparent ability virtually to equate the means and methods of acquiring financial wealth with the same set of attitudes and approaches that he used in acquiring works of art. Morgan struck everyone as forceful, but even more as consistent; he was built not to waver. Like his peers, he relied on the words of experts, at least on most occasions. But he was known for his propensity to buy an entire collection just for the satisfaction of owning one or more singular items that it might contain. He also had nearly boundless confidence in his ability to tell the genuine from the fraudulent. Operating with bountiful shields of privacy, he protected his plans and predilections from all those who might profit from the "information signaling" that he had brought to bear in his financial dealings. This meant that he constantly traded in gossip, in leaked information, even in coded correspondence, often sent by wire hours before a crucial sale or in response to the harried urgings of a dealer who was offering prized objects in a controlled timeframe. All this created a need for expertise and connoisseurship.

One of the events that influenced Morgan's dealings with art experts was his encounter with the reputation of Bernard Berenson. Along with his wife, Mary, Berenson made available his services as an expert in attributions of paintings—especially by Renaissance Italian masters—as he traveled to all the major centers of art and culture, amassing fees from wealthy collectors. These masterpieces of vision and technique were enjoying a great increase in popularity among American collectors, which was both the cause and the result of Berenson's reputation. His expertise was based on his prodigious memory, formidable learning, and a series of art history books that were filled with detailed studies that revolved around questions of attributions. Berenson became a virtual prototype of the connoisseur, but while on occasion he made available his services at the behest of Morgan, the two men never really formed a deep relationship. For his part, Morgan diversified his consulting experts, open to many opinions and persuasions, but always decisively asserting his own judgment.

The world of experts and millionaire collectors overlapped, however, to such an extent that the major figures of each realm eventually dealt with one another, by reputation or by specific arrangements. Sometimes the dealings took on a very sharp edge. In 1903 Frederick Rhinelander, who had become the Metropolitan Museum's treasurer in 1871, was serving as the president of the board of the museum; in fact, he was Morgan's immediate predecessor in that position. Rhinelander, eager to upgrade the museum staff, had begun a campaign to have Berenson made the Met's director. But Joseph Duveen, by this time one of the most prominent art dealers in the world—and hence a dominant middle man between the millionaires and the expert—was apparently willing to cast a shadow on people's reputations. He may have honestly suspected Berenson of having engaged in dealings with an unscrupulous forger (Duveen didn't actually meet Berenson until 1906). But since he had considerably increased his own wealth through arranging many of Morgan's purchases, he wanted to keep Morgan from being burned and subsequently was overly suspicious of other dealers and connoisseurs. So in 1904 he went to Morgan and suggested that Berenson was not altogether above reproach in his business transactions. Morgan, at least as cautious as Duveen, decided to block Berenson's appointment until such time as he, Morgan, could succeed Rhinelander.[15] When the time came for Morgan to become president of the trustees, and so to be in a position to influence the selection of a director of the Metropolitan, with Berenson out of consideration, several other experts would be available and other machinations would follow. Eventually, Duveen's maneuver involved considerable irony, as Berenson and Duveen entered into a secret partnership in 1912, which guaranteed that Berenson would provide the authentications that would most increase Duveen's financial advantage. This secret arrangement—involving an actual signed contract—was decidedly ethically compromised and was not discovered until years later.[16] It is unlikely that Morgan knew of the arrangement, and whether his sense of moral probity would have condoned or condemned the situation is hidden from view.

## THE ARRIVAL OF BELLE DA COSTA GREENE

Morgan, having impatiently waited as the Library on which much of his future fame would rest neared completion, turned in another direction for a different form of assistance. He realized that he needed someone who could not only catalog his new acquisitions but also help him in evaluating and purchasing yet more material, for he essentially continued on a buying spree for the final twenty-five or so years of his life. A person who could satisfy such a need would have to combine the skills of a secretary, an advisor, a bibliophile, and a confidante. With a portion of luck so rare that it seemed like fate, he met Belle da Costa Greene.

In 1905, Greene, then only twenty-two years old, was introduced to Morgan by his nephew, Junius, who had come to know her when she was working as a librarian at Princeton University. Her father, Richard Theodore Greener, was the first African American to graduate from Harvard University; he had married and then separated from a light-skinned woman who decided to pass for white, along with her children. Greene's mother changed the family name from Greener to Greene, and then Belle Greene went further and added the vaguely distinguished middle name of da Costa, often claiming Portuguese descent. Greene mastered the difficult field of illuminated manuscripts and knew several languages. But it was her sangfroid in handling importunate dealers that impressed Morgan, as did her willingness to stand up to the banker himself. Greene remained a single woman throughout her life, dying in 1950 after managing the Morgan Library for almost four decades.

One of the more memorable triumphs that helped seal her place in Morgan's estimation occurred when she attended the auction of the estate of Lord Amherst in London in late 1909. Meeting with Amherst the day before the auction, she offered her price for sixteen volumes printed by William Caxton, one of the earliest of England's great producers of illuminated books, and one of Morgan's special favorites. She also let Amherst know that if he didn't take the offer then and there, she would refrain from bidding the next day and thus lower the ultimate price among the other bidders. Greene's abilities as a negotiator may have derived in part from her experience passing as white, as well as her experience maintaining control over her self-presentation in the social world to which she had access because of her closeness to Morgan.[17]

Greene impressed Morgan many times and in many areas. She was described by a *New York Times* interviewer as "one with a vivacious laugh, with brown eyes and rosy cheeks, who speaks delectable French, and who picks up a musty tome as gracefully as a butterfly alights on a dusty leaf." But what Morgan may not have known about her was the long-term intimate relationship she had with Berenson.

Belle Greene and Berenson had met in 1908 when he and his wife, Mary, visiting America, were invited to a tour of the Morgan Library. Berenson had earlier told his patroness, Isabella Stewart Gardner, that he thought Morgan's holdings in his London residence at Prince's Gate, which he viewed in 1906, looked "like a pawnbroker's shop for Croesuses." But his tour of the Library changed his view somewhat, and he wrote Gardner that he was "duly impressed."[18] Berenson enjoyed not only an acid tongue but also possessed a snobbish attitude toward many of the millionaires with whom he bought

*Belle da Costa Greene: Morgan's most intimate, trusted, and effective employee, Greene (1883–1950) unstintingly admired Morgan as both a financier and an art collector. She continued to manage the Library for years after Morgan's death.*

and sold paintings. Whether Berenson's admiration was won by Morgan's impressive collection or Greene's sensuous sophistication, the connoisseur definitely became entangled.

Despite her amorous and idealized attachment to Berenson, which was expressed through a passionate correspondence, Greene corrected him on the subject of Morgan's character and inner life. Berenson had offered Greene some negative gossip about Morgan only to have her answer, "please don't jeer at my dearly-beloved Boss." Using sincere testimony about Morgan's generosity and paternal feelings for her, Greene insisted that Morgan had shown himself to her "in a unique way." She continued: "there is an honesty of thought between us—a soul-oneness which makes it possible for him to tell me things." She spent many years living in a social world peopled with those who would often slavishly seek Morgan's approval and access to his wealth. Still, her closeness to him seemed always to be built on true feelings. "I wonder how many other people know, as I do, of the utter loneliness of his life?" This closeness to him was the basis for her fidelity, and she went on to offer a most sober estimation (perhaps not realizing how discrediting it would sound to some) that "the things he stands for . . . are not his art collections, be they good, bad, or indifferent—they are after all but his amusement, as are his yachts, his Belle-dames, his game of solitaire and his game of finance." Greene handled her affairs, and her benefactors, with striking aplomb. It is unlikely that she and Morgan were intimate, but with Berenson the situation was different. He clearly included her among his several mistresses, many of whom were known to his wife, Mary.


ONCE BELLE GREENE HAD BROUGHT HER CONSIDER-able talents for management and negotiation to bear on Morgan's art collection, it freed Morgan to redouble his involvement in his cultural pursuits. Much of this new energy went to controlling the affairs of the Metropolitan Museum of Art. His own tastes and willingness to spend large sums determined the shape and content of many of the museum's holdings. Two purchases stand out, among many others. Morgan greatly admired Chinese porcelains. James A. Garland, a banker who had drawn on Duveen's expertise in assembling two thousand pieces, owned one of the most impressive collections of these artifacts. He had put the collection on loan to the museum, and the Met assumed eventually it would receive the collection as a gift; however, in 1902 Garland died before making any such arrangement. Duveen responded quickly and bought the collection for half a million dollars. Morgan then purchased it from him for six hundred thousand dollars and gave it to the Metropolitan. In the same year Morgan purchased an additional $200,000 worth of more porcelains and gave them to the Metropolitan. No other collection of Chinese porcelains of comparable quality exists.

A similar set of sales and purchases occurred in what was to become the museum's Department of Arms and Armor. (Indeed, Morgan called the department into being when he became president of the trustees in 1904, as part of a major reorganization of the institution.) A society friend of Morgan's wife divorced her husband, the Duc de Dino, a French aristocrat, who in turn needed to sell his collection of armor. Morgan enlisted the aid of a trustee, Rutherfurd Stuyvesant, who secured the collection with a floated check (covered by Morgan) for $240,000. Morgan assembled the trustees, encouraged them to join in with their contributions, and after settling the finances, he accepted the shipment of the armor. He then proceeded to hire an expert, Bashford Dean, who spoke seven languages and came by his expertise from his studies of armored fish, to set about installing and cataloging the material. Unlike the Chinese porcelain, armor was not one of Morgan's deep interests. However, he did own a famously beautiful armored helmet, made for Francis I by Philip Negroli, known as "the Michelangelo of armorers." He donated it to the museum, and it stands out as one of the most striking objects in the collection. So Morgan's activities in building the Metropolitan's holdings and reputation were not always limited to areas that greatly interested him. But he definitely displayed a tendency to equate his taste and judgment with that of the museum's collective leadership.

As for Morgan's deepest interests and desires, they were often most actively engaged when he traveled throughout Europe. He made a European trip in 1902 that was notable for the amount and variety of the art he purchased. (In 1903 he was overseas only for five weeks, but bought a good deal of art even so. There were also later purchasing tours of the Continent that were equally abundant in their rewards.) Clinton Dawkins, one of his business partners, said in 1902 that Morgan showed an "inclination to pull out of business," and that he could absorb business matters only in "small concentrated doses like patent medicine."[19] Just days after he hired McKim to design his Library, Morgan left for Europe, having appointed his nephew Junius to oversee the details. The list of Morgan's purchases included among other items the following: a tapestry ($340,000), a marble bas-relief of the Virgin and Child, attributed to Donatello ($74,000), a Gainsborough portrait ($150,000), a collection of bronzes ($64,000), and the manuscript of John Ruskin's *The Stones of Venice* ($82,000). He indulged another of his penchants when he bought an entire collection, this one a masterly library owned by William Bennett of Manchester ($700,000). Meanwhile the estimated cost of the McKim library was $850,000, but in four years it rose to more than a million dollars.

Obviously buying on this scale not only demonstrated the incredible extent of Morgan's wealth, it virtually shaped the market in which he operated. One of the bankers at Barings, the London banking house, whom Morgan had dealt with when buying a steamship line (one of his rare business failures), wrote to a colleague that Morgan's "operations in pictures, tapestries & curios have done him more harm with the general public than steel or shipbuilding." The general populace would respect the complex decisions that went into the making of Morgan's industrial fortune, but were likely to consider the large amounts of money spent on his artworks the sign of mental imbalance, at least according to this observer. He cites this example: Morgan came across a receipt for a bronze bust of Hercules and inquired of Belle Greene where the statue was; she wrote back that it was in his Library, "where it faces you when [you're] sitting in your chair. It has been there about a year."[20]

Morgan maintained a lifestyle that dazzled everyone, and despite his best efforts to stop its coverage of him, the press followed him constantly. His personal traits and activities were of consuming interest to many. However, his favorite pastime was playing solitaire for hours at a time. The nettlesome newspapers did supply one constant special feature: the dockside interview that he was purported to give the crowd of reporters every time he sailed from New York or returned. The contents of the interviews, which duly appeared in the next morning's paper, were often totally fictitious. His travels and business dealings exemplified the old saw that the most expensive item a supremely wealthy person will need to buy is his privacy. In 1902, Morgan enjoyed what was for him a rather ordinary whirl of events. In London he had purchased several collections of antique silver and bronzes, one of them known as the Gutman collection. His son-in-law, Herbert L. Satterlee, describes the events of a not atypical few days: "[F]rom Paris he went down to the Riviera to join *Corsair* [his custom built yacht], and they cruised to Venice. This was not only the first visit of the *Corsair* to Venice, but the first time that several of the party had been there, and every day of the week that they spent was filled with incidents never to be forgotten. From Venice the yacht cruised down the Adriatic, and on June 8 landed the party at Brindisi, and they all left for London by rail via Paris."[21]

In London, Morgan had but two days to prepare for a dinner given by Ambassador Whitelaw Reid, where the special guests were King Edward and his wife, Alexandra. Satterlee adds tersely, "The King and Morgan had been friends of long standing."

In the early years of the twentieth century, Morgan enlarged his stature as a cultural leader in many ways. He was instrumental in founding the American Academy in Rome, helping the institution financially and arranging for its purchase of a choice location on the top of the Janiculum. As was often his practice, he influenced others to make sizable donations, and such influence was seldom unavailing. In the last month of 1903 he was elected as the first vice president of the American Museum of Natural History. The next year he became president of the Metropolitan Museum's board of trustees. From there he would be able to influence the museum's growth and policies as could no other of his peers. He contributed money and advice to the permanent organizing of the Peabody Education Fund, a fund started by his father to improve schooling in the South after the Civil War. He also helped fund the medical college at Harvard. And of course he continued to make extraordinary gifts to the Metropolitan Museum. The scale of his wealth and philanthropy combined

*"The Pied Piper" cartoon expressed what Morgan's detractors felt about his unchecked influence in the industrial and financial markets. Those "magnetized" by Morgan's influence also included people from all sectors of society.*

with the force of his will to make him an obvious candidate for president of the museum. When Morgan had become vice president of the museum in early 1904, it was only a few months later that Frederick Rhinelander, who had served as trustee since the incorporation of the museum, and president since 1902, passed away. The line of succession allowed for no blurring, and Morgan was voted in unanimously by the trustees.

One of his first decisions as the newly installed president was to hire away from the Victoria and Albert Museum its director, Sir Caspar Purdon Clarke. (To the surprise of many, Clarke even applied for American citizenship.) Assembling an expert staff—including chiefly the director and the head curator—would become the most important part of putting the Metropolitan on a professional footing. It was a task that Morgan undertook with his customary strength of will. Operating with the full compliance of his fellow trustees, and a readiness to exercise his philanthropy, Morgan clearly relished the opportunity to see himself expressed and reflected in America's foremost museum.

The *New York Times* of January 22, 1905, took notice of the appointment of Clarke, naming the members of the "special" committee in charge: Charles McKim, Rutherfurd Stuyvesant, Elihu Root (all trustees), and Robert De Forest (secretary for the museum). The decisive meeting was held at Morgan's residence, and the salary was "understood to have been $10,000." The *Times* went on, spelling out the policy behind the appointment: "It is understood that under the direction of Sir C. Purdon Clarke the work of the museum on educational lines will be greatly enlarged and extended at the same time that the methods of the institution as a museum will be widened in accordance with the ideas of the new President, Mr. Morgan." There was also the information about the Victoria and Albert Museum that would appeal to the American readers, namely that "Its object is not only to exhibit masterpieces of art but to educate art teachers and to further art education."

Morgan was in a position where his ideas and plans about the museum's policies and future could be directly implemented without serious questioning. His power as a collector continued to grow. With his Library recently finished and his rare books and manuscripts soon to be organized by Greene, his unchecked desire to meld and regularize and reformulate the things he controlled—his preeminent ability to "Morganize"—could proceed at full speed. When he became president of the Met he was sixty-seven years old. There were still many business struggles left to settle, to be sure, as the public mood for antitrust legislation and litigation had grown considerably. But when 1905 arrived, he could look into the museum's future and see only the brightest of prospects.

# CHAPTER II

# THE ESTHETIC EDUCATION
# OF AN ART CRITIC

## *Roger Fry*

ROGER FRY WAS AN ESTHETE, BUT HE WAS NOT A stereotype. The center of his life rested on his sense of beauty. For him, beauty often served as an end in itself, providing moments of what he came to call "aesthetic emotion." But at the same time, he saw it as creating an urge to something yet more valuable, namely a life enriched and enlarged by a spiritual force. The late-nineteenth-century English culture that formed his personality nourished his estheticism, while maintaining fairly strict bounds to it, bounds he often found intolerable. What this culture also provided him, one could almost say burdened him with, was a felt need to explain the beautiful. Such an explanation would certify and share the emotional experiences art could offer. In a sense Fry was able to re-contain the skills and values of the paternally approved professions he rejected—science and the law—in his quest to put art criticism and art history on a footing that would be undergirded by logic, precision, and focused argument.

Fry's first commitment to pursuing beauty as a way of organizing the purpose of one's life came when he resolutely chose a vocation as an artist over the career, strongly favored by his father, of being a scientist. This conflict, between values and facts, between the choice of self-making and parental submission, served to give hundreds of works of fiction in the late nineteenth century their organizing themes, but remained in force in Fry's life. As for his father, Fry couldn't but be proud of the man's public accomplishments in the law, even as the father might easily have been viewed as a failed scientist himself. As a judge who earned considerable distinction, Edward Fry was also, and especially through his Quaker faith, a rich source of Roger's morality.

Fry's early adult years recapitulated a well-rehearsed pattern, that of the artistically sensitive son who must break away from the respectably bourgeois father. Of course in Fry's case weighty particulars added their shadings and gravity to the narrative, which entailed conflict but also mutual affection. Edward Fry eventually enjoyed a knighthood for his valuable jurisprudence, while Roger helped set the artistic agenda for the portion of the British public who found a need to appreciate and understand modern art. For the father, his strong Quaker sentiments set him apart from the typical Victorian sage, and he succeeded in imparting a special sense of personal morality to his son, which was amply reflected in Roger's personal ethics and complexly registered in his esthetic views. Even in his university years, Roger attempted to secure a balance between his father's endowment of character and his own personal desires. Few art historians, while still in university, have published a scientific paper in biology, but Fry accomplished this because he was already disposed toward the scientific vocation his father urged him to consider. But the years at Cambridge exerted a different shaping force, as friendships with esthetes and philosophers brought to bear a strong set of beliefs and commitments. For him, art posed and answered questions in ways different from science, offering instead a world of emotions and forms that had to be addressed with their own distinctive values.

Fry went up to Cambridge in 1885, at the age of nineteen, after four years at Clifton College, a boarding school in Bristol. His first plans at the university included a study of the natural sciences, abetted by his having won an "exhibition" prize on the basis of the results of his entrance examination. His honors would eventually include a double first in science, and he was fairly confident that he could have secured a fellowship at King's College as a teacher of botany. It was only in the years following his work in science that his interests were decidedly drawn to literary and artistic matters. King's College, Cambridge, with its impressively beautiful chapel, marked the distance from Clifton, with its persisting sense of loneliness and repugnance at the boys and their brutalities. His earlier days of home schooling were spent equally distantly from the Backs at Cambridge, with their lush rolling lawns running down to the river Cam. So King's stood as Fry's first chance at seeing in education something beyond mere discipline or family obligations. In the fall of his third year there he would say, "it was the only place in this wicked world where a man is permitted truly to live."[1] Virginia Woolf echoed the thought when she later reported in her biography of Fry that he dated everything from his years at Cambridge.[2]

One letter to his university roommate Charles Robert Ashbee lends a striking tone to the way Fry would approach his experiences in the esthetic realm. He reports that he doesn't think that "we have been wont to lay enough stress on the value . . . of pure aesthetics as apart from the emotional end. I am also still very much mixed about its relation to morality."[3] The conflict of esthetics and morality conjures up the melodrama of late Victorian intellectual life into which Fry was plunged. He manages to wrestle his way out of this difficulty by insisting that art should be moral, but only "from the point of view of its intrinsic beauty" and not its goodness. He equates beauty and goodness, or at least makes them cognates, not unlike John Keats's famous formulation: "Beauty is truth, truth beauty." Much of this frame of mind, structured around the Ruskinian equation of morality and truth, would need to navigate through the egoistic shoals of Wildean estheticism. Already in the late 1880s Fry was attempting to see through the lens of Victorian esthetics with its notion that poetry—and art—should increasingly take on the features and functions of religious belief. The letter to Ashbee goes on: "I am fully persuaded that the aim of all art and all life is ultimately the worship of God in its broadest sense." Coupling "all art" with "all life" indicates how Fry and his Cambridge classmates sensed that the value scales of the metaphysical and the esthetic had somehow to be harmonized, if not equated.

The distinctive character of King's College, and Fry's shift to esthetic concerns, were both cemented by friendships that would stay with Fry for decades afterward. None was more formative than that with G. Lowes Dickinson. Bearing the rather florid first name of Goldsworthy, Dickinson was known to friends and associates as Goldie. His father was an accomplished painter and provided his son

*Fry's portrait of Goldsworthy Lowes Dickinson: Known as "Goldie," Dickinson (1862–1932) was one of Fry's closest Cambridge friends, sharing with him long discussions about philosophy and art. He later worked for the cause of world peace.*

with an excellent education that allowed him to be an exhibitor, that is, a student who did well enough on the entrance exams to be provided with a partial scholarship. This distinction he shared with Fry, who was four years his junior, and by Fry's fourth year at Cambridge the two star pupils had become exceptionally close. Prior to his meeting Fry, Goldie had finished his undergraduate studies—capped with a prize-winning poem—and traveled in Germany for a year before returning to Cambridge. He wrote poems throughout his life, often using the elaboration of a sonnet sequence to memorialize his romantic longings and express a transcendent curiosity about how humans should build their relationships with each other, and their ties to the higher world.

Dickinson's closeness to Fry was more than indelibly sealed with their common membership in the Cambridge Apostles, officially known as the Cambridge Conversazione Society. It was in this secret society that the issues of the day were fully examined, and Dickinson relished sharing with Fry his admiration for the idealist philosophy of that time and place. This philosophy featured a strong emphasis on ethics, shaped by the work of G. E. Moore and J. M. E. McTaggart, the latter of whom shared a room with Fry. McTaggart, who would later be employed as a fellow in philosophy at Trinity College, Cambridge, busily pondered the metaphysical issues, dwelling on thorny problems like the nature and existence of time. His work attracted Moore, who, as a classicist-turned-philosopher, won a First in classical studies when he graduated in 1896. Moore's important treatise *Principia Ethica* (1903) stressed that the ethical goods that presented us with the most important values were moments of love and dedication to close friends, and the intensity of esthetic insights and experiences. (Some have pointed to it as the foundational text for the Bloomsbury Group.) Moore asserted that ethical values could not be paraphrased or logically explained; one could only indicate the good in its manifestation as an event or thing. He eventually moved away from McTaggart's idealism, but he continued to mistrust empirical tests for truth. Working in the tradition of idealist thought that Moore had championed early on, Dickinson, through the agency of his impressive dissertation on Plotinus, the Greek idealist philosopher, was able to win an appointment as a fellow at King's. So began his long academic association, in 1887, which was the final year of Fry's stay there. Though Fry left Cambridge and Dickinson remained behind, the two in a sense never parted company.[4]

Dickinson revealed in his autobiography (published nearly four decades after the deaths of Fry and Dickinson) his passionate love for Fry, though their friendship was never sexually consummated.[5] Dickinson returned to Cambridge after his graduation and a year abroad with the ostensible purpose of studying medicine, with his father's support, but as happened with Fry, his interests soon turned in another direction. He excused himself, so to speak, when he confessed "the belief in metaphysics as the method of knowledge persisted with me for many years, and no doubt obstructed any useful pursuit of science."[6] He went on to a distinguished academic career at Cambridge, becoming influential in support of the campaign for international peace, including work that led to the League of Nations. His academic career at Cambridge spanned more than three decades as a professor of political science, and also a period as the King's College librarian. His published works, highlighted by books on a myriad of historical and political subjects as well as classical studies, such as *The Greek View of Life* (1896), made him a popular writer throughout England. Dickinson resembled Fry in that both men turned their belief in higher values to a public accounting, hoping to make their learning and their traditional training serve as the sounder basis of a common culture and a shared comity. Fiercely committed to the idea of humane progress through enlightened policies, Dickinson possessed the highest and most impressive sort of academic mind, and his inspiring effect on Fry's intellectual development was singular and solid.

Another shared activity that united Fry and Dickinson, even beyond their college days, was their work as extension lecturers. Dickinson, in addition to his Cambridge teaching, lectured at the London School of Economics for fifteen years. Demonstrating their commitment to education beyond the elite and restricted numbers of students available at Cambridge, both men managed to apply their academic training without becoming typically hermetic professors. Many decades later Fry's lecturing skills would be recalled by Frances Partridge, a Bloomsbury figure who published several volumes of her memoirs (and who lived to be 104, dying in 2004): "Anyone who heard Roger Fry lecture on art must owe him an immense debt of pure pleasure, for he had the rare gift of conveying his own love for paintings, even when their attractions were not obvious, even when the slides were put in upside down."[7]

Added to this somewhat general depiction there is another, more detailed, crafted by Virginia Woolf. Referring to the hanging sheet onto which were projected the illuminated paintings being discussed, she detailed Fry in operation: "As the next slide slid over the sheet there was a pause. He gazed afresh at the picture. And then in a flash he found the word he wanted. He added on the spur of the moment what he had just seen as if for the first time." Fry had mastered a technique—rhetorical and dramatic—used by many lecturers trying to propel their presentation. But he may have had more genuine effusiveness than technical premeditation. Woolf continued: "That, perhaps, was the secret of his hold over his audience. They could see the sensation strike and form; he could lay bare the very moment of perception. So with pauses and spurts the world of spiritual reality emerged in slide after slide—in Poussin, in Chardin, in Rembrandt, in Cézanne—in its uplands and its lowlands, all connected, all somehow made whole and entire, upon the great screen in the Queen's Hall."[8] This quality—a desire to reach a "spiritual reality," a spontaneous self-correcting—stayed with Fry all his life, not only while spending many hours addressing extension students, but also as he came more and more to see his vocation as one that involved teaching the broadest possible English public.

The transition from the cloistered atmosphere of Cambridge to the more open world of a modern mass urbanized society can be tracked in Fry's case by one of the earliest essays he published, this in the undergraduate journal *Granta*. Though founded in 1889, a year after Fry left Cambridge, the magazine had editors who reached out to their recently departed classmate. They meant to enlist his aid in attacking one Oscar Browning, the butt of many jokes because of his inflated ego and arch manner, who had tried to steal the thunder of *Granta* with a rival journal that he was planning to edit. Nathaniel Wedd, a friend of both Fry and Dickinson and a fellow Apostle, would play a key role in the episode by opposing and publicly mocking Browning.[9] Wedd used the pages of the recently established *Granta* to publish a series of four articles called "What Men Do When They Go Down" (i.e., graduate), and Fry wrote the third in the series, entitled, "III- Art." Keen to have Fry stir things up with his contribution, Wedd urged his fellow Apostle to make the article "grotesque & don't mind distorting facts." Behind Wedd's iconoclasm were not only a dispute between him and Browning, but all the over-plotted outrages against decorum favored by typical undergraduates. Fry was happy to join in, and sent along an account of his recent days in London that Wedd pronounced as "*distinctly* smart."[10]

Fry's essay opens a window onto his early ambitions and makes it clear just how thoroughly resolved he was to pursue a career as a painter and to leave the sciences behind. "That the English are a nation of Philistines and that we live in an age of commercialism are commonplaces and the stock-in-trade of the lowest evening papers. But art is not dead—there are twelve thousand artists in London alone." Having introduced a note of hyperbole, Fry allows himself a bit of waggishness. "Why, I doubt if there were twelve thousand artists in Italy in the fifteenth century. Think of the pressure of genius to the square mile in London!" He then turns to the testament of experience. "These facts seemed sufficiently encouraging to induce me, after leaving Cambridge, to become the twelve-thousand-and-first artist in London. I accordingly investigated the various schools of art." Two things stand out here: first, that Fry seems almost resigned to the commercialism of society persisting in its negative effect on art, and second, the scope and function of artistic training remains the way to infer the esthetic health of the metropolis. Art's place in society would be a site of contestation.

What follows, however, is less a serious analysis than a collegiate romp through a number of various satirical portraits. After contrasting the main art schools, in Paris (which he had not yet visited), London (the Royal Academy School, where the "authorities . . . pursue the method of exhaustion"), and Chicago (also not visited, but presented as buffoonishly provincial), Fry focuses on his contemporary situation. Here, leaving his choice of art school unnamed, he tauntingly finds some grounds for satisfaction, if not high praise: "But in one thing this new school resembles unavoidably the pre-Raphaelites of the last generation. It, too, is hated of the Academy. It contains the youthful enthusiasm of the rising generation, and receives quite the usual share of snubbing from the effete cynics of the last. But perhaps it will soon be unsafe to scoff at them. Let us make the most of the present opportunity." Fry's dedication to helping the "rising generation" rests in part on his own ambitions, while affirming the value of innovation, even allowing an oppositional role for culture, if only to counter the "snubbing" of the elders.

Then in conclusion Fry gives his waggishness full play as he decides that all the alternatives must be rejected in favor of a truly radical—but historically, or dialectically sanctioned—individualized pursuit. He playfully leaves behind any meaning of "school" as an art school, and refers instead to a school of painting, not one he might attend as a student, but one he "founded" as an artist. "I accordingly founded a new school. It was an impressive ceremony. I had some difficulty in finding a name, but I bethought me of the

Hegelian dialectic (no household should be without one), and called it the Impressionist-Pre-Raphaelite School. It consists, up to the time of going to press, of one member; but the strength of a school does not lie in its numbers. Its productions have not yet galvanized the art world; but that is not to be wondered at, because they have not been produced. But time will show." There is more than a bit of historical irony here, as Fry's later reputation will be built to a large extent on his naming and canonizing a new school, the Post-Impressionists, in a way that at once heroicized their innovatory skills and combined with their historical self-awareness. But his postgraduate brio drove the humor of his essay even as he gently mocked his own ambitions.

The years at Cambridge and the friendships he formed there gave Fry a full sentimental education. What he constructed as another demanding level of education resulted, over the following decade or so, from his becoming an expert in art history, one who, within two decades, earned a national reputation. This expertise developed at the same time that the young man worked hard to establish himself as a professional painter. His work on his lectures to his extension students counted importantly toward an increase in expert knowledge, while lecturing led him to confront the difficulties of putting into words the esthetic experience his education had suggested could not be verbalized. At least not readily so. The combination of his efforts to be an established painter while learning about the history of art and teaching it to a broad audience suited Fry's temperament. He was at once solitary, quite independent in his thinking, and not at all reluctant to confront authority and popular opinion. At the same time he clearly allowed his idealizing impulses to support a social conscience, not least by continuously presenting high art as a guide to a fuller life.

As for the workaday life Fry pursued after his Cambridge days ended in 1888, it began with his living in his father's house in Broad Walk, near Kensington Gardens. Sir Edward was already a well-known judge by this time, and would slowly reconcile himself to Roger's vocation. Three years after leaving Cambridge, Fry shared lodging in Chelsea with Robert Trevelyan, son of the famous Whig historian George Trevelyan. "Trevy," as the Bloomsbury Group nicknamed Robert, was a poet and translator, and also an Apostle at

Cambridge, and was known among his very wide circle of famous friends as an eccentric. At this time Fry established yeoman skills as a writer about art, bent on preparing his lectures. But it would be a few years before he experienced appearances in print, eventually becoming the art critic for a newspaper called *The Pilot*, and placing reviews and short notices in various journals such as the *Monthly Review* and the *Athenaeum*.[11] Pursuit of a vocation as a self-sustaining practicing artist meanwhile led Fry to an art school that was recognized as progressive—in that it shunned sheer academicism—and at first it barely satisfied Fry's taste, though he had perhaps chosen it in a compromise with his father.

Located in Hammersmith, the school was run by H. Francis Bate, himself a very reputable traditional painter, mostly working in landscape. Bate enjoyed his many honors and exhibited in a wide array of galleries such as the Grosvenor and the Royal Society of British Artists. Well established by the late 1880s, Bate wrote a book, *The Naturalistic School of Painting*, that went through two editions. At the end of 1889 Fry wrote to Dickinson to record his first, qualifiedly positive impressions of his new teacher: "I've just finished my first day's work with Bate—it was quite as dull as I expected but not more so, and I think he teaches well—he has ideas—he teaches you more how to analyze your impressions than how to move your pencil," and then added, "this seems to me the right way to begin."[12] As much as Fry may have learned from Bate, he remained committed to a more adventurous approach. In the last decade of the nineteenth century, as far as painting went, such an approach would lead inexorably to Paris.

In 1891 Fry set off for what Walter Benjamin called the capital of the nineteenth century. The trip to Paris would be the first of many sojourns in France, and this one also included peregrinations throughout Italy, where he was rather horrified at the hygiene but impressed with the art, especially that of Raphael. His hours of daily sketching matched the time spent traveling. His esthetic education remained his focus. In Paris, he enrolled in the Académie Julian, the art school most welcoming to foreign students. Founded thirty years earlier, the school would become famous because of the many successful students who attended; in fact, it eventually opened a number of branches around the city, and even challenged tradition by admitting female students. When Fry arrived the group of students then among the most prominent were the Nabis, who counted Pierre Bonnard, Maurice Denis (whose essay on Cézanne Fry would later translate and publish), and Edouard Vuillard among their bellwethers. These painters had already accepted many of the standards of the generation beyond the early Impressionists, and so could be regarded in the line of development that led to Fauvism and Cubism. Many features of modernism—such as a bold palette, the use of lithography and other non-easel media, and a concentration on a design sense indebted to Art Nouveau and Japonism—led the Nabis to be prized as daring innovators. At least for a time. By the middle of the twentieth century most critics regarded them as conservative. Fry absorbed very little of their concerns and stylistic techniques, and more importantly, according to Alfred Werner, he failed to see any works by Cézanne.[13]

Sooner or later, however, Fry had to return to England and continue working toward some commercial success as a painter. This was dictated not only by his own ambition, of course, but an unfailing need to demonstrate to his father that he was both serious and more than competent. Spelling out a long firm argument, Fry attempted to convince Sir Edward that recurrent travel abroad in pursuit of special advanced skills was not a frivolous matter, indeed it was "solid hard work all the time."[14] Fry turned up the rhetorical heat by appealing to his father's own professional identity. "To stay at home permanently and work up connexions would be as though you, when a barrister, had thrown aside your law books and devoted yourself to nursing solicitors, and you know how short-lived and unsatisfactory is a reputation that is supported by such means." He added a pragmatic reason to the argument, pointing out that such travel made him a better-qualified and better-paid lecturer, and so in one system of accounting the trips paid for themselves.

Throughout the 1890s, Fry dedicated his time to learning about Renaissance art, learning how to draw, lecturing on art history, and continuing to attempt to demonstrate his professional accomplishments to his family, especially his father. The milieu he entered was one shaped by various interests and groups. Fry was familiar with them all. Speaking comprehensively, one critic put it this way: "in the long nineteenth century the art market was in fact a multi-actor network: a tapestry of intricate interdependencies between artists, dealers, critics, collectors, patrons, institutions, and the public, relationships which were increasingly mediated and then significantly transformed by the press as the nineteenth century progressed."[15] Fry's considerable energy was devoted to increasing his expertise in virtually all of these areas. During several trips to Europe he was occupied with visiting the annual French Salon (generally coming away unimpressed), spending time in Italy and working, for example, at a very detailed level in the Uffizi to form his ideas about identifiable styles, his rankings of historical and artistic worth, and the complexities of schools and influences, and occasionally meeting other tourists. In Florence, for example, in the summer of 1891 he met John Addington Symonds, the poet, literary critic, and collector of pornography, and Frederic Cope Whitehouse, an American engineer known for his discovery of an elaborate ancient water system in the Nile basin. Polished as his manners were, and increasingly less shy, Fry nevertheless spent most of his time in London, where the basis of his vocation lay. Social acceptance and economic independence would never be easy to achieve, but he was diligent and committed to becoming a practicing artist. As he had earlier quipped, there were twelve thousand artists in London, and he aimed to become the twelve-thousandth-and-one.

In 1885 a new institution had appeared on the London scene with the establishment of the New English Art Club (NEAC). Meant to be a strong and progressive alternative to the Royal Academy, complete with juried exhibitions, the club featured many prominent artists, such as John Singer Sargent, James Abbott McNeill Whistler, and Walter Sickert. Sickert especially drew Fry's attention, and he identified Sickert as the main power at the club. During a visit by Sickert to Fry's studio, he remarked that he felt he had at first underestimated Fry's work and was now more impressed.[16] This was in 1894. Reporting this positive appraisal to his father, Fry added, "it is the opinion of one's fellow artists that tells in the long run."[17] However, only six months earlier he had written to his father that "I have grown cautious of saying I am *going* to exhibit anywhere, for I thought these [submitted paintings] were safe for the N.E.A.C." In the same letter he avowed, "I still think it the best place to exhibit in England,"[18] adding that Bate agreed with this evaluation.

One exception to Fry's frequent frustrations at being rejected by galleries and exhibitions came about in 1894, when he painted Edward Carpenter, poet, socialist, gay activist, and one of the founders of the Fabian Society. Fry had been drawn to socialist thought, or at least strongly left-wing politics, while at Cambridge, largely through meeting people like George Bernard Shaw and Carpenter himself. Fry's striking rendition of Carpenter shows a very worldly man, posed in a nondescript room with a full-length mirror behind him. The mirror generates depth, and Carpenter's pose, standing with hands in his overcoat pockets, slightly twisted back to his right, suggests a measure of impatience, hauteur, and even defiance, as his gaze is off to the viewer's left and just slightly elevated. Fry eagerly reported to his mother that he had begun the portrait and referred, teasingly, to Carpenter's "very anarchist overcoat." Fry stops short of heroicizing Carpenter, but he vividly conveys his sense that the political activist was driven by high purpose. The picture enjoyed success in many quarters, and eventually was placed in the National Portrait Gallery in London.[19]

Several accounts of Fry's life and career describe him as beginning to write articles about art in 1892. This view was probably fostered by Woolf's biography, where she referred to a sheaf of articles that were from the pen of Fry.[20] But diligent research by Fry's bibliographer, Donald A. Laing, demonstrates that in fact between 1893 and 1899 Fry published nothing about art or art history. It was not until 1900 that he began writing steadily for *The Pilot*, and his first article for the *Athenaeum* appeared in 1901.[21] Fry's high reputation is sometimes explained by the claim that his art writing was deeply informed by his own practice as a painter. On the other hand, however, there are few direct links between his paintings and his expertise in art history and analysis. The decade of the 1890s was full of his efforts to make a career for himself as a painter. It may also be filled with his deep study of the visual arts as a field demanding historical insight and analytic rigor. In any case, though he continued diligently to labor at his easel, his gifts were to be more and more concentrated on his writings about art.

Fry's writings for *The Pilot* and the *Athenaeum* form an extensive record of looking and thinking about art across a wide range of periods, styles, media, and techniques. Laing's bibliography has been slightly corrected to support the claim that in the six years following 1900 Fry contributed almost 500 separate pieces. Most of these were short reviews, running to about 2,000 words on average, along with a few longer essays.[22] The dutiful criticism Fry offered in these two outlets resembled that of an increasingly broader and more informed art journalism that had grown up in the late Victorian era. Coming as it did out of his extension lectures, Fry's art writing was aimed at the educated middle class, and it pursued with some rigor the ideas that would eventually form his major theory, "aesthetic formalism." This theory involved concentrating on a detailed looking at features that separated art from anecdotal subject matter or the standards of verisimilitude. Fry's practice as an art writer favored the stance of Sidney Colvin, the Slade Professor of Fine Art at Cambridge and the director of the Fitzwilliam Museum there. Colvin focused on what was intrinsic to a single painting, say, rather than pursuing the mode of John Ruskin's esthetics, which favored a rhapsodic connection to a matrix of the larger cultural values. Equally important as his affinity with Colvin, however, was Fry's habit of intensive and protracted looking, for he repeated countless times thereafter that his intention as an art critic was to focus on what he would come to call "aesthetic emotion." This could only be experienced when in the presence of the art object, in a way that both the object and the viewer were detached from the dailiness of routinized looking.

## FRY'S TURN TOWARD THEORY

Not long after the turn of the century, Fry published an intriguing essay that contains some of his earliest reflections and theorizing about high art and, moreover, shows him working with themes that would reappear often in his later writings. "Art and Religion" assembles a short argument with lengthy consequences.[23] It begins with Fry reversing the usual perspective: instead of asking how religion views art, he wants to consider how art views religion. Only an ideal world is acceptable as a focus for the fine arts, so religion can indeed supply the material. This doesn't mean, however, that religion continues to operate at an idealized level. To the contrary, the church's need for art produces "a straight-forward well organized trade," if only because the church has large appetites and widespread needs. This contrasts pointedly with modern art, which is made in order to fill up exhibitions, to please a public, not rich patrons. Where the church restricts its appropriate subjects and confines the artist's imagination, modern art allows for virtually limitless subject matter and themes. But in any case, what the artists must do is explore the natural world up to "its furthest point," where it impinges on the supernatural. Here Fry sounds like the prototypical Romantic artist whom he often criticizes, claiming that it is impossible for "artists to understand the natural without reference to the supernatural."

Speaking, as he often did, with the tacit authority of a practicing artist, Fry turns to the question of subject matter. Here he again gives the nod to the traditions of religious painting, especially in the fifteenth century. The Bible contains a wealth of stories, and some—such as the Annunciation—lend themselves to obvious structural patterns, as the angel and the Virgin Mary can be shown together in different alignments and expressing differing states of mind. Additionally, the Renaissance incorporated variations on pagan mythology, utilizing allegorical traditions, so that, for example, Venus could be seen by Botticelli as symbolizing a version of pantheism, which the church otherwise overruled as heretical. But with this welter of stories and personages both biblical and classical, Christian art was able to become fully dramatic.

Fry here tends in a rhapsodic direction, invoking Giotto's spirit, borrowed, in Fry's version, from that of St. Francis of Assisi. Then, in a rather startling coda, Fry launches into a jeremiad against the contemporary art found in English churches, which he regards as deplorably vulgar and uninspired. Pushing further, he suggests that he himself could lean in a spiritual direction if somehow the church and contemporary artists could rediscover the symbiotic relationship that art and religion enjoyed in the Renaissance, and bring truth to people in a manner that would delight and instruct. But even as he formulates this clearly counterfactual and un-historicist speculation, he catches himself, and ends on a thoroughly negative note, realizing how remote is any such possibility. "If to clothe the abstract truth in exoteric symbols means to lose sight of the truth itself, then we must be content to go on in the sordid and revoltingly ugly surroundings which are the distinguishing characteristics of the past hundred years of our civilization." Like other clear-eyed modernists, Fry accepted the Enlightenment legacy of a thoroughly secular approach to truth, even at the cost of a measure of disenchantment. Mass urbanized society, resting smugly on its industrialized basis, offered little magic by way of a commitment to the esthetic realm.

But there lingers in this essay a sense that Fry could fully appreciate the approach Ruskin took to art, namely that it was always tied to the moral dimensions of experience and was valuable only to the extent that it kept other spiritual values forcefully alive in social relations. Fry, by now no longer an active believer in organized religion, was continuing to thrash out the issues that he had raised in that letter to his roommate Ashbee a dozen or more years earlier. Those long evenings of philosophical discussion and debate with Ashbee, Dickinson, and his other Cambridge friends had raised the issues of art, morality, and religion in a way that left definitive answers even harder to grasp, while the problems now again announced themselves in the paintings of fourteenth- and fifteenth-century Italians.

Fry would transform his many hours of looking at Italian paintings during the 1890s into a firm expertise that grew only sharper and more contestatory in the first years of the twentieth century. This transformation took place in a significant way under the shadow—and the tutelage—of Bernard Berenson. He and Fry came to be quite close for a relatively brief period, sharing an energized friendship that was based on the deep interests they shared, though often troubled by disagreements and competitive feelings. They knew several people in common, perhaps most importantly Robert Trevelyan, with whom Berenson occasionally traveled throughout Europe.[24] "Trevy" may have been the person who introduced them, for he had shared rooms with Fry after their time in university, and had come to know Berenson through the latter's visits to London and Cambridge. By this time—the late 1890s—Berenson had already been acting for several years as the advisor to Isabella Stewart Gardner in her pursuit of Italian paintings to fulfill her plans for a personal museum. This particular activity on Berenson's part was in effect the beginning of a practice of using connoisseurship to foster commercial interests, as Gardner remained intent on spending large amounts of money on acquiring only masterpieces accredited by experts. Many others, especially American millionaires, followed in her style. Thus Berenson could support himself as an artistic consultant by the enjoyment of commissions on those paintings he located and arranged for Gardner to buy. Fry himself soon became adept at the same blending of connoisseurship and commercial savoir faire.

It was in 1890 that Berenson had met the man who was crucial to the early development of connoisseurship, Giovanni Morelli, a doctor turned art historian, who was then over seventy years old.[25] For the previous fifteen years, drawing in some ways on his scientific and medical training, with its eye on the telling and symptomatic fact, he had used what he called the "hand" to identify artists and attribute their paintings, largely on the basis of distinctive details. Himself strongly anti-academic, Morelli was able through his studies to influence not only Berenson but also many other art historians of the time. His genuine skills carried an aura of scientific accuracy, but his method was met with considerable skepticism and charges of subjectivism, despite resting on claims of objective assessment.

Morelli, however, fully earned a reputation for himself as extremely argumentative, and while not alone in displaying in his work rather uncharitable attributes, to say the least, he gave to the field of connoisseurship at the turn of the century a tone of sharp combativeness.[26] Fry occasionally suffered from this tone, but in the pursuit of careful estimations, for he felt that in public one should be both more tempered and more skeptical than a scholar like Morelli. In 1904 Fry attempted to mediate between Morelli and other experts, maintaining an avowed balance in his allegiance to both Morelli's methods and those of a pair of scholars very well known for their expertise in Italian painting, Joseph Crowe and Giovanni Cavalcaselle. Their popular two-volume study, *A History of Painting in North Italy*, of 1871, was especially valued by English readers and tourists, but in it the authors disdained Morelli's work, and he returned the favor.

The publishers of the book trustingly approached Fry in 1904 to edit an updated version, but when Crowe's widow heard of the publishers' choice, she protested vehemently, keenly aware of the intense rivalry between Crowe and Morelli (and their respective supporters). She was convinced that Fry was a "partisan" of the Morelli approach, and so was likely to distort and discredit her husband's accomplishments. Fry wrote plaintively to Mrs. Crowe's son to set the record straight. "I confess I am astonished at the entirely mistaken notion that I belong to any camp which could profess antagonism or disrespect to Crowe and Cavalcaselle's work," Fry protested. He claimed to "have studiously avoided any ground for imputation that I belong to any camp. I hate the whole business of politics in matters where the love of truth should be the only object." Feeling that "anyone who instead of listening to partisan statements had studied what I have written would be forced to admit that I have never been a partisan."[27] Despite his protestations, most of which stressed his belief in balance and judiciousness in claiming final judgments, Fry was rejected as the editor, resulting in a loss of remuneration that he sorely needed at the time.

By late 1901 Fry, somewhat in the dual role of acolyte and close friend, was writing long, detailed letters to Berenson, discussing Italian painting and attributions and chronologies that were being researched by several experts, all of whom both men knew and held firm opinions of concerning the validity of their expertise. In 1902 Fry painted a wedding tray—he referred to it as a *desco da Sposalizio*—to celebrate the wedding of Berenson and his wife, Mary. An accomplished art historian in her own right, Mary, recently widowed, married Berenson in 1900 in the chapel at their home in Florence, Villa I Tatti. Berenson and Fry sharpened each other's axes when it came to judging other art historians. Fry, for example, expounded contemptuously when telling Berenson about a recently published volume by James M. Hoppin, a professor at Yale: "He's no conception of one thing being more important than another, of any standard or relation. He's equally interested in everything that has been said or can be said. It's the queerest mixture of childish in-

*Bernard Berenson (1865–1959) had a troubled relationship with Fry,
as the two men competed in the development of their connoisseurship.*

competence and senile decay without a spark of feeling or perception and yet he's well read, deucedly so, only it's made no difference
to his native incapacity to understanding anything. Of such, I suppose is the new Kingdom of Heaven they are preparing."[28] Fry apparently felt unsteady enough in Berenson's eyes that he had to display his high, indeed sometimes blinkered, standards of judgment in
order to be taken seriously, at least in the privacy of their correspondence. A more benign approach to Fry's rhetoric would stress that
the new methodology of verification was still proceeding in an infant
stage and so polemics were unavoidable.

Typical prickly exchanges between experts took place, of course,
even before Berenson became fully acknowledged throughout the

world as a leading expert, especially by the world of billionaire art collectors.[29] Writing to his friend Trevelyan, Fry corrected an impression that his estimation of Berenson was negative. "I have always rather believed in him," Fry wrote, using the "rather" as a way to hedge his opinion. At this point, however, in 1898, Berenson, born a year and a half before Fry, had produced work much more copious and substantial than Fry's, as far as connoisseurship went. Berenson had recently published his *Florentine Painters of the Renaissance* (1896) and was well on his way to becoming recognized. It was preceded by a similar study on Venetian painters, and followed by one on Central Italian painters. His innovative monograph *Lorenzo Lotto: An Essay in Constructive Criticism*, which appeared in 1895, served as an early model for the monographic study of single artists. In 1903 came the monumental three-volume *The Drawings of the Florentine Painters*, generally considered his masterwork.

Later in the same letter to Trevelyan, Fry opined more securely: "What is wanted now in the way of criticism is someone who will make appreciations as finely and imaginatively conceived and take them into greater detail as well. Perhaps Berenson will get to this if he gets over his theories." In the next two decades Berenson's "theories" would, according to some, virtually establish the field of attribution and its relationship to art history and esthetics.[30] Fry's stance here, however, contains an implicit opinion that connoisseurship needs more than an empirical basis, and only by relying on opinions "finely and imaginatively conceived" can the expert arrive at his special vantage point. In an important sense, what Berenson and Fry held as believers in the rightness of connoisseurship was not at all the same. For Fry it was a cognitive faculty that operated behind every emotional esthetic experience (deeply felt and hard to define) and always allowing for error and correction. For Berenson it was a faculty long in development, prized in its rarity, unassailable in its rectitude (warranted by the expert's reputation), and ultimately based on a complex sense of the artist's identity and personality.

The intellectual debt that Fry owed to Berenson became evident when Fry published his monograph, *Giovanni Bellini*, in 1899. In the preface Fry recorded "with great pleasure my indebtedness to

Mr. Bernard Berenson for his generous encouragement and learned advice at the outset of this undertaking." Shortly after the first appearance, the slim volume went through two more editions.[31] At the time Giovanni Bellini did not enjoy the overwhelming prestige that would eventually attach to his name. But the attributions of his paintings stood on relatively firm ground, and the development of his skills and conceptual brilliance stood out among Venetian Renaissance masters. Fry could rest easy on the first score, and he demonstrated his sharp insights into the latter. Indeed, Fry's study of Bellini is noteworthy for its sturdy learning and its deft analysis. Fry begins by sketching the culture and social history of Venice, before going on to a discussion of Bellini's father, Jacopo. The father brought to his work the influence of painters from Padua, such as Pisanello, and along with his other son, Gentile, played a notable role in the official court art of Venice. But Jacopo's work concentrated on naturalistic details and was somewhat limited in its incorporation of classical ideals. Giovanni's art changed all that, and Fry stresses the artist's control of emotions and empathetic imagination to distinguish what he accounts as a much superior accomplishment.

The study then goes through, decade by decade, the paintings that made Bellini famous and influential among the artists of Venetian distinction, anticipating the high level of Titian and other later masters. Sometimes it is the general quality that takes Fry's attention. Though contending that "it is no doubt rash to argue from the artistic temperament to the temperament of real life," Fry praises Bellini's early works in which "the feelings of pity and love are expressed with such frequency and such intimate intensity, as to make any other construction of his character impossible." (The caution against directly linking life and art may be aimed covertly at Berenson.) Sometimes Fry introduces a purely technical point, as when he explains how the use of oil pigments over tempera allows Bellini to create an atmospheric effect, a technique borrowed from Antonello da Messina, but brought to perfection by Bellini.[32] There are also moments where Fry employs a poetic strain to convey Bellini's skill in painting landscapes: how "surprising is the way in which the eye is led down the valley to free spaces of luminous air, of sunlit sea and hill." Most impressive of all, Fry's medley of contexts, points of interest and varied methodologies constitute a convincing overview and a lastingly valuable piece of art criticism.

Fry also corresponded in the early years of the century with Berenson's wife, whom he addressed as Mariechen, using her familiar nickname. In fact, beginning in 1904 Berenson declined to correspond with Fry, leaving all such matters to Mary. This rebuff resulted from a dispute about an article that Fry and Berenson had planned to publish together. Fry proposed shaping Berenson's source notes for the article in a way that displeased Berenson, for Fry invoked the expertise of Herbert Horne, a largely self-taught scholar in Italian Renaissance painting. Horne's deep expertise made him a crucial figure in the relationship between Fry and Berenson, serving to triangulate the envy and suspicions that eventually arose among the three men. It seemed that Berenson felt more challenged by Horne than by Fry, but in any case, much confusion resulted.[33] The relationship between Fry and Berenson could henceforth never be considered fraternal, and much later in his life Berenson continued to record in his journals negative feelings toward Fry.[34]

Fry nevertheless proceeded with his correspondence with Mary as if he rated her expertise as equal to that of her husband, but later told people that she was merely an echo chamber for her husband's imperious opinions. But the business of connoisseurship was like a game played for nearly mortal stakes. Another example of how such business was conducted exists as a postscript in a letter from Fry to Mariechen in March 1903.[35] At stake was whether a painting, then owned by John Stogdon of Middlesex, was by Lorenzo di Credi or Piero di Cosimo. Fry rather abruptly inserted himself into the dispute because he had discovered a tondo in a dealer's shop and felt sure that it was by Piero "all over," though from an early period, in fact "a schoolpiece." Fry wanted to announce his discovery, which would help substantiate Berenson's conclusion, with a note in the *Burlington Magazine*. Fry hesitated to publicize his opinion so widely, however, since first Mary would have to approve, so as to ensure that Berenson would not be "rob[bed] . . . of his discovery." Fry readily assumed Berenson would agree with his attribution of the work to Piero, even as he was solicitous of Berenson's vanity. Ironically, though Berenson came to make the attribution to Piero, the painting was eventually credited by Berenson to Tommaso. For John Stogdon, the matter concerned his wealth; for Berenson, his reputation and pride; for Fry, his need to embellish and solidify his credentials.

All in all, from the last years of the nineteenth century to the early days of the twentieth, Fry and Berenson were colleagues—if not pacific equals in expertise—who were defining connoisseurship in ways that would continue down to the present. A unique set of skills, partly forensic, partly subjective, could be gained only by innumerable visits to museums, galleries, and dealers; with an erratic mixture of elements, connoisseurship formed the central part of this new field of academic art history. Here Berenson obviously had the advantage on Fry, since Fry had spent hours lecturing and pursuing his own painting, whereas Berenson had traveled more extensively and over a longer period of time, unimpeded by any academic chores. Berenson also had what could be called a special advantage because he was acting as an agent who negotiated the acquisition of important paintings, usually held by gallery owners and sought after by wealthy collectors, often American millionaires. The dominant example of this was Berenson's efforts on behalf of Isabella Stewart Gardner's collection, which would eventually be housed at her personal museum in Boston. Fry, too, acted as an agent for buyers, and so needed to be generally accredited with deciding correctly on the attributions of paintings that were often four centuries old.

As connoisseurs, Fry and Berenson could not avoid being competitive, because considerable sources of income were at stake; however, as scholars and historians of art, they needed to rely on one another to some extent. Fry was able to maintain at least a sense of disinterest when it came to Berenson's rising reputation as a scholar, a reputation built in large measure on the publication in 1903 of *The Drawings of the Florentine Painters*. Berenson's biographer suggests strongly that Berenson's "nervous irritability" was aggravated by Fry's review, which appeared in two parts in the *Athenaeum* in November and December of the same year.[36] Fry called the book a "monument" and said its very conception—using drawings as a special lens for refining points of attribution and historical import—marked it with a "certain greatness." At the same time, Fry clearly was occupied with striking the right balance of praise and demurral. The conclusion of the review demonstrates this unmistakably: "One is charmed, amazed, indignant, irritated by turns, but boredom or a mere sleepy acquiescence is out of the question." Fry's inbred skepticism seldom acquiesced completely.

In 1907 Berenson published another important study, *North Italian Painters*, and again Fry reviewed it, in 1908, in the *Burlington Magazine*. Fry began in the complimentary mode: "To have visited so many galleries in all parts of the world and to have kept track of even unimportant pictures in their many wanderings through salerooms implies an energy and method for which the student of Italian art must ever remain gratefully indebted." Then there followed the tail with the mild sting: "And if, as we are sometimes inclined to think, Mr. Berenson with his love of order and constructive design errs on the side of definite classification where other critics might be inclined to leave a picture in the limbo of anonymity, even this is an error which makes on the whole for knowledge."[37]

Fry's skill in balancing his judgments with praise and fault-finding here controls the overall view, enacting a modulated skepticism even as he chides the absence of it in Berenson's rather imperious method. Berenson's penchant for erecting too large a historical and stylistic scaffold told against him in Fry's view. For example, he complains that Berenson "has tried to find some kind of formula which may be applied uniformly to the artists of North Italy as he applied the formula of 'tactile values' to the Florentines and 'space composition' to the Central Italians." Fry makes it explicit when he adds that Berenson's "endeavour to keep constantly in view this general formula has, we think, led to a certain amount of distortion and exaggeration." Part of what Fry was holding out for, so to speak, was that sense of an esthetic experience which, though it might be refined by a nearly scientific weighing of countless comparisons, finally could only be shaped by its singularity.

There should have been no surprise to Berenson when he read Fry's review, though there was likely very little good cheer. Five years earlier, in 1903, Fry had written to Mary explaining in some detail, and with a touch of self-justification, how he navigated the question of his own expertise, pointing out that because few in England had the level of expertise he did, he was often pushed forward and made to come up with shaky attributions that "B.B. would settle definitely."[38] The same letter contains Fry's honest self-evaluation while also staking his claim to address Berenson's work in a direct way, saying he knew that Berenson realized that "I differ respectfully and not dogmatically." The prickliness of Berenson would hardly vanish before such a claim, however, so Fry continued. He felt that "such differences should be tolerated and even welcomed, for it is what helps, in so far as it is intelligent, to keep the subject alive." He also felt strongly that one should provide for "keep[ing] a subject from getting isolated from the general current of educated opinion." This separated him, temperamentally and intellectually, from Berenson, and it marked a key aspect of his character and his work. Tonally the letter remains gracious, but firm. Near the end of it Fry even suggests that he and Berenson collaborate on an article about an important collection of paintings owned by Sir Hubert Parry that was eventually part of a bequest to the Courtauld Gallery. In the end Fry wrote the article himself and published it in the *Burlington Magazine*. He wrote to Mary, however, before it appeared to explain just how he had mentioned and credited Berenson's various attributions, and asked for "charity" in any criticism of the piece, which he averred did not "go as deep as B.B.'s" would have.

However, Fry did not always remain as loyal to Berenson, and to his methods, as when he began.[39] A quarter century later, Fry had the occasion to review yet another book by Berenson, in which this time the connoisseur sought to justify what he had done to professionalize the field. Fry creates the illusion of detachment as he relates how Berenson describes his method: "He represents this [process] as the application of a scientific method in which, by consideration of details of architecture, costume, pose and facial type, he gradually tracks the picture in question to its place and date of origin. He then considers in turn the authors which those indications render available and chooses finally the author whose name was to be discovered." The passive voice in the passage's final phrase connotes an air of inevitability. Then, however, Fry slowly peels away some of the honorific gloss of the word "scientific." Claiming there was nothing new in the method, Fry added specifics: "All attributors have made appeal to details of architecture, costume, etc., to substantiate their guesses or demolish those of their rivals. What Mr. Berenson gives us is a far more imposing array of comparisons, based on special details; and he represents the chase for the author as being so elaborate that in this particular case we have to go through fifty pages of argument before we are allowed to do more than say that the pictures in question are Veronese and painted between 1480 and 1490. Then and only then may we mention the name of Domenico Morone which, to tell the truth, Mr. Berenson must have arrived at long before a tenth part of these facts had been clear to his mind."[40]

As this review proceeds, empirical study remains the focus, yet Fry, having raised the specter of Berenson's well-stocked mind, turns the screw gently, suggesting that the subjective "facts" are equally present, albeit not fully addressed. Berenson has recounted how he examined one picture in particular, and Fry continues by offering a gloss: "For some reason, which is not apparent, the author seems to have an almost personal objection to the picture. His mere choice of words in describing it betrays this. Mr. Berenson frequently finds a difficulty in preventing his powerful personality from intruding into the spectator's field of vision, and here he seems scarcely to make an effort against that." From Fry's first meeting with Berenson, in the late 1890s, to a time in the mid-1920s when he, Fry, had left the narrow field of connoisseurship, the two men took sharply divergent paths, which led to quite different audiences. They would rely unabashedly on both scientific facts and subjective experience, but the question of the proper use of both realms, and their syncretic force, would separate the two experts.

Arguments with Berenson and others helped hone Fry's ability to express his ideas about art in a distinctive way. His professionalization as a writer in the first decade of the twentieth century led him to the practice of producing voluminous amounts of art criticism out of financial necessity, of course, and it was also likely spurred by his recognition that his reputation as a painter was not steeply ascendant. The *Pilot* and the *Athenaeum*, his main outlets, published large numbers of "notices" of exhibits, book reviews, disputes about attributions, and somewhat academic studies (such as his monograph on Giotto), many running to little more than 2,000 words.[41] There were several formats for such pieces, determined in part by the projected audiences for the differing forms of publication. One critic has divided the range into magazines designed for the academy, for the popular press, and for the art market.[42] Fry's work stood out because he was adept at satisfying each idiom; again, his work as a lecturer increased his fluency. Equally important, these writings—while based to an understandable extent on the reigning esthetic values, categories, and judgments—led him to display and develop his pragmatic and adaptive temperament in fresh new ways.

Fry also frequently resorted to the pages of the *Monthly Review* to display many of his opinions and discoveries in the early years of the twentieth century. Often this meant more short pieces on a range of exhibitions, but occasionally, by working up his lecture notes, a broader range of reflection and analysis became possible. His two articles on Giotto, for example, appeared in the journal in December 1900 and February 1901; based on his lectures, they brought him considerable positive notice. Fry reprinted them later, combining them as one of the essays in his *Vision and Design* (1920). This book, especially in its paperback version, was the first title to bring Fry's work before a larger audience. He gathered together twenty-five articles that demonstrated, among other virtues, the wide range of erudition and taste that would be his trademark as an art critic.

In the reprinted version of the Giotto study, Fry used a footnote to explain that the chief focus of his analysis was Giotto's use of the "dramatic idea," a focus he described as "at variance with the more recent expression of my aesthetic ideas." This referred to his important adoption of the principles of esthetic formalism, beginning around 1910. With this marked shift, and with almost all of Fry's later work, formalism meant an increased interest in pattern, form, and design, while at the same time avoiding any stress on the narrative and ideational aspect of painting, what Fry called the painting's "associated ideas." In the footnote, Fry announces his new view very clearly: "It now seems to me possible by a more searching analysis of our experience in front of a work of art to disentangle our reaction to pure form from our reaction to its implied associated ideas." But the Giotto piece remains remarkably engrossing, combining a keen sketch of broad socio-historical background, a carefully wrought

Cover of the Burlington Magazine: *Fry's role in founding, editing,
and raising money for this serious art journal demanded time and energy
but was a vital part of his education as an expert.*

version of Giotto's development, and a number of sensitively observed details. All this Fry managed while pursuing and celebrating the spiritual element in the painter, as he expressed the qualities of his favorite subjects, the life of Saint Francis of Assisi and the Virgin.

At the same time as the frequency of his periodical publications increased, Fry remained busy with various kinds of public speaking, such as a public lecture series at Cambridge, and talks—he referred to them as "preaching"—for audiences like the Church Crafts League. To this group of clerics and artisans he urged that "the Church must furnish forms for the imaginative life of the people once more," an argument that formed the core of his essay on "Art and Religion." While he sought a wider audience in a mass-market journal such as the *Monthly Review,* he also kept his sights on a more polished and elitist journal, in which he played a major editorial role, namely the *Burlington Magazine*.

In 1902 Fry and others began to plan the founding of the *Burlington Magazine*, hoping to supply the educated British public with an approach to art that was serious, scholarly, and comprehensive. Because it thrived for many years—despite some personal conflicts and rough financial periods—the magazine set a high standard in a way that gratified Fry, even as it drained his energies. One of its many historians has summarized it: "[T]here was one institution with which Fry's association could hardly have been closer or more enduring, and that was THE BURLINGTON MAGAZINE. He was intimately concerned with the plans for the new journal in 1902, he was a hyper-active member of its Consultative Committee from the first issue in March 1903 until his death, he was co-editor from 1909 to 1919, and he almost single-handedly saved the Magazine from financial ruin in 1903-06."[43] The "hyper-active" figure continued as a painter and a lecturer, frequently traveling to Europe, and he increasingly demonstrated how he was able to appreciate, create, and analyze many different kinds of art. The *Burlington* encompassed an ideal place for Fry to hone his expertise and build a more educated art spectatorship at the same time. In its first years it would take up editorial stands on a number of important issues. He was pleased with what he had done, and said so; in March 1911 he told his mother about his feelings toward the *Burlington*: "although it pays me very little it is getting to be a more and more important work and one that I have much at heart."

The magazine drew its strengths from an elite class, and Fry was able to contribute significantly to this outlet for serious art history and criticism because of his understanding of the role of the connoisseur, a role to be justified only if it added to the general store of learning and appreciation. Drawing on his friendship with men whose wealth and social position were greater than his own, Fry won the respect of the backers of the magazine even as he worked very hard to make sure its funding was both sufficient and removed from any attempts to influence the content of the articles and the direction of its editorial policy. Years later, one of the chief backers of the magazine, Sir Charles Holmes, would record Fry's energy and commitment to making the *Burlington* the great success it became. Indeed Holmes suggested that Fry stood at the head of all those who brought the *Burlington* to the highest point of British art criticism, and so avoided the doldrums into which it had lately fallen. "Fry was almost alone in recognizing in that crisis the germ, the chance, of a magazine which should do for English art scholarship what the *Gazette des Beaux Arts* and the *Repertorium* were doing for continental reputation." But equaling the quality of the leading European journals was not the work of a single day. Some people took time to praise him. "To make this ideal a reality," Holmes continued, "was no light matter. For four months, September to December, 1903, Fry was indefatigable in interviewing creditors, liquidators, solicitors, and, of course, the financial vultures who collect round any such promising carcass. Scheme after scheme was weighed and found wanting . . . And all the while Fry was not only struggling with ill-health at home, but was busy begging his friends to advance the capital required for a fresh start."[44] This encomium, offered by Holmes on the occasion of Fry's passing, may have some inflation because it was part of a eulogy, but the detailed record of Fry's daily and strenuous efforts speaks for itself.

Fry's role in the founding of the magazine makes him the obvious choice to have been the author of the unsigned "Editorial Article" in the inaugural issue. (We can only surmise, since the archives of the internal correspondence at the *Burlington*, from the early 1920s and earlier, no longer exist.) This was one of the earliest public occasions where Fry considered the relationship between commerce and art. Fry's sensibility projects through the discussion of how wealthy collectors honor a noble instinct, but one that can readily be corrupted, since "the desire to collect in the abstract—the mere collecting for the sake of collecting—is one of the crudest of instincts." Fry was strongly of the opinion that "this crude form is even worse than purposeless; it makes in the opposite direction to the finest appreciation of works of art, since the pleasures of legal possession come to seem more positive than those of a disinterested appreciation. Further, the evil is aggravated by the possibilities of collecting at one and the same time works of art and money." Though this was written in the pages of an elitist magazine, it was heartfelt. In many ways it derived from the Quaker ethic of Fry's youth. Though buffeted and abraded at times, his social conscience led repeatedly to a continued profession of a deep sense of how the spiritual side of art—which for him came more and more to be felt simply as its esthetic core—must always be present and centrally acknowledged. He went on in the editorial to discuss the workings of commercial values and class structures. "To collectors of this class, rapid alterations in the values attached to particular works are as important as the fluctuations on the Stock Exchange are to the broker." The result of such fluctuations was far from benign: "The atmosphere becomes tainted, and the study itself acquires ill-repute by the presence of these knowing ones, these tipsters of the sale-room. Such we shall discourage, though we may use them so far as they will serve our turn." Fry, however, singled out those he felt supplied the more than saving grace, praising "the collector who is also a sincere amateur, a true lover of the arts, [who] has our whole-hearted sympathy; nor will we forget that some who come merely to collect remain to admire."[45] The gracious closing note harmonized with Fry's feelings of propriety, and indicates why so many of his friends thought of him as forthright and honest.

Fry, while editorializing about wealth and art, found time to inaugurate another heartfelt project. This was his idea to found the National Art Collections Fund, a plan to collectivize the effort and expense of keeping artistic masterpieces in England. It began with considerable momentum in early 1903, but it, too, produced its own string of conflicts. Bringing into reality the idea of protecting England's cultural patrimony, rooted in Fry's sense of public education, demanded (like the *Burlington Magazine*) a level of energy that left Fry occasionally exhausted but his friends constantly impressed. Motivated by a belief that government support of museums was woefully low and that English-owned masterpieces frequently left the country because of the monetary needs of their owners, Fry instituted a charitable plan to draw on contributions that would make funds available for the purchase of high-quality art to be kept and shown in English museums. This plan was consonant with other such efforts to address and resolve a nexus of problems in the English art establishment. These problems not only beset Fry and his contemporaries, but many have persisted until the present day. As one historian identified them in 2003, "The subjects treated [in the press]—the loss of art works to foreign buyers, the need for reform in the national museums, the British government's parsimony to the arts, the mismanagement of the Chantrey Bequest, the National Art-Collections Fund, the role of regional museums, the preservation of buildings—have changed little in a hundred years."[46] The storms of financial distress continued unabated as far as the funding for the *Burlington* went, and Fry's domestic funds were far from overflowing. An unusual opportunity to buy, and then resell at a profit, two unrecognized Giovanni Bellinis (in a deal brokered in part with the help of Berenson), netted a welcome dividend, though he had to borrow from his father to make the purchase in the first place.

The second half of the year 1904 found Fry nearly overwhelmed. He wrote his wife in July that "things are very thick just now, I feel as though it was a very critical moment for me." Just a few weeks earlier his nomination to be the Slade Professor of Fine Art at Cambridge ended in rejection. Fry presumed that the cause for the rejection involved a controversial public appearance he had recently made. At issue was the Chantrey Bequest, administered by members of the Royal Academy, which was intended to support the purchase of works by contemporary English painters for the National Gallery. It originated with the will of Sir Francis Leggatt Chantrey, who died in 1841; however, the funds in the trust were only made available after the death of Chantrey's widow in 1877. Fry had gone before a committee of the House of Lords to testify that the Chantrey funds were not being well used by members of the Royal Academy, as no good paintings by contemporary British artists were being purchased.[47] The committee voted in favor of an inquiry, which would eventually produce some reforms. Fry, though satisfied with his own testimony, yet had enough vitriol to remark on the appearances and implicit attitudes of members of the Royal Academy. Some had appeared as witnesses to defend their actions, and Fry told his friend Trevelyan that they had "come out miserably," and though he had never seen them before, they were "physically mentally and morally on the level of small tradesmen."[48] His dislike of academic art hardly needed seeing academicians in order to intensify. His appearance before the inquiry tested his powers of persuasion, however, and in this instance soon joined his social conscience, and both were put at the service of his commitment to great art. It would not be the last time Fry undertook an action that some—including his father—would consider Quixotic.

Fry proceeded to say in public what he wrote to Trevelyan, and his voice was joined with others in attacking the hidebound and self-serving administrators of the Chantrey Bequest. He used the pages of the *Athenaeum* to rally the art world against what he saw, an inexcusable breach of a public trust. The magazine published a brief note in May 1903, a longer essay in July of the following year, and then a third piece, which was an examination of the report by the committee of the House of Lords that had investigated the matter.[49] In the July essay, Fry built his argument by invoking a long historical context, one that reached back to the Middle Ages and the artistic guilds that had been a prime feature of cultural life for centuries. With this context, he sharpened the contrast between the guilds, and their putatively honest dealing, and the academy with its "pretensions." Fry's judgment was unrelenting: "Though the Academy is the lingering representative of the idea of a guild, it no longer performs its functions, it no longer represents even the average, still less the most scholarly, opinion among artists."

Fry continued attacking, invoking the "Royal" modifier in the group's official title, and claiming that this officially sanctioned organization was "descending as low as its less favored, and therefore more excusable, rivals in the bid for cheap and lucrative popularity." The next essay to appear used its analysis of the committee report to tighten yet more the frame of judgment, declaring that the academy "understands to perfection the supreme power of masterful inactivity." While Fry commended the suggested reform that would create a three-person panel to decide on where the resources should be spent, still it would be better to have one person to make the decisions—such as was the arrangement with the Keeper (curator) of the Tate Gallery—because "compromise is fatal to art." Fry rounded out the argument by insisting that the individualism of the modern artist meant that the predictable actions of a committee, drawn inevitably to weak compromises, would always be a "serious blow to genuine art."

The three articles in the *Athenaeum* were not a mortal wound to Fry's reputation among the privileged classes, but as his increasingly public role repeatedly led him into the issues that made modern art such a contentious subject in England, for many he represented a radical voice. At or near the center of his character and his beliefs lay the paradox of one who was fiercely individualistic and at the same time driven by the urgencies of a public-minded consciousness. In the next three decades he would find—almost without seeking them—several occasions to throw both his private and public values against the windmills of official taste and power.

### HELEN FRY'S ILLNESS

As his experiences, some plotted, some circumstantial, led Fry closer and closer to being a prominent public figure, his personal life was under increasing strain from his wife's recurrent bouts of mental instability. Two years older than Roger, Helen Coombe was born in 1864. While studying art she became a dedicated artisan, working with Arnold Dolmetsch, the famous student of the clavichord. Dolmetsch, a singular figure in popularizing early music, had his workshop in Haslemere, Surrey, and Helen spent time there working on the instruments. She worked very hard at her own studio, deeply drawn to the esthetic of the Arts and Crafts movement and the example of William Morris, along the way bolstering Fry's interest in the same issues.

Roger and Helen married in December 1896, within a year after they met. Almost immediately Helen's health became an issue, however. At first it was trouble with her lungs, briefly treated by a restorative trip together to Italy in 1897. But then she endured a severe bout of depression a year later. This instability became chronic, and increasingly intense periods of her anger and depression made it difficult for Roger to know what should be done. Hospitalization would be followed by periods of relative health, the alternation and length of which were unpredictable. However, the couple had two children, a son, Julian, born in 1901, and Pamela, a daughter, a year later. Margery Fry, Roger's unmarried sister, would eventually take over the

*Roger Fry, with his wife Helen (Coombe): Married only a year after they met in 1895, the Frys shared a high esthetic sense. Helen was afflicted with bouts of mental instability shortly after their wedding. Photograph of Roger Fry and Helen Coombe, c. 1896, photographer unknown. Copyright © Tate, London 2015.*

management of the household as Helen became increasingly incapacitated. By 1910 Helen had to be committed to an asylum, where she remained until her death in 1937. Only then, three years after Roger's death, was it discovered through an autopsy that she had suffered from a condition which had caused her skull to progressively thicken.[50]

Helen's illness threw the domestic life of Fry into near chaos, but it seemed only to have strengthened his love for her, as shown by his very tender letters to her. He seems to have felt that marriage must not become an *égoïsme à deux*, as he told Dickinson, who had once described Helen as "the wittiest woman he had ever known."[51] Trevelyan shared this high opinion, and offered Virginia Woolf a verbal portrait of Helen to be included in her biography of Roger: "It is often so hard to distinguish charm and intelligence from beauty. Her movements were always graceful and unhurried and her way of talking too. She had a beautiful and expressive voice, and a quiet, humorous, often rather satirical smile. I think it was Roger who first put it into my mind that she was like the Spring of Botticelli's Primavera."[52] Trevelyan's portrait idealizes Helen, in part, of course, to compensate for the pain her illness must have caused her and all those close to her. For his part, Roger drew upon his own idealized view of his wife, and also on his Quaker sense of pious duty. During the two and a half decades he lived without her, Fry had a number of intense romantic and sexual involvements with other women, but he chose never to divorce Helen.

Virginia Woolf offered a summary judgment of Fry's relationship with Helen, one that is consonant with her high estimation of his sense of rectitude: "Roger Fry, it can only be said, did all that he could to help his wife; his patience and sympathy were indefatigable, his resourcefulness beyond belief. But her obsessions increased. And finally, when they came back to England in the spring the blow fell. Madness declared itself. 'I was a fool to be happy yesterday,' he wrote to R. C. Trevelyan."

Woolf probably refers here to the time in 1898, when, after the trip to Italy, the full weight of Helen's illness was being felt. Fry wrote to his father in June that "I cannot even now realize what it would mean to me to lose Helen—she has given me a new sense of confidence and hopefulness in life." And six months later he told Trevelyan that "I shall go every day [to see Helen in hospital] unless it seems to excite her too much. It is difficult to keep up a one-sided conversation for three hours; in fact at the end I feel utterly done."[53]

As resourceful as Fry had to be in dealing with his wife's illness, he also needed to consider how to go on earning a living when he had a family to support. The early years of the twentieth century were altogether similar to the ending years of the nineteenth when it came to Fry's income. He continued to be largely dependent on his lecturing fees and the small but numerous payments for the various reviews and essays he continued to publish. His tastes in personal matters were simple, if not altogether Spartan. But he felt the pressure to show his father, and others, that his career was not a ragged, catch-as-catch-can operation. Through all this he continued to work on his own painting; his first solo exhibition took place at the Carfax Gallery in London in 1903. Trips to the Continent stirred his urge to create, and his sentimental education was far from complete. As he told Dickinson, "a place like Rome so bowls me over with its complexity and the insistence of its purely sensuous presentations that I can't get away from it." His commitment to sensuous complexity always operated under the aegis of painted canvases.

As his own knowledge about and experience with oil painting and its European history constantly increased, and as his friends continued to reflect their admiration for his intellectual gifts, he turned more of his attention to the wealth and stability of institutions—museums, chiefly, and also a serious magazine with a broad readership. He was always looking to broaden his capacity for expert knowledge; his trip with Helen to Italy in 1898, for instance, led to his great enthusiasm for the work of Piero della Francesca.[54] So there were lengthy studies that might be written, the opening of new areas of scholarly work to be pursued, and the further development of the two areas where his labors in the next few decades could be concentrated: the study of attributions and art history, and the role of the museum in guiding public betterment through the intense appreciation of esthetic experience.

EVENTUALLY ROGER FRY, IN THE MIDST OF MUCH PERsonal and institutional wrangling, would devote three decades to the *Burlington*, and his changing views of art were often first made public in its pages. However, one key moment in the story of the magazine—and in Fry's life as critic and connoisseur—can be readily summarized.

The years 1904 and 1905 saw Fry working tirelessly on the *Burlington*. Thinking he had been invited to New York on *Burlington* business in January 1906, he was, in fact, "lured to America by a group of influential collectors hoping to install him at the Metropolitan Museum of Art." When he learned the real reason for the invitation, "he did not scruple to use it as a lever to raise further capital for the Magazine" from J. P. Morgan, Henry Clay Frick, J. G. Johnson, Henry Walters, and others. The added benefit, though one that was hardly unmixed with considerable disappointment, came in the form of an offer for "his appointment as curator of paintings at the Metropolitan, which in turn prevented him from becoming Director of the National Gallery in London."[55] One name in this list of multi-millionaire collectors stands above the rest: J. Pierpont Morgan. It was especially through his relationship with Morgan that Fry's views on art were to be challenged and his "ceaseless" work in opening the educated public to great paintings would suffer strong resistance. Meanwhile, his virgin trip to America exposed him to a violent mid-ocean storm and "abject misery" in the waters of the Atlantic. But still more stress awaited him when he debarked.

# CHAPTER III

# THE METROPOLITAN MUSEUM

## *Acquisitions and Expertise*

IN LATE 1904, ROGER FRY WAS BEING CONSID-
ered for a position at the Metropolitan Museum of Art. By early 1905,
he had met J. Pierpont Morgan, who offered him an appointment as
assistant director of the museum. But the relationship between the
two men quickly grew complicated. By 1910, they were no longer involved in any mutual activity. The difficulties in their relationship
grew out of differences in temperament and values, and reflected as
well changes in the institution that served for a while as their common ground. Meanwhile, that institution was itself the arena for extensive and conflicting changes.

Also in 1904, after several decades living abroad in Europe,
Henry James, now sixty, returned to America for a short but intense
visit. After taking a full measure of fresh observations, he wrote *The
American Scene*. In it, he described the Metropolitan Museum's new
commitment, "without regard to cost," to what he called "'Education,' with a capital 'E,'" to denote its nearly deific power, a power
that was going to "seat herself in these marble halls." He knew in his
bones—New Yorker that he was—that the growth of the museum
meant more than an extensive physical alteration. This was James exercising the mode of prophecy. But earlier in the passage about the
change in the museum's status, he recalled its early years, and he
wrote more in the mode of elegy. The embodiment of the museum
he had known thirty or more years earlier had been housed in the
Douglas Mansion at 128 West 14th Street. Now it was in the new

structure alongside Central Park. Out would go all the questionable collections—mainly those brought to the museum by General Cesnola, its first director—and in would come others to replace them, chiefly the gift of a benevolent Mr. Henry G. Marquand, who, with his "rare munificence," provided the template for gifts and bequests for decades to follow. Marquand was, according to one historian of the museum, "without a doubt the most discriminating collector and art patron of his time," namely the last third of the nineteenth century.[1] James saw this new patronage as both loss and gain. The earthshaking change would be viewed by everyone, all those who would come to visit the museum and know they were watching something extraordinary: "the visitor takes in two or three things—first, perhaps the scale on which, in the past, bewildering tribute had flowed in; second, the scale on which it must absolutely now flow out; and third, the presumption created by the vivacity of these two movements for a really fertilizing stir of the ground. . . ." The museum would soon be enlarged by an outlay of wealth that would provide a great many new objects. James commented, drawing attention to the expenditures involved:

> *Acquisition—acquisition if need be on the highest terms—may, during the years to come, bask here as in a climate it has never before enjoyed. There was money in the air, ever so much money . . . And the money was to be all for the most exquisite things—for all the most exquisite things except creation, which was to be off the scene altogether . . . The Museum, in short, was going to be great.*[2]

In the overall curve of the amazing passage, James moves from elegy to prophecy. The museum would in fact become great, though not without a struggle between past and future, in a field of great dramatic and historic developments.

James, by a turn of historic irony, was able to bear witness to profound changes in America—he had been residing in England for more than the past twenty years—just as Morgan and Fry were joining forces. Few of these changes would be more dramatic, more expensively achieved than the Metropolitan Museum's greatest period of expansion. The growth resulted from a dialectical conflict between commerce and art, wealth and beauty. For nearly five years, the conflict could be seen as centered on two men, Morgan and Fry.

Behind the conflict in which Fry and Morgan typified the forces at work, the museum was undergoing a fundamental transformation. The early stages of the museum's identity as a leading cultural institution culminated in a struggle to shape a beneficent balance between and among philanthropic missions on the part of highly wealthy men, civic prestige in the form of esthetic monuments, and educational programs that would justify the political forces that were needed to sustain the museum's funding.[3] The city fathers and the legislators in Albany had built into the charter for the museum a high-minded statement of purpose. This charter, as was typical in American habits of constitutional governance, combined a pliable sense of interdependence between private and public monies.[4] But the interdependence was occasionally unsettled by matters large and small. In 1891, for example, there was a dispute over whether the museum would be open on Sundays. It was the era of the six-day workweek, and Sunday was the day off for the city's large laboring class. The trustees were opposed, as it meant an increase in the attendance by this class. The politicians were in favor, for it justified the expenditures by the city council in the subvention of the museum's yearly budget. This political consideration extended to new pressures to highlight and improve the museum's educational programs, increasingly attended by the lower-class members whose support the museum staff valued.

Indeed, the Sunday opening was a relatively small (but symbolic) issue, and its expenses were borne by funds from the city's tax levies and by private contributions, mainly from philanthropists. This extension of the melded support by private and public sources would in turn inevitably continue to shape the outlook and mission of the museum in many areas. A commitment to working with the city's public schools, in 1905, demonstrated a willingness to think in terms of a large and continuing common weal. In some senses, the museum had to serve two masters. Its first obligation remained to the wealthy citizens whose generosity and cultural taste it embodied. As it grew in size, thanks to the gift by the city of public land for expansion and yearly support for its operating budget, however, it came more and more to resemble a department of civic services. It did not go as far in this direction as some years later did the National Gallery, whose founder, Andrew Mellon, saw his philanthropy in terms different from those of Morgan. Still, the Metropolitan Museum was obliged to combine differing purposes: not only the preservation of valuable and rare masterpieces but also an educational and entertainment function for the entire population of the city that supported it and drew on its cultural prestige.

Managing the museum became exponentially more complex. The decades at the end of the nineteenth and the beginning of the twentieth century at the museum saw a change in the reins of power and authority, as more and more the trustees ceded, often reluctantly, their authority to a professionalized class of managers, art historians, and educators. The difficulties in managing an increasingly large institution were further made burdensome by this division of authority between the philanthropists—whose gifts had largely founded and thoroughly enriched the museum—and this newly professionalized class, from the director down through a phalanx of specializing curators and others, in charge of the physical plant as well as the educational and cultural mission. Trustees were qualified by their wealth and social position; directors and other staff were expected to mold their practices according to the policies approved by the trustees.[5] In a sense, some of these problems were obviated by Morgan's immense fortune, even as they were intensified by his dominance. Roughly, the decade from 1904 until 1913, the year he died, was a period in which Morgan's will sternly expressed itself in virtually all the details of the museum, and in its larger scope and purpose as well. This rather titanic figure, though operating in a collective institution, only too willingly took over at a crucial time with firm leadership, knowing that he was *primus inter pares* among a small class of men of great wealth, most of whom held him in respect, if not awe.


## THE APPEARANCE OF THE EXPERT

In the years leading up to his accepting a position at the Metropolitan Museum of Art, Roger Fry enjoyed an ever-increasing reputation as an art expert, in ways that made him thoroughly qualified for leading a museum. This reputation put him at the forefront of that professional class of staff members who would redefine the social, political, and financial nature of the twentieth-century museum. What marked Fry's off from other reputations, however, was that it grew in at least two different areas. Beginning with his first article, the study of Giotto that appeared in the *Monthly Review* in 1900, up to his annotated edition of *The Discourses of Sir Joshua Reynolds* in 1905, his expertise brought him to the attention of museum directors, dealers in fine arts—especially European masters—and the educated public. Here his renown would begin at least to compare to that of Bernard Berenson, with whom he began to correspond in 1901 about Italian art. Berenson, already well known to American millionaire collectors, typified the highly knowledgeable expert whose ability to authenticate masterworks gave him access to wealth and influence; at his death in 1959 his name was a byword for connoisseurship in the arts. Fry, however, maintained that he didn't mean to set himself up as an expert equal to Berenson, telling Mary Berenson (who handled all her husband's correspondence) that he "never had the patience or the opportunity for his [Berenson's] kind of study."[6] Fry's expertise had behind it an educational commitment, and he had developed a public face in a manner not shared by Berenson.

In the second area where his reputation flourished, his increasing success as a lecturer in the Cambridge University Extension series, he enjoyed a popularity among the more serious lay audience, made up largely of a prosperous and literate middle class. This aspect of his reputation would eventually culminate in the Omega Workshops, while his work on journals and magazines such as the *Burlington* combined scholarly expertise and an ability to popularize that in many ways embodied a high-minded Victorian ethos. The *Burlington*, by adding a mix of scholarship and popularization that distinguished it from other publications, typified Fry's approach to the task of gaining a wider and more educated audience.

These two areas of Fry's reputation did not always mesh successfully, however. At a minimum, they drained his energy in considerable measure. There persisted a felt tension as well in his resistance to Berenson's too-imperious attitude and an equally negative view of any attempt to popularize in ways that were vulgar or mercantile.

Behind both areas, however, and fed by his Quaker commitment to a higher vision, there operated a seriousness of purpose. This he steadfastly maintained by his love of instruction and his quest for a full and accurate rendering of esthetic experience. What could be called Fry's intellectual style rested on a mixture of pedagogy and a modern (and eventually a modernist) melding of the moral and esthetic realms in the service of a call to a higher form of civilized sensibility.

This intellectual style led Fry, as an English subject, to a concrete plan to realize significant purchases of art as a way to strengthen the national patrimony. The dispute over the Chantrey Bequest left him with bitter feelings, and at the same time impressed upon him the need to rally financial and moral support to maintain England's depth and sophistication in the arts. In the fall of 1903, he was exceptionally busy forming the National Art Collections Fund. Fry was worried, telling his mother, "If we don't get such a society formed all our national treasures will drift across the Atlantic."[7] Using the prestige of David Lindsay, the 27th Earl of Crawford and the 10th Earl of Balcarres, as the chairman of the committee, Fry sought to amass private funds from wealthy Englishmen dedicated to conserving what was often being auctioned off to satisfy various financial needs. Lord Balcarres more than fulfilled the model of an impressive peer who could achieve great things, since he himself possessed a reputation as an art historian of some note, having written on Italian sculpture and authored a book on Donatello. While serving as an MP he used his considerable learning and interest in arts administration to push for reform in the South Kensington Museum; his committee reformed the museum into the immensely popular Victoria and Albert, the world's largest museum of arts and design. Balcarres, by being both a sophisticated student of the fine arts and a high-ranking public servant, combined political and esthetic experience in a striking way. Fry would obviously view Balcarres as standing in sharp relief compared to Morgan, an American far removed from inherited titles and refined tastes certified by history and social privilege.

The National Art Collections Fund stood in mute but stunning contrast to anything operating at the time in America. This contrast heightened starkly when put alongside the model of how robber barons would sponsor the museums in America's largest cities.

The fund operated as a volunteer organization, which grew to eighty thousand members, all of whom contributed toward the purchase of great art. This often meant art by British artists, though one of the most noteworthy paintings, acquired by the fund in 1906, was Diego Velázquez's *Rokeby Venus*, prized in large part because it was bought from the English family who owned it. Nationalist sentiments were therefore involved, but not only in the most narrow sense. The fund envisioned its mission as shaped by the artistic needs of the nation and its subjects, and so thought of objects like master paintings as repositories of qualities higher than nationalism. Fry participated in the fund's work and spent long hours in shaping its mission. These efforts were both like and unlike what he had already begun to do— and would only devote yet more and more time to such an enterprise—in using the marketable exchanges of great works of art as both his vocation and his sustenance, physical and spiritual.

The intellectual part of Fry's work had begun to express itself in a real way in the pages of the *Burlington Magazine*. This sometimes involved Fry in distinguishing levels of knowledge that would pose a challenge to the "common reader." The status of expertise itself was often at stake in what might be seen as minor matters. In early 1903, Fry wrote to T. Sturge Moore, a poet and graduate of art schools, and the brother of the famous ethicist G. E. Moore. At issue was whether or not Sturge would be willing to review a book about Old Master drawings in the collection of the Duke of Devonshire. The book stood out as an item in the very thick of the world of artistic masterpieces and aristocratic wealth. Fry proceeded cautiously, explaining to Moore that while the book had "one or two obvious howlers in the matter of attributions," it was important to signal such errors, or "it will appear we haven't found them out."[8] Fry clarified further, invoking two experts on Italian Renaissance art, Berenson and Herbert Horne: "I only want to show the kinds of lines on which it would naturally be treated in the *Burlington* which as Berenson, Horne and I are Italian advisers will, I suppose, go in for attributions so far as they count for esthetic appreciation." Fry's persisting hope was that the framework of esthetic worth rather than monetary value would determine how the works would be discussed.

Fry, Berenson, and Horne formed a triumvirate of experts who

*Portrait of Herbert Horne: Painted by Henry Harris Brown in 1908,*
*this shows Horne (1864–1916) as the committed esthete whose work on*
*Italian Renaissance painters rivaled that of Berenson and Fry. Fry and*
*Horne maintained a friendly correspondence for several years.*

contributed significantly to the notion of connoisseurship, especially
as it related to early Italian painting. Fry, however, was in temperament closer to Horne than to Berenson. Horne, like Fry, was an esthete. He began a life focused on the arts in his twenties. Oscar Wilde
and Walter Pater became his friends and influences, as his private life
combined elements of decadence and dandyism; he was known by
many figures in what was called the Yellow Decade (named after the
*Yellow Book,* a quarterly magazine focusing on estheticism and decadence), but little recognized by a wider public, choosing to become
more and more reclusive as he grew older. Working as an amateur
architect, he soon joined his skills with those of two students of John
Ruskin, Arthur Mackmurdo and Selwyn Image, the latter a poet and
designer of stained-glass windows, who became the Slade Profes-

sor of Fine Art, a title Fry would achieve many years later. (It was Mackmurdo who introduced Fry to Helen Coombe, who became his wife in 1896, shortly after they met.) Mackmurdo, Image, and Horne were active in establishing the Century Guild of Artists, committed to "render[ing] all branches of Art the sphere no longer of tradesmen but of the artist," and so "would restore building, decoration, glass-painting, pottery, wood-carving and metal-work to their rightful place beside painting and sculpture" and "emphasize the Unity of Art." The guild set up the *Hobby Horse*, a London-based journal edited by Mackmurdo and Horne and dedicated to the innovations and excellences of the crafts of publishing and printing.

Fry would have been in sympathy with such artisanal ideals, and would later build his Omega Workshops based on them. Horne, having discovered the pleasures and graces of Italian design, made his first trip to that country in 1889.[9] He took ardently to Florence in the early 1890s, soon spending half of each year there, and began to exercise fully a life-long devotion to the Italian Renaissance. At first he acted as a guide to the masterpieces of that highly endowed city, offering his services to Mary Costelloe, who would marry Berenson and begin the formation of a salon built around her husband's refined taste and studies. Horne had probably earlier met Fry and Berenson in London around the same time, in the late 1880s.[10] His dedication to painting flowered into a rich self-taught expertise, capped off by his publication of his monograph on Sandro Botticelli.[11] This densely researched but plainly written monograph about an individual artist is the model of a work that would eventually become a standard offering in the discipline of academic art history.

The book opens with a detailed account of how Botticelli, born Alessandro Filipepi, came to be apprenticed to Fra Filippo Lippi; the account builds on and corrects that of the most famous biographer of Italian artists, Giorgio Vasari. Horne also had models closer to home, such as Giovanni Cavalcaselle and Joseph Crowe, the co-authors of the most famous books in the late nineteenth century on Italian paintings. Their three-volume study, *A History of Painting in Italy* (1864), was followed by their popular two-volume study, *A History of Painting in North Italy* (1871). These experts, too, receive gentle but firm corrections. A long digression about Fra Filippo's scandalous indulgence with a Florentine beauty and the consequent father-ing of his child with her also uses many contemporary sources, at the mastery of which Horne excelled. Such details and a scrupulous crit-ical reading of contemporary accounts do not, however, mean that Horne ignores the esthetic issues. He describes in great detail Botti-celli's "naturalism," its sources and nuances.

After the introductory background, Horne deals separately with forty works by Botticelli, mostly oil paintings and altarpieces, from private collections and museums such as the Uffizi Gallery in Flor-ence, utilizing various forms of argument and analysis to arrive at a comprehensive and particularized treatment of each work. All the works are treated lovingly, and the questions concerning attribution and provenance are mustered in order to establish and reaffirm Bot-ticelli's greatness. It all constitutes a demonstration of art historical expertise of a high order. Horne asserts the work was written over the span of several years, marked by rigorous concentration and de-termined confidence. Still the notes of communal and even trans-generational values assert themselves, as Horne concludes his "In-troduction" by asserting, in a Fry-like key, that "until every field of research has been duly explored, any attempt at reconstruction must, of necessity, to some extent or another, prove to be of a provisional character."

Horne's elitism freely acknowledged the protracted and self-correcting labor of an academic criticism, and he shared such val-ues with Berenson and Fry, though not without a sense of rivalry. Fry and Berenson found their motivations directed in considerable measure through the shifting activity of the art market, Fry, how-ever, for a shorter period than Berenson. But all three men, as well as their colleagues in the field, could be prickly if they felt their discov-eries and demonstrations were being slighted. Horne's outlets were various, but he took great pride in the scholarly essays he contrib-uted to the *Burlington*, and valued Fry's sensibility and character, and the two men enjoyed an affectionate correpondence.[12] In 1905 Horne thanked Fry for sending along a copy of his edition of Reynolds's *Discourses*, but complained about Charles Holmes's selection of ar-ticles for the *Burlington* (probably as lacking scholarly rigor). Some-what gently Horne asked whether Fry's friendship with him would lead Fry to overpraise a translation of a biography that Horne had published: "I would wish no more than that the book should deserve all you say about it." When it came time for Fry to review Horne's Botticelli book Fry was quite balanced in his assessment, which appeared in the *Burlington*'s May 1908 issue, but he concluded that the study "has the air of a classic." Horne died in 1916, yet his fame as an expert did not persist and increase, as did that of Fry and Berenson.[13]

Just as the Metropolitan Museum began to modify its sense of a mission by introducing the idea of a professionalized staff, so, too, did the critics and art historians such as Fry, Horne, and Berenson reshape what a curatorial career might look like if equally rigorous standards were adopted. Such a career meant a set of new skills, to be used in recognizing, interpreting, and appraising the highest levels of artistic genius. The concern for the question of attributions, which laid at the heart of connoisseurship, carried enormous weight, of course, as it at one and the same time gained notice for the expert appraiser's skill and probity and set the monetary scales firmly in place. The mingling of esthetic and commercial values would, however, become increasingly vexatious.

The *Burlington* stood as an important pivot in making the new skills manifest to a broader readership. For its inaugural issue, in 1903, an article, written by R. Langton Douglas, a reputable expert who later briefly served as director of the National Gallery of Ireland, had been accepted. Fry hadn't yet read the article before its acceptance, and the journal's editor, Robert Dell, worried that it cast some aspersions on Berenson's expertise. Fry wrote to Mary to calm what looked to become quite troubled waters. He chose to do this by recommending that the magazine proceed with publishing the already accepted article, and then have Mary answer it by correcting its errors, and decline all further submissions from this particular reviewer. (Fry disliked Douglas and his work but felt that the support Douglas garnered from "well-meaning gushers and idiots" was even more "nauseating.") He went on, however, to urge that the *Burlington* not become a mere mouthpiece for Berenson and his supporters, which would cause all the other cliques to turn away. "It is very important that it shouldn't be said that the *Burlington* belongs to B. B.'s clique," he wrote, adding that "surely it is still more important that

B. B. should not have it said that he is capable of political scheming to ring-fence Italian art."[14] Fry pleaded with Mary to have her husband ignore the lesser experts and so find "peace of mind," arguing not on a personal but on an abstract basis.[15] This ability, this peace of mind, that Fry offered to the expert Berenson would mark him as an elitist, but Fry was at the point where he was beginning to wear his elitism, and his expertise, rather more lightly. He would surely need a light diplomatic touch when he began his discussions with the Metropolitan Museum.


## THE FIRST TRIP TO AMERICA

Fry sailed to New York for the first time during January 1905, and on the sixth of the month he relayed his incipient seasickness to his wife with the peremptory opinion that "the ocean is simply disgusting." His trip was in response to an invitation to meet with potential financial backers for the *Burlington*. He had two weeks earlier told his fellow artist William Rothenstein that he was going to New York "on *Burlington Mag.* business," hoping to find some financial security for the new but costly undertaking. No sooner had he landed than apparently he realized that the offer was not merely to support the *Burlington* but to take a position at the Metropolitan Museum of Art. As J. Pierpont Morgan had recently become the chairman of the museum's board of trustees, the fate of both men would soon be joined. Fry had sniffed out the larger scheme in advance, and had his guard hairs at the ready. It was William Laffan, one of the museum's trustees, having begun his journalistic career writing art criticism before going on to own the *New York Sun* and other newspapers, who would serve as the museum's interlocutor.[16] Laffan had been able to purchase the *Sun* with Morgan's financial help, and his papers often printed flattering accounts of Morgan, so he clearly was Morgan's choice to act as agent in the negotiations that followed. Unbeknownst to Fry at this time, Morgan often preferred to work through emissaries rather than by immediate face-to-face discussions. At this time Laffan was rumored to be having an affair with Belle da Costa Greene, Morgan's assistant, and so was not only close to Morgan's world but thoroughly cognizant of all the machinations involved in the restricted circle of wealthy collectors.

But now Fry had entered the thicket of relationships. He reported to Helen: "It is e'en as I thought; I go tomorrow to the Metropolitan Museum to meet the great J. P. Morgan to see whether he and I hit it off and whether I shall suit them for the post of Director." Fry sensed that it was "evident that I am Laffan's man for the post and he means to get me. Well, we shall have to think it over," he concluded. Wariness spilled over onto his estimation of Americans, and he found in New York a "mixture of extreme progress and hopeless barbarism." In the same letter he told Helen that "the people look to me rather terrible—types I don't understand the meaning of at all, never quite squalid like the Londoners but much more heartless and indifferent." He was to be met with a full salvo of wealth and pretension as the forces in Morgan's control set out to make the offer irresistible. A medley of impressions threatened to overwhelm Fry's sense of balance, focused by the fact he had arrived in New York under false, or at least misleading, assumptions.

What followed, in what could fairly be called the courtship period between Fry and the various members of the Metropolitan Museum organization, became a rather elaborate onset of misperceptions on a number of grounds. To begin with, Fry was clearly flattered by the way he was treated, and he probably assumed, reasonably, that meeting his salary demands would not present any difficulty to Morgan. Morgan, for his part, operated for decades with an attitude toward his employees that was often distant and severe; in addition he had a notorious reputation for never stooping to bargain about prices. As for the various people in between Fry and Morgan, they all had difficult negotiations to conduct. Sir Caspar Purdon Clarke, whom Morgan had recently hired away from the South Kensington Museum in London, suffered from poor health and homesickness. (After an extended leave, he would resign in 1910, to be replaced by the assistant director, Edward Robinson.) The board of trustees would clearly do Morgan's bidding even as to details. But they, too, had a stake in the way things might develop. Some, for example, collected American artists, and they may have understandably feared Fry would emphasize European painters when it came to expensive acquisitions. Though Clarke was British, there was a current of xenophobia among some trustees; they had sensed the resentment of other British officials and collectors, many of whom felt Americans were overly acquisitive and not fully cultured. Fry himself remained thoroughly British and seemed at times to face America and its citizenry with a mixture of bemusement and condescension.

Fry, of course, met some people that he admired, chief among them John G. Johnson, a lawyer and astute collector of art from Philadelphia who served as Morgan's attorney. He had read all of Fry's unsigned writings for the *Athenaeum* and told him they were most impressive. The two became close friends. Fry visited Johnson in Philadelphia on January 9, and Johnson told Fry he should take the Metropolitan Museum job, "for the good it might do" in America. Saying to Helen that he was "inclined to accept" the post, Fry considerably softened his view of the national character when he added that "there are heaps of really nice interesting people . . . and the intellectual society is very friendly and accessible." He also had a visit arranged to see the Widener Collection, which would eventually go to America's National Gallery when institutions in Philadelphia, such as the Museum of Art, failed to secure it. Eventually a sort of climax of the trip was reached, as the actual position at the museum was named, though without a full roster of details. Meanwhile, upon his return to New York from Philadelphia, Fry was told he was being considered for the deputy director position, under Sir Caspar. Clarke was described as being a mere figurehead, and Fry was told the post of director would come to him when Sir Caspar retired.

The next day something like a victory progress occurred. On January 11, Fry was in "the great J. P. Morgan's own private observation car tacked on to the end of a special express" on his way to Washington, DC. The vast wealth of America at this period was beholden to the growth of railroads to such a degree that the trip could not have felt neutral. Fry often complained to Helen about constantly being entertained at evening meals. He mused that meeting a dozen or more fellow diners was a strain, but especially if he had earlier met some of the same people at a previous dinner but retained no memory of them. Regrettably, he told Helen, they had failed to make any impression on him. Eventually, however, his negative sense of the shal-

*John G. Johnson: This pen-and-ink drawing (1901) by Floyd Campbell shows the man many considered the best lawyer in America. Fry and he became good friends, and Fry advised Johnson (1841–1917) on the purchase of paintings. Courtesy of the Philadelphia Museum of Art.*

low American businessman or socialite would transform into an acceptance of new possibilities for himself, especially in the framework of the museum as a source of genuine learning and cultural deepening. Moreover, the dinner in Washington was to be on a much larger scale than any other, and the fame of many of the guests meant their names were easily recalled.

Morgan, perhaps out of bluster, had said the dinner would include meeting the president, Theodore Roosevelt—which led Fry to tell his wife "It's alarming and interesting"—but there were to be many other notables as well. The official occasion, whose attendees included senators and cabinet members, was the meeting of the American Institute of Architects marking the initial stages of fundraising for the American Academy in Rome. Henry Walters, the millionaire art collector from Baltimore, had donated $100,000 to support the academy, and Morgan matched the gift. Among the guests were famous artists, such as John LaFarge, Augustus Saint-Gaudens, and Henry James, university presidents, and a Supreme Court justice. Charles McKim, having recently finished the building of Morgan's library, wrote to Saint-Gaudens that "Henry James is coming; in fact *everybody*, and *more* than we want!"[17] Though the Arlington Hotel, where the dinner was served, didn't allow women at its formal events, it made an exception for the president's wife, Edith, as well as Morgan's sister Anne, and his mistress, Adelaide Douglas.

However, one of the most impressive of the guests there—besides Morgan and Roosevelt, who sat together at the high table—was Elihu Root. He was the main speaker for the evening, and in his remarks he lauded the effort made by many of those in attendance to tour Europe and take in "the great examples of art in the ancient and modern world, [and] have come back with new standards." He also spoke of his idealizing desire to see such art become the art of "our whole people."[18] Fry identified Root to Helen by relaying the widespread belief that Root's public image was so favorable that he had a good chance to become president himself. Most recently Root, who had become a trustee of the Metropolitan in 1900, had served as the secretary of war under Roosevelt's predecessor, William McKinley, impressing everyone with his reorganization of the army and the enlargement of West Point. After Root returned for a brief period to his private law practice, Roosevelt chose him to replace John Hay as secretary of state, in which position he refined the Open Door Policy, greatly increasing American trade with China. Equally impressive were his skills as a negotiator, and after helping settle a number of international disputes, he was awarded in 1912 the Nobel Peace Prize, which President Roosevelt had won before him in 1906. In several important legal disputes involving Morgan and the museum, Root served as legal counsel, clearly trusted by many important and wealthy clients. During his term as senator from New York, and most significantly, he also helped pass the law that lowered the excise tax on the importation of artworks—an exercise of legislative power of great interest to Morgan. Known as thoroughly honest and highly effective in his work in government positions, legal matters, and business arrangements, he epitomized a small class of men who harmonized business ethics and government policy. Fry could easily have felt comfortable with such men, as his experience in England often included interactions with nobility and people of great wealth; at the highest levels of power and influence, America and England shared common ground. In a sense, possessed of immense power and influence, Root was a member of the American nobility, fulfilling a public role that was the analog to Morgan's private one.

But it was meeting Morgan himself that heavily marked the temper of the trip for Fry. At the Washington dinner, the two men talked for the first time. Morgan promised monetary support for the *Burlington*; he also told Fry of his desire to buy a Botticelli, though the particular painting he had chosen ended up in the collection of Benjamin Altman, eventually coming as a gift to the Metropolitan in any case. Morgan utterly dominated the conversation. Fry observed that, as he "sat next to him [Morgan], like a courtier who has at last got an audience," all the while he must behave tactfully. Still, "for a few minutes," Fry felt he himself had "wielded absolute power." His portrait of the plutocrat contained some broad strokes: "Morgan, rather jovial and making jokes, which I parried, about my becoming an American. After lunch a cigar called the Regalia de Morgan. The whole thing regal and yet how infinitely provincial." Morgan promised Fry "a free hand with the pictures," and since Morgan had "complete control of the whole thing," this was a form of reassurance. Fry also used his visual imagination to describe Morgan to Helen, comparing his face to that of the man in Domenico Ghirlandaio's *Portrait of an Old Man and a Boy*, indicating just how Morgan's rosacea caused his nose to be inflamed and misshapen. Fry's summary view was unflinching: "He [Morgan] behaves not as a host but exactly as a crowned head and everyone else behaves accordingly." He bravely looked for some ameliorating stance or gesture and confided to Helen that Morgan had "not got anything but money to intimidate you with."

To see the after-dinner talk with Morgan as both regal and provincial indicates just how unable—or unwilling—Fry was to separate his own sense of values from the world of limitless finance and social power. Such a conversation, as well as the ride back to New York with a head-spinning cohort of famous and powerful men, would have left anybody of average means intimidated or bewildered, or both. In a sense, as later events would prove, the dinner in Washington was the high-water mark of Fry's exposure to American wealth and its relationship to culture. He was facing, perhaps without fully realizing it, a force field made up of currents of power that flowed in every direction, but emanated most often from Morgan. Fry continued to be keenly committed to protecting his own status while realizing this meant a measure of financial security he had not yet enjoyed, and a likely immigration to a culture different from the one he embodied. All the limits, of his salary, his opportunities, and his duties, remained yet to be set. At the same time he might very well have felt that he had entered a situation where the limits seemed almost nugatory.

The train ride back to New York sparked in Fry considerably higher spirits than he had enjoyed when he first arrived in America. He was able to connect with "really fine intelligent men all working together with a big idea of the future of art," and their plans included "proposing to unite with the University" (presumably Columbia) in a "big scheme for artistic education." How much all this was meant to flatter Fry, who surely let his own views on art education have a full airing, and how much was part of the museum's redefinition of its aims and social obligations, is hard to say. Fry intended to "discount most of the polite speeches," but he asserted that "the bigness of the job, the *élan* and real confidence in the future . . . fascinate me and this climate is exhilarating, no doubt." All the cultural stereotypes about America's bigness and the ability to start again in the New World and build beyond the apparent horizons were now taking on palpable and present form.

But no sooner had his spirits rose than he came against the grain of Morgan's willfulness. At first the annual salary for the position at the

Metropolitan was set at £1,600. But when Fry went to discuss the salary with Morgan, he took Laffan with him, hoping to use his advice and presence to temper any of Morgan's force. Fry thought £2,400 a fairer sum. Morgan was offended and even briefly withdrew the offer to support the *Burlington*. But at this point, Morgan absented himself from further negotiations. Laffan reassured Fry that his demeanor had been acceptable, but the hiring process came to a halt. Laffan perhaps reasoned that, since Morgan was unlikely to increase the salary offer, it would be better to draw back on the scope of the position. So he came up with the idea—which at a later time was put into practice—of having Fry serve as an advisor to the museum on the purchase of European paintings. Fry was tempted to sail home immediately, but talked himself down, telling Helen that he had "set out to do this thing and I mustn't leave a stone unturned." The retainer fee as European consultant might be "the best of all," but he wasn't prepared at the time to "build on it." All this soured him again on the American character. He formulated a condemnation of sorts for "this hard, calculating American world," mixed as it was with its opposite: "They are as sentimental as you like but as hard as nails, and their sentimentality prevents their knowing how hard they are."

Fry, clearly disturbed by the turn of events but bound by economic and other considerations, decided to delay his return to England until the first of February. When this delay occurred, he arranged a trip to Boston to meet Mrs. Isabella Stewart Gardner in her museum and to talk with Denman Ross, a curator at the Boston Museum of Fine Arts, about his theories of color. At first Gardner, whose attachment to Berenson dictated most of her purchases, seemed reluctant to let Fry view her collection; he assumed that she feared he might have pronounced some as fakes. But at the last moment she relented and when he ended by praising her Mantegna *Sacra Conversazione*, she was greatly pleased. When he left Boston he went straight through to Philadelphia, where he hoped to secure support from Johnson for the *Burlington*. Luckily Morgan relented and kept his promise, giving £1,000, and when others joined in, Fry was able to gather a total of just over £5,000. So despite the present failure of the offer of a post at the museum, the magazine, which meant so much to Fry, was at last able to achieve a solid financial footing. By February 21, Fry was back in Hampstead, at a distance advising Johnson on his purchase of three paintings by Hieronymus Bosch and a *Virgin and Child* by Bellini. There were other patrons and collectors to advise, and many paintings to be discovered and assessed. Fry, after much worry and homesickness, was returned to his element, for the time being.

## FRY AND FRICK: AN INTERLUDE

During his first trip to America, Fry also had the pleasure of meeting one of the country's most successful collectors of art, Henry Clay Frick. Like his competitor Morgan, Frick would eventually encase his formidable collection of masterpieces in a jewel-like New York City mansion built in a neoclassical style, specifically for the purpose of displaying the art. After earning the popular title of "the most hated man in America" because of his role in the Johnstown Flood (1889) and the use of armed Pinkerton agents in the Homestead Steel strike (1892), Frick decided to move to New York City from Pittsburgh, where his steel and coke companies were based. With his ownership of companies related to steel, Frick had formed a friendship with Andrew Carnegie, and the two men competed with Morgan, not only for monetary wealth but also for prizes in the area of art collecting. By 1905 Frick had transferred his paintings to New York City, and was still actively pursuing European masterpieces. Indeed, his collection is often considered the best of those that had been amassed by the likes of Morgan, Carnegie, and other robber barons.

When Fry was drawn to America by the men in charge at the Metropolitan Museum, chiefly Lannan and Morgan himself, he was able to meet Frick for the first time.[19] Their working relationship would prove very satisfying to Frick, and especially remunerative to Fry, whose finances were often at low ebb. Frick had also contributed to the support of the *Burlington*, so Fry had ample reason to continue their relationship. In the summer of 1907 Fry helped Frick obtain *Pietà with Donor* by Antonello da Messina, which Frick then put on loan to the Met. (This painting was later judged to be by an unknown artist, and based on an earlier painting by Konrad Witz, an important

Swiss master.) This was followed by Frick's request to Fry that he inspect and evaluate a portrait by Anthony van Dyck, which Frick also eventually purchased after Fry declared it "authentic and fine." Then came the coup de grâce. In April 1910 Rembrandt's haunting masterpiece *The Polish Rider* came up for sale, and an offer for £60,000 had been made. Fry sent a wire to Frick, who responded quickly, allowing Fry to proceed with the purchase: "You have authority to do as you think best in all matters."

At the time the painting was in the possession of Count Ladislas Tarnowski, who was willing to sell it. The count's brother, however, wanted to know what might be the fairest price and approached the Carfax Gallery in London for an independent estimate. Fry had shown his work at Carfax, and it was through this connection that he came to know of the painting and its availability, as well as Frick's possible interest. Writing to Frick to say that he found the count "a good natured rather rustic gentleman with the obstinate suspicions of a peasant type quite unused to business," and though he was "extremely difficult to deal with," Fry was able to conclude the sale. This happened, however, only after Fry made the two-and-a-half-day journey to Poland to see the painting, as the count insisted he must.

The Carfax Gallery received a fee of £1,400 for its services, and Fry asked for, and Frick paid, a commission of £3,000. The sale became a news story, covered by both the *New York Times* and the *London Times*. The former listed the price at $300,000, and the latter could not resist recording that the painting had been purchased by "Mr. Frick of Pittsburgh and New York, one of those competitive millionaires on whose dollars so many impoverished European aristocrats are now living." Fry praised the painting for its "quite exceptional beauty," describing it as "the most romantic thing Rembrandt ever did and [it] stands quite alone." Frick, once he had the painting in his possession, sent Fry a final cable in which he declared himself "Enchanted." This incident stands as one exemplum of how America's wealthiest people went about acquiring works of the very highest quality. The process, at once based on both commercial and esthetic values, was possible only for a relatively short historical period, as the fabulous wealth eventually leveled off to some degree, and the supply of Old Masters was always limited. It was also in this short period that connoisseurship became more highly disciplined and practiced with remarkable consequences.

Frick's thorough satisfaction at obtaining an impressive Rembrandt has been matched over the years by visitors to his museum, where it remains one of the collection's most popular paintings. Fry, too, was satisfied, and he wrote to his mother about the experience, pledging her to secrecy before the sale was final, as the "picture is so important that when it becomes known it will create great excitement." Fry seemed fatigued at the very thought of the required trip to Poland, but steeling himself, he complained that "It's tiresome and rather hateful work but I couldn't refuse to do it." Possibly some benefit would appear, as he hoped "Mr. Frick will be more decent to me than his fellow millionaire. At all events I ought to get handsomely paid for all I have done and indeed it comes at a critical time, for I am just at the end of my resources and have been feeling very anxious of late as to how I can possibly meet expenses. So that this thing is a godsend."[20] Fry clearly meant the phrase "fellow millionaire" to refer to Morgan; as for "all I have done," this refers to the trip to Poland, and also the task of following the painting to Paris to unpack it after its arrival from Poland and repack it for shipping to America. The core of expert knowledge that made Fry an essential part of the transaction had nevertheless to leave room for more mundane skills. Though Fry's relationship with Frick never soured, it just dwindled; however, even at its best, Fry's employment as a guide to masterpieces for millionaires would seldom be free from a substantial amount of "tiresome and rather hateful work."

## THE SECOND INVITATION TO AMERICA

In 1905, after returning to England from his first American trip, Fry continued his work as an art historian and connoisseur. There was the *Burlington* to manage now that it was becoming debt free, and a book to publish, as he brought back into print *The Discourses of Sir Joshua Reynolds*, with his own introduction and annotations. This was Fry's attempt to instill a sense of the painter's excellence, and to show that English painting had a valuable tradition of its own that could contribute to contemporary artists. Believing deeply in the need of a sense of history as a source of value, and respecting lines of descent by which living painters drew on the past masters for their visions, Fry would later rely on such a historical consciousness to form in important measure the content of his esthetic.

Being back in England also entailed trips to the Continent, and Fry went to look at paintings in Vienna, Prague, Frankfurt, and Budapest, among other places. Requests for advice about prices and attributions came from several quarters, including from Morgan himself. Fry wrote several times to inform Sir Caspar Purdon Clarke about various issues in ways that could help the Metropolitan Museum. He also quipped that his English compatriots thought he might be working at odds with the National Arts Collection Fund by drawing great works out of England (which in a sense he was). In early December he offered his advice on a Lorenzo Lotto and a Maître de Flémalle, both of which were acquired by the Rogers Fund, the museum's chief source for purchases. His work in this regard, he would soon claim, saved the museum several hundred pounds in fees. But clearly more was at stake than Fry's advice emanating from European cities. Talk about his assuming a position at the museum had seriously restarted in the autumn. He told his mother in December, however, that he wouldn't sail again to America unless the questions about salary were settled beforehand. His naïveté when considering economic issues had clearly wrecked the first attempt to find a place for his expertise; from now on he would rely on written offers and responses. At the end of the month he spelled out what he felt were fair terms in a letter to Sir Caspar. In the midst of all this there were persistent rumors that he was being considered for the post of director of Britain's National Gallery. In a letter to his father he downplayed his chances, and yet was willing to ask for paternal help, if it were possible, to exercise any influence in the matter. Here he knew that he had offended many with his part in the Chantrey Bequest, and behind the scenes such offenses were slow to be erased.

But eventually, against the odds, the Metropolitan position had again become the glittering prize. Morgan had done almost all he could to impress Fry during the first visit. But now, by the time that

*Sir Caspar Purdon Clarke: A popular director of London's South Kensington Museum (later the Victoria and Albert Museum) for many years, Sir Caspar (1846–1911) fared less well at the Metropolitan Museum, from which he resigned in 1910. He and Morgan got to know each other when Morgan lent some of his paintings to the South Kensington Museum.*

1905 would draw to a close, it was as if a new campaign had begun, with other pressures and impressions as part of the process. The long and frequently tortured tale of the working relationship between Morgan and Fry first resumed momentum in earnest in May 1905. Louis Ehrich,[21] a prosperous art dealer with a distinguished gallery at 8 West 33rd Street in Manhattan, had worked closely with Bernard Berenson and others, and had met Fry and knew of his rising reputation. Willing to go a bit further in pursuit of his goals, Ehrich wrote a letter to Sir Caspar recommending that the Metropolitan employ the services of Fry. The luster Fry's expertise would bring to the Metropolitan, at the time urgently in need of reform on several levels, would be a move both practical and wise. Clarke's cosmopolitan experiences, of course, readily allowed him to form a full appraisal of Fry's growing renown. The letter from Ehrich, however, helped move Clarke to take action.

In the first weeks of January 1906, however, before Fry and Morgan would again come face to face in New York, Clarke, with little more than a year's experience as director of the museum, found himself in the role of mediator. Corresponding with Fry while the latter was in England gave Sir Caspar a chance to literally spell out the terms of Fry's salary, and he succeeded to the extent that Fry willingly made his second visit to America. During his first visit, Fry had been struck by Clarke as "the most lovely example of mid-Victorian taste that ever was made." On the level of the practicable, Clarke did call on his considerable managerial skills to try and find a middle way between Fry and Morgan, as well as satisfactorily managing many other details, but he was also aloof and passive, accepting Morgan's domination. Fry, however, couldn't help but see him in English terms (though Clarke was born in County Dublin), comparing him to the heavy-drinking Mrs. Gamp, a character in Dickens's *Martin Chuzzlewit*, satirized for being too comfortably ambivalent, equally at home on occasions of births—"lying in"—and funerals—"lying out." Sir Caspar brought out the waggish side of Fry, who shared with Helen, under a solemn vow of secrecy, a verbal portrait in museological terms: "He [Clarke] ought to be preserved in a glass case in our Museum with a label 'circa 1850, probably made for the Great Exhibition of 1851 by a member of the Royal Family.'"[22] As for the American Edward Robinson, who would soon replace Clarke, he was twelve years younger than Sir Caspar but eight older than Fry. Fry referred to him as "the Greek man," and saw him as "a real brick, a man of solid sense and capacity." More impressed by the American than the Englishman, and the younger rather than the older man, Fry was indirectly expressing his forward-looking attitude toward the educational rather than the merely archival side of the museum.

Morgan had known Clarke for some time while he served as director at South Kensington (later the Victoria and Albert), where Morgan often visited to discuss and sharpen his acquisitive desires for elegant museum objects. Clarke's background in the arts and museum work was striking. At sixty, he already had had a full career as the "supervising architect to the crown," having designed the ventilation and heating systems for the Houses of Parliament, as well as various government buildings in the service of the Empire. What was as important, if not more so, he had the ear of Morgan. Sir Caspar epitomized the values of the British Empire, refined by dutiful and effective service, and trusting to the inbred sense of justice and manners. His fellow subjects were dismayed to lose him to an American institution, and a wry joke circulated that said Morgan had not only bought valuable objects that the Victoria and Albert would have liked, he also bought its director. Clarke would serve as the Met's chief negotiator—though Morgan of course remained in control—in the rather tangled discussions with Fry.

Meanwhile in London and in Europe, Fry continued to undertake tasks for Clarke, including trying to make the new director commit to a Rubens portrait being offered for sale by King Leopold of Belgium. At the same time Fry urged a quick resolution to the prospect of his appointment, and he asked Clarke to send him a catalog for the museum, so he could assay what his burdens and possibilities might be if he decided to join the Metropolitan's staff of experts and curators. Clarke had clearly gotten permission to once again sound out Fry's interest in a post of some sort. Fry mentioned the possibility of facing the "dread [that] would be the promiscuous entertainments" should the position require his being in New York and entering the world of formal evenings, one of the more onerous of the museum's attendant social obligations. Fry was indicating here that his constant presence at the museum, especially at long formal dinners, was not something he was prepared to accept as an obligation. The purposes of Fry's employment were clear, but the amount of time he would need to fulfill them was uncertain. It was one more example of a missed signal. Eventually some rough chapters would appear in this part of the narrative.

But Fry's interest in the position became more substantial, and Clarke began to feel pressure to finish the negotiations. He wrote Fry a telegram in late November of 1905 saying that it was "advisable you come at once New York answer." Laffan acted to second Clarke's efforts and followed up quickly with a letter.[23] The trustees had "unanimously authorized an arrangement" for an appointment that carried an annual salary of £500, plus allowance for travel. Laffan's letter came with a letterhead from his office in the New York Sun Building, itself a symbol of how the question—on whose authority was the current offer being made?—would bedevil the negotiations and eventually lead to countless corrections and misunderstandings. Laffan was probably closer to Morgan than Clarke was; he had not only acquired one of his newspapers with financial support from Morgan, he made sure to use all his editorial powers to advance Morgan's interests. This time it was likely that Fry fully appreciated whose interests he was dealing with.

Now the issue became how Fry and the museum would handle the customary "finder's fee." Two weeks later, leaning toward acceptance of the offer, Fry insisted to Clarke that "I have given out that the only way to gain favor is to deal absolutely with the Museum." This meant that he would not act as an independent agent and do what other agents and appraisers had become accustomed to doing, namely inflate the commissions on sales to museums. Fry more than once took on a stern tone, derived in part from his Quaker upbringing, in an attempt to guide the discussion in a way that preserved not only his independence, to the extent possible, but his generally high sense of morality where money and art mingled.

Behind Erhich's recommendation to Clarke lay the belief that Fry would be adept at spotting forgeries and fakes, a problem that had begun to afflict America's millionaire collectors in a way that seemed contagious, if not epidemic. However, Fry's self-praise about his own probity in such matters was slightly offset by his additional, rather suppliant claim that he had already saved Morgan £500 in the preceding months by bringing valuable works to the museum's attention without unduly profiting by commissions. As with many negotiations for employment, the question of money often dominated the discussion, and though Fry remained in financial need, he felt psychologically bound not to accept anything below the mark he set for his services. Of course, everyone knew of Morgan's wealth and his extensive collection, and it became increasingly clear, or at least ardently hoped, that he might willingly bequeath large amounts of it to the museum. Fry had to deal with a nearly immeasurable estate and ego in his relationship with Morgan, yet simultaneously keep his eyes on the main objects—securing a place where he could make a difference in the world of fine art, and securing his family economically.

In the same letter to Clarke where he mentioned his desire to "deal absolutely with the Museum," Fry revealed that he had discussed the salary for such a position with the director of the British Museum, who opined that £1,000 would be a "fair salary." At the same time that the salary question remained unsettled, Fry told Clarke that he couldn't sail to America because of pressing business matters, but added that it was also the case that he couldn't come over in any "speculative capacity." Clarke passed this letter on to Laffan with the annotation, "Fry announces we will want his future services and therefore [he] requires a larger salary." In answer, and with perhaps a bit of exasperation added to his relief, Laffan replied to Clarke, "the matter should rest wholly in your hands henceforth." Clarke wasted no time and four days later dictated a three-page letter to Fry pressing for an answer. He explained to the Englishman that the museum must do its budget punctually in order to ensure the proper amount of New York City support in the form of tax-levy funds. However, he added a note to the letter saying that it was not an "official" offer. The framework of possible misunderstandings remained in place.

The letter from Clarke, dated December 14, nevertheless contained what would become the gist of the offer. It defined the post as having Fry "be commissioned as our agent and representative in Europe." Further, though Clarke agreed that the annual salary of £1,000 was fair, the trustees were divided, and instead offered £500, with the stipulation that further compensation would come in the form of a commission on those pictures bought by the museum on Fry's recommendation. Clarke said that architects, when contracting services for the museum, operated on such a basis, and Fry should be willing to do the same—and Clarke explicitly mentioned that the architects were trusted not to run up prices. This may appear as if the museum was taking on Fry as something like a gallerist and dealer in residence, one whose financial relation to the institution was underpinned by individual monetary transactions, though it was his expertise that allowed Fry to receive the cash benefit. The elements of the annual salary and the title of agent modified this arrangement, but did not alter it substantially. It was a substantial falling off from the post of director, or even assistant director, however.

Fry was in no position—or at least no strong one—to bargain. Unable to commit himself to long periods in New York, not least because of Helen's situation, he realized that this sort of unspecified time-and-place commitment would be acceptable. He countered with a different financial framework, writing Clarke on the last day of 1905 that to ensure the museum's "trust" in the arrangement he would accept a 5 percent commission on paintings sold to the museum below £5,000, and 3 percent for those above that figure. Putting the rate of commissions in writing would help reassure the anxious Fry and maintain his probity. After adding that a one-time sum of £250 would cover the expenses he had already incurred in providing Morgan and the museum with information and advice concerning valuable paintings entering the market, Fry conveyed his readiness to come to terms. He listed five points in his letter: the salary was set at £500, per year, for which he would give the museum first choice on any painting he identified as authentic and valuable; that the commission he would receive from the museum's purchase was as he had spelt it out (i.e., 5 percent or 3 percent); that he could recommend to others any painting first recommended to the museum that they declined to purchase; that he could take 10 percent commission from the seller on any painting he brought to the attention of the museum; and that his travel expenses should be covered. He sent Clarke a telegram ahead of this letter to alert him to how close the parties were, saying, "post terms suggested[;] letter [follows] to explain delay in sailing."

Fry's being occupied with various paintings and possible sales caused the delay in sailing. Within three weeks, Laffan wired the museum on January 23 to second Clarke's offer, recommending "closing arrangements [F]ry thousand pounds." His urgency was driven by news that he also mentioned: it was "quite likely new government may appoint Fry National Gallery." Not only did an imminent offer from the National Gallery in London change the temperature of the negotiations, the salary offered Fry had suddenly doubled. This came about through an apparently unforeseen development, one that was as positive as it was conclusive. George Storey, then the curator of paintings at the museum, had suddenly decided to retire. The trustees quickly responded to this news by offering Fry the title and the same salary, $5,000 (£1,000), that Storey had enjoyed, namely, what had been recommended in Clarke's offer. After considerable back-and-forth discussion, the best part of the offer had sprung up fortuitously, yet this apparent good luck concealed difficulties that later would spring up with less grace.

## ACCEPTING THE OFFER

Two days after Laffan's telegram mentioning the National Gallery's intention to offer Fry a position as its director, he again telegrammed the museum to say "Closed Fry he intends sail Baltic [January] 31st." And sail he did, though he immediately regretted the exceptionally rough crossing that left him thoroughly seasick to a degree he had never experienced. While he was on board the *Baltic*, the trustees held a special meeting and agreed on an annual salary of $5,000, altogether fair in terms of the exchange rate, which was then five US dollars to the pound sterling. By January 26, 1906, he announced to his mother that he had "accepted the post of Curator of Paintings at the Metropolitan," describing the race between them and the National Gallery as "a very close one." To his wife, while he was already at sea, he cabled that he acknowledged it "an honour" just to have been considered by the National Gallery, but added that he couldn't "go back on [his] word to Laffan and my letter without appearing a brute." Almost three decades later he would be offered the position of Slade Professor at Cambridge, and he was then able to accept. But for now he told Helen that the mist of the sea and the tooting of the ship's horn made him "jumpy."

Clearly Fry's initially negative impressions of Americans—or at least what he saw on his first trip as the "indifferent" look in the eyes of New Yorkers—began to change further as he met colleagues like Robinson, as well as highly successful but cultivated men like Elihu Root and John G. Johnson. The presence of Clarke also mediated the tension Fry felt between the "civilization types" of the

Americans and his native Englishmen, though Fry's assessment of the man's character rose very little, if at all. Many people in England had been dismayed to hear of Clarke's going off to America, and he rather intensified that feeling when he at first declared his intention to take US citizenship (a vow he eventually failed to keep). In any case, he appeared ready to work with Fry in remaking the Metropolitan Museum.

By early February 1906, Fry was staying at the Wolcott Hotel on Fifth Avenue. A blizzard pounded the city and made his hotel rock like the steamship *Baltic*, obviously a hyperbole invoked in the shadow of his seasickness. Fry had already gotten his first look at America on his earlier visit and knew what Morgan represented by way of character and social style, so there was little left for him to do now but start work. The Metropolitan presented a challenge to those who would remake it into a more professional museum, one containing more and greater masterpieces so that it would be on the level with others such as the Louvre and England's National Gallery. This meant not only acquiring—at whatever the increasingly burdensome cost—more oil paintings of impeccable provenance and unmistakable esthetic excellence but also creating a set of relationships between its managers and its public. "Already the rich and fashionable ladies are getting together to form a society to help the Museum," Fry crowed, though he added he had no idea such a force was "only asking to be directed." Some members of the administration thought Clarke would be spinning out ideas for new plans, but so far he had not come forward. So others quickly turned to Fry, who took up the challenge by proposing a new gallery in the museum where he could set up his own exhibition. He predicted to Helen he could have it set up in a month. The museum's *Bulletin*, recently started in 1905, would carry an article in its fourth number in which Fry explained his esthetics and his sense of the purposes of a museum, with the new gallery as its embodiment. Committed to the educational role of the museum, he remained firm and ready to shape policies.

The title of Fry's essay, "The Idea of a Gallery," signaled an attitude usually associated with manifestos. On a humbler level, the essay represented Fry's effort to inaugurate a program of educational values by adopting a new model for the museum. Certain idealizing moves, however, were involved in setting out the lineaments of the modern museum. Chief among them for Fry was a sense of historical continuity that supported—and was supported by—a firm esthetic orientation. As is the case with political and social manifestos, it is the optative mood that dominates. What the Metropolitan needed in 1905 was fairly simple to declare—a selection of masterpieces representing, to adopt Matthew Arnold, the best that was thought and pictured in the visual arts. Nothing like this, however, was easy to realize. Fry would bring with him to the Metropolitan his firsthand experience as a painter, a historian, and a teacher imbued with a taste for the greatest of the Old Masters. What carried the article to its fullest height was a feeling for a theoretical formulation that would advance his ideas but also give the museum a way to move forward while yet keeping to a sense of artistic standards worthy of the effort and the expense. Fry would say it simply and boldly: the only effort worth the effort would be to secure "the establishment of standards of truth and beauty, and the encouragement of a keener discrimination and a firmer faith." The elision, so to speak, from "establishment" to "faith" marked out the path, if not the graded steps.

Fry opened his description with a democratizing gesture: "What does the 'man in the street' expect when he leaves the street to enter a picture gallery?" With only this glancing reference to the issue of taste in a democracy, Fry suggests a range of answers, from trifling amusement to an exercise of historical imagination to "food for a deeply and intense imaginative life." These possible aims, however, don't answer the key question, which concerns what a public gallery like the Metropolitan should look for; Fry has an answer in mind:

> *Which of all these desires should a great public institution like the Metropolitan Museum endeavor to gratify in its public, and how should it set about doing it? The private collector can set before himself a certain aim and within the limits of his purse he can realize it; the guardians of a public institution have no such complete freedom. None the less they may do well to formulate ideals even with the full knowledge that they will always remain ideals, only imperfectly translated into fact.*

Clearly Fry aims at the ideal while relying on his own recent appointment to sharpen the contrast between private and public, as he was all too familiar with private collectors and would soon be in the thicket of a very public undertaking. The ideal, especially elusive at the Metropolitan, had to be conjured up in the context of a collection that is "the result of generous and public spirited impulses springing up in the minds of very diversely gifted benefactors." In this context diversity did not function as an unmixed strength. Fry tactfully refrains from stressing the Metropolitan's then random and rather inexpert selection of paintings and their arrangements. But he does make it clear that "the uninstructed visitor can scarcely hope to acquire definite notions about the historical sequence of artistic expression, nor can he hope to increase his susceptibility to the finest artistic impressions by a careful attention, fixed with all patience and humility, only upon the works of the great creative minds. And yet these are surely the two great educational ends which justify a city in spending the money of its citizens upon a public picture gallery." Either the historical sense or the exposure to the workings of great minds will do to justify the museum's exertions, though its greatness would consist in its support of both. Again, art should delight as well as instruct, and its latter function could not be achieved casually.

Fry then shifts to positive examples, describing in some detail other museums and the rationale for their approach to hanging their galleries. In doing so he calls on a mass of scholarship that had proliferated in the field of art history, most of it generated in academic contexts.[24] Indeed, the task of translating this scholarship into the actual physical space of walls and rooms and passageways in and through a modern museum was a form of pedagogic discipline that would eventually come to rival the breadth and depth of art history itself. The work of rearrangement at the Brera in Milan, one of Italy's greatest galleries, was undertaken by Corrado Ricci in a way that fulfilled Fry's high standard, as did the National Gallery and the Louvre, though even with these latter two there are rough passages in some galleries. But then Fry returns to the Metropolitan, to lament that "we can only present isolated points in the great sequence of European creative thought. We have as yet no Byzantine paintings, no Giotto, no Giottesque, no Mantegna, no Botticelli, no Leonardo, no

Raphael, no Michelangelo." His standards were high, and he applied them strictly; one can only guess at what the more sensitive trustees and benefactors thought of this newly appointed voice.

It would be impossible to obtain great examples for every artist on the list Fry set out, but he consoled the possible visitor to the museum that he—and the museum—would proceed "with the intention of acquiring as many of the connecting links of the kind as may come into the market." The new arrangement would stress the fact that some works are more worth serious attention than others, and "It is only by some such emphasis upon what has high and serious merit, that we can hope in time to arouse an understanding of that most difficult but most fascinating language of human emotion, the language of art." Fry describes this language as one that must be valid "in all times and in all countries," but it must be learned. This perplexing combination of what seems both universal, hence natural, and yet artificial, and so easier for some to master than others, keeps the bar high, and so the essay concludes with a highly placed reward: "At all events the aim we should set before ourselves is the establishment of standards of truth and beauty, and the encouragement of a keener discrimination and a firmer faith." The last phrase connotes a spiritual dimension, which Fry had always in mind and eagerly shared. Exalted as the language is, Fry was here attempting to take on the real and present burdens of museum-centered education, and at the same time accept and define the highest goals of his new position.

# CHAPTER IV

# THE METROPOLITAN
# AND THE CONFLICTS
# OF A NEW VISION

MORE THAN A TOUCH OF IRONY EMANATES FROM the fact that Fry's essay on his ideal gallery is flanked in the museum's *Bulletin* by two rather different efforts, both of which indicate the low level of expertise that was often on display. Preceding his essay is a laudatory description of several American paintings, from the collection of George Hearn, a trustee, and all given by Hearn to the museum. One landscape, of New Jersey's Passaic River, by F. Ballard Williams, merited praise for the way it "embodies his taste and power of transfusing ordinary things into a world of his own, where all nature sings in one eternal harmony." The article that follows Fry's offering was about various busts, taken from life, of Benjamin Franklin. The author, of an antiquarian turn of mind, eagerly reiterated and refined detailed observations from a piece he had published three months earlier in the bulletin of the New York Public Library. At once, both articles come encased with a measure of nationalistic pride and reflect a level of amateur art appreciation that may have charmed Fry, but would certainly fail to impress him. Before long, in keeping with the growth of professionalism at the museum, the contributions to the *Bulletin* would reflect higher esthetic and art-historical standards.

Meanwhile, for Fry the winter months had continued to bring in a flood of social obligations, "dinners at clubs and private houses." The secretary of the museum, Robert Weeks De Forest (who would later become the museum's director), was in his view a "gentleman," a "brick" who "pulled things right again." Laffan, on the other hand, had so far failed to write out a letter or memo stating all the terms of the appointment precisely. The failure to arrive at a signed contract had been one of the many negative consequences Fry faced in his first visit. To go much further without one would signal a gap between his expectations and the institution's commitment. There was, in addition to the monetary considerations, the nagging question of residence. Fry felt it was up to him to decide, along with his colleagues, just how much time he would spend in New York. As for his colleagues Caspar Purdon Clarke and Edward Robinson, Fry inclined to see them now as "really decent" and wanted them to help him draw up a job description, a "charter" that would "prevent Morgan from having power to call me across [the Atlantic] at any odd moment." With an unblinkered view, one could easily regard the situation as a continuation of the back-and-forth of the transatlantic negotiations. One trustee had written to De Forest enquiring whether Fry was indeed curator of "paintings *in* the museum," the preposition containing a possible trapdoor. For a while during the first visit, the limits of time and power seemed ignorable, but now they were making themselves fully felt.

For the time being Robinson took over the unpalatable job of trying to harmonize everyone's views of just what Fry was to do and not to do, and he needed to draw on his previous experience as a museum administrator in Boston. This meant a six-page letter to De Forest, who in his position as secretary would presumably bring it up before the executive committee, and then the board of trustees, for approval. The letter, dated February 24, 1906, recapitulated all of the proposals and suggested changes that passed among Fry, Laffan, Clarke, and others. The summary listed three items that had to be completed in 1906: the arrangement of the experimental gallery that Fry had proposed; the selection and appointment of an assistant curator; and the completion of an inventory of paintings that had been started earlier. In addition, in the fall of 1906 Fry would have to start preliminary work on a Rembrandt exhibit, and to make arrangements for redecorating and rehanging the painting collection. Fry cosigned the letter, describing it as giving the "clearest and fairest expression to my views." This document also represented a contract that would in effect commit many people to put the museum's painting collection

*Edward Robinson: Robinson (1858–1931) became the museum's
third director following the resignation of Sir Caspar Purdon Clarke.
His relations with Fry were sometimes contentious.*

on a new and more rigorous art-historical foundation. The contract
spoke volumes about the need for a new museological vision for the
Metropolitan, and also embodied a great deal of trust in Fry's expertise and practical abilities. For the moment, though not all the details
were spelt out and agreed to, the working terms and conditions appeared set.

A sense of relief surely settled on both sides of the often cumber-
some negotiations. Robinson told De Forest at the end of 1906 that
"we have come very close to losing Fry within the last few days,"
referring to the fact that the offer to Fry from the National Gallery
was still open. That Fry gave up the offer from the British institution
led Clarke to feel a greater obligation to satisfy Fry. By the second

week of March De Forest could telegraph Laffan that the "Fry incident [is] satisfactorily closed," and a week later the secretary's report recorded that the appointment was "ratified and confirmed" by the Trustees—this last action coming with an air of haste and prompted by a letter from Robinson sent from his redoubt at the Jekyll Island Club, off Georgia's Atlantic coast. The club included Morgan among its distinguished and very wealthy members.

### THE CLEANING SCANDAL

No sooner had the six-page letter served as a contract and brought the negotiations to a conclusion than another nettlesome affair arose, again involving a three-way tension among the parties. This came to be known as the "Cleaning Scandal" when its details were featured in the newspapers, bringing considerable unwanted attention to Fry at a time when he was burdened with fulfilling his first round of obligations to the museum. George Hearn, the museum trustee whose American paintings had been self-servingly described in the *Bulletin*, along with Fry's essay on his ideal gallery, grew convinced that Fry's restoration methods were egregiously destructive. He wrote Robinson an imperious letter in April asking for the names of all the paintings "to have suffered through [Fry's] treatment." This treatment involved the use of alcohol in cleaning a Rembrandt, one of the tasks Fry took in preparing for the exhibit he had promised to hang. In his role as self-appointed expert, Hearn contended, without clear evidence, that the methods Fry used were in fact greatly at odds with the approved standards; he soon added to his list of charges that a Rubens painting, the *Holy Family*, was "artistically and commercially injured," and the same might be said about a Manet and a Masaccio on which Fry had worked. The reference to "commercial" injury underscores Hearn's business ethos, for he clearly saw the museum as in an important way exercising a fiduciary responsibility. Some, however, may have suspected that Hearn was acting out of pique, and even a measure of jingoism, resentful or jealous of Fry's stature, and determined to assert his own influence as trustee, patron, and collector. By going to the newspaper, Hearn virtually guaranteed that the affair would be aired in less than sophisticated terms.

Part of the dispute arose because Fry did indeed use alcohol in his restoration, but, contrary to Hearn's claims, he did not apply it directly to the canvas. Instead he employed a technique in which a painting was suspended, face down, over a box partially filled with alcohol. Once the alcohol was heated, the fumes from it loosened the accumulated grime and dust from the surface of the painting. The trustees and other collectors and experts chose sides, and as usual in such "scandals," the issue seemed as if it would turn on who could gather the most like-minded experts to support his opinion. The museum director and his assistant took the whole affair very seriously, as it threatened to retard, if not block altogether, the forces that were trying to professionalize the institution's standards. Something definitive and beyond the reach of petty feelings was called for. So Clarke and Robinson had the trustees appoint a committee to investigate Fry's work and Hearn's charges, and to produce a written report.

By the end of April, Clarke and Robinson submitted their signed report to the trustees. The key sentence voiced the report's conclusion unequivocally: "We do not find that in any of the pictures treated [by Fry] the original was in any way affected."[1] Whatever feelings beyond that of vindication that Fry may have enjoyed, he did not give expression to them after the outcome. Yet it is hard not to conclude that, whatever negative feelings he harbored against the esthetic outlook of a man like Hearn, these unfounded—and rather amateurish—charges only solidified them. For his part, Hearn did not bear a huge grudge toward the museum itself, since in 1911 he bequeathed, in memory of his son, several paintings and $100,000, the funds to be used to purchase works by living artists who must be "citizens of the United States of America, or by those hereafter born, who may at the time of the purchase have become citizens thereof."[2] The nationalistic note continued to sound distinctly, as the commercial one had done earlier. The incident also likely reverberated with Fry because of his earlier efforts in contesting the administration of the Chantrey Bequest.

Exactly how much animosity toward Fry showed through in

the unfolding of the cleaning scandal is hard to measure, but it certainly did not help the museum's administrators to take him at face value going forward. Surviving the abrasions of the scandal and enjoying the comfort of the report was one thing, but to enjoy widespread trust was something else. Morgan's control of the trustees and his grand hopes for increasing the reputation and influence of the museum would only strengthen and expand in the years ahead. Fry meanwhile had arrived at the Metropolitan Museum but had not been fully welcomed.

Though Fry's name was cleared in the cleaning scandal, it had nevertheless for a time been sullied in the minds of some people associated with the museum. Out of what was a tense and overly public imbroglio, however, there came at least one very positive note: Fry's reputation and expertise were defended by John G. Johnson, who was, among other things, Morgan's lawyer. Johnson had impressed Fry on the Englishman's first visit to America, and Fry had happily and effectively continued to advise Johnson on artistic matters for the next year. Johnson reciprocated by not only giving generously to the support of the *Burlington* but offering Fry wise counsel on his dealings with the Metropolitan.

Johnson was much more than Morgan's lawyer. Born in Philadelphia in 1841, in humble circumstances, he became, according to his *New York Times* obituary, "in the opinion of some well qualified judges, the greatest lawyer in the English speaking world."[3] After serving briefly in the Civil War, he went on to a magnificent legal career as a single practitioner, dealing with property and corporate law and highly wealthy and well-known clients, which made him—to quote the *Times* again—"probably less known to the general public in proportion to his importance than any other man in the United States." He had befriended Fry during the Englishman's first trip to America, and the two were to become and remain quite close, while Fry put all his expertise at Johnson's disposal in forming his impressive collection. Fry would later write an obituary for Johnson, who died in 1917, in which he subtly pointed out the contrast between the Philadelphia lawyer and Morgan. Speaking of the style and taste that Johnson exhibited in acquiring his collection of European master paintings, Fry wrote: "He never bought like the great millionaire who accepts the celebrated and duly authenticated at its face value, who follows in the footsteps of the Popes and Princes of past ages."[4]

Johnson established his sterling reputation by arguing 168 cases before the Supreme Court. Two presidents—James A. Garfield and Grover Cleveland—offered him a seat on the Supreme Court, but he declined in both instances. In addition to Morgan, his clients included Henry Frick, Andrew Carnegie, and Pierre S. du Pont, for whom he handled antitrust cases that helped set patterns in the business world for decades. Despite the wealth and prestige of his clients, Johnson was unfailing in his avoidance of the public eye, giving no interviews for the last three decades of his life, yet becoming known as someone whose fees remained incredibly modest. In some circles he was known as the least expensive lawyer in Philadelphia. He spent his summers traveling to Europe, where he bought the 1,200 paintings he eventually bequeathed to the city of his birth. After the house where the collection was kept after his death became unsound, the collection was moved to the Philadelphia Museum of Art, where it attracted a tenfold increase in visitors. Eventually, after considerable legal maneuvering, it became the core of that museum's holdings in European masters, including Jan van Eyck, Rogier van der Weyden, Botticelli, el Greco, Edouard Manet, and Claude Monet, among many others.

In the obituary for his friend, Fry especially praised the fact that Johnson was able to grow in his taste and appreciation, even to the point of admitting his early purchases were inferior, and in fact he scrapped all of them before going on to procure works of much higher esthetic value. There was in addition for Fry the praiseworthy fact that Johnson did not "stick to the highways of the great central traditions of Italian and Flemish painting, but was one of the first to see that the Burgundian, Provencal, and Catalonian schools were deserving of investigation." These two facts, and others as well—especially his sense of economic fairness and personal modesty—would have been attractive to Fry in a deep and sincere way. If one recalls Johnson's interest in contributing to the financial support of the *Burlington*, one can easily see him as the ideal interlocutor for Fry's dealings with the Metropolitan Museum. Johnson himself ventured into esthetic criticism when in 1892 he published a forty-page pamphlet on

*Sight-seeing in Berlin and Holland Among the Pictures.* It represented an amateur's approach, but his discussion of how paintings were best to be displayed and lighted reflected a sophisticated eye and an alert sensibility. Clearly, Johnson was not only an extraordinary lawyer and citizen but also a unique collector.

Speculation flourished concerning Johnson's collection as to whether or not it would end up in Philadelphia or New York. It ended in the former, of course, but unlike Morgan's the bequest remained essentially a civic gift rather than becoming a personal monument. Very high among the many regrets that can be drawn from Fry's experience at the Metropolitan must be reckoned the missed opportunity that kept Fry and Johnson from being the two main principals in deciding the future of the collection as well as the museum's future public role. Johnson possessed many of the attributes that Fry himself admired and would wish to emulate. Yet there were marked differences in their stations in life, and Johnson became, shortly after Fry's time at the Metropolitan Museum, a member of its board of trustees. The further irony endures that Johnson's legal work served the class of finance and industrial capitalists epitomized by Morgan, yet in the esthetic realm his values and experience rendered him the veritable opposite of Fry's nemesis.

A CHANGE OF TITLE

Hardly capable of ever biding his time, Fry went to work on his other projects at the museum. Soon overwhelmed by the work he found to be necessary, his burden was lightened somewhat when, in 1906, the museum hired Edward Robinson, who had been the highly professional curator of classical antiquities at the Museum of Fine Arts in Boston. Robinson, with a distinguished academic and museum background, was named assistant director, and would eventually succeed Clarke as director in 1910; together Fry and Robinson did laudable work in raising the level of expertise and renown accorded to the museum. Later developments put Robinson in a delicate position as he tried to make suitable arrangements for Fry's continuing employment at the museum. Fry would even find himself in a situation where he did not fully trust Robinson, but at the beginning of their association they worked well together. There was no question, however, but that Robinson's expertise elevated the professionalism of the Metropolitan's staff.

Fry continued to meet various American collectors and patrons, and even managed to enjoy their company on occasion. In November he wrote to Helen to describe a weekend in the country, at the Connecticut home of the Pope family, who happened to be ex-Quakers, as he described them. Fry felt the high-toned rural setting was Tuscan in flavor: he admired "the woodwork house, with a huge *loggia*, on a hill overlooking a wide valley." It seemed "a queer phenomenon" to Fry that Alfred Pope, a "man of business who used to live in Ohio, suddenly with no antecedents," had become a serious collector of what was still at the time highly innovative painting. Pope had become friends with James McNeill Whistler, part of an esthetic education in which he had "fall[en] in love with Monet and from him [went] to Whistler, Manet and Degas." Not only did he have "really superb examples" of each artist, but he and Fry "talked all day delightfully and never once was the price of anything mentioned, a rare treat that."[5]

Whatever softening of his attitude toward rich American businessmen took place—and with Pope it was his taste in European painters that was thoroughly redemptive—Fry in some ways remained a stranger in a strange land. Eventually whatever national differences and esthetic tastes separated Fry from the American scene, it appeared that his main opponent over and over again came to be Morgan.

But on the other end of the relations between employer and employee, Fry encountered resistance to his frequent absences from the museum. By July 1907 Fry and Clarke had already begun discussions as to how Fry's salary might be adjusted. Fry clearly had no desire to accept less. But that month he did write to Clarke that he would willingly change his title from "Curator of Paintings" to "European Advisor on Paintings," and thus would no longer be "primarily responsible for the care of pictures in the Museum." Clarke held off any firm decision and, clearly not keen to renegotiate terms and conditions of employment for Fry, replied to the suggestion by saying that nothing could be done until the board of trustees met in October.

In November, however, Fry was still negotiating with Laffan about the title of curator and about having the power to withdraw what he felt were weak or frivolous paintings. He told Helen, perhaps overstating things to avoid troubling her, that "I think they are really quite pleased with me," but he was having trouble getting approval to buy a Velázquez, made more difficult, he said, because Morgan was not interested in it. Morgan's acquisitiveness would become the major obstacle for Fry, and complicating matters further, the budgets for new purchases would be administered stringently, even as Morgan continued to spend freely on his own collection with a rapaciousness much remarked upon.

By the end of the year 1907, the board of trustees saw fit to approve the change in Fry's title. They in all likelihood reached this decision through Morgan's pressure. Almost a year earlier, an adjustment to Fry's position was being contemplated. Near the end of 1906, Fry observed that "Mr. Morgan, though annoyed that I refused to stay longer in America, admitted that there was work over in Europe, that someone was needed there." In February 1907, Fry wrote to tell Clarke that "I gather Mr. Morgan and Mr. Laffan are coming over [to England]" and so "we may be able to effect a satisfactory arrangement."[6] Behind these possible changes in title and function lay what became Morgan's rather more positive opinion of Fry, formed in large part during their tour of European cities, which took place over several months in 1907. Fry would now spend more time with Morgan during this tour and could observe the magnate's purchasing style close at hand. Under such circumstances, Fry's ambivalence did not abate.

## THE 1907 TOUR WITH MORGAN AND FRY

The year 1907 began auspiciously for Morgan the collector. Although he was suffering with a terrible cold, he purchased Vermeer's *A Lady Writing*, one of the Dutch master's finest works, bringing to five the total of this newly popular artist's paintings in the United States. But his spending on art had become so extensive and constant that it alarmed his son, Jack, Jr., who warned his father that such consumption drew so heavily on the family's finances that the family bank was feeling the effects. The son spoke, hesitantly, to his father, "not asking for apologies or excuses on his part." He told one of the bank's partners that Morgan "did not object to my mentioning it, which surprised me somewhat."[7] Morgan's business concerns at this time—his indecision about financing the Russian government after its loss of the Russo-Japanese war, for example, and the fervor in America to somehow or other bust up the trusts that people felt were controlling the economy for the benefit of a few multi-millionaires—made some whisper about his age and his acumen. Perhaps while the one was growing inexorably the other was suffering a diminishment. But as he had done several years running, Morgan planned a European trip, which was essentially an art buying tour.

The biggest coup of the year—and one of Morgan's most astonishing purchases—was when he bought, prior to the Europe trip, a large portion of the Kann collection. Rodolphe Kann, recently deceased, was a German resident in Paris; he had a passion for Dutch and Italian art, but had collected widely in other areas as well. Joseph Duveen arranged to buy his entire collection for $4.5 million;[8] Morgan decided to put up half, with the proviso that he could choose for himself at least thirty of the paintings. He chose well, and how could he not have, given the stellar quality of what Kann had collected: Ghirlandaio, Andrea del Castagno, van der Weyden, Hans Memling, Gerard David, Salomon van Ruysdael, and Gabriël Metsu—a list of masterpieces that would substantially reshape the Metropolitan's holdings. However, some never ended up at the Met, as many were sold by Morgan's heirs after his death. The other "missing item," so to speak, was Rembrandt's much-heralded *Aristotle with a Bust of Homer*, which for some reason Morgan declined.[9]

This purchase demonstrated all too clearly that Morgan used a number of agents, such as Duveen, who were in turn also working for other collectors. Fry may have been close to a number of important sales, but he was only one of many people who influenced Morgan, and by extension the ultimate placing of various masterpieces. Duveen, who had seized the upper hand, had promised to offer to Isabella Stewart Gardner the Castagno, *Portrait of a Man* (which features one of the most riveting stares in the Italian Renaissance). As was his style, Berenson, urging her to buy quickly, described it at the time as "the grandest surviving work of one of the greatest figures in Italian art," but Mrs. Gardner couldn't afford it. The Panic of 1907 had left her short of funds. The event distressed her greatly: "Woe is me! Why am I not Morgan or Frick? I am wretched about it," she told Berenson. Duveen also managed to sell one of Kann's Vermeers, *A Maid Asleep*, to Benjamin Altman, who later bequeathed it to the Metropolitan.

In April 1907, Fry began to face a simmering complication that would not come to light until later. It was serious, especially because it concerned Fry's prospects and Morgan's buying habits. Still, Fry may have hoped to resolve it through the process of a tour of Italian cities, where he and Morgan were to be in each other's company for several weeks. Fry, however, needed timely advice and support, and so he turned to his Philadelphia friend Johnson shortly before the European tour began. Writing to Johnson to complain first of a change in policy at the museum, he related how the trustees "have cut down the fund . . . to a small figure and say they wish to save up for great and sensational things." Such a policy went against what Fry had argued for in "The Idea of a Gallery." Worse than this, though, was Morgan's sense that both Fry and the museum should be at his disposal, and that Morgan should have something like the right of first choice in any acquisition the museum might be contemplating. Fry elaborated on his unpleasant situation to Johnson: "I have found several other Italian pictures which I wanted for the Museum, and on my calling Mr. Morgan's attention to them he secured three for himself and expressed a pious hope that the Museum might be able to buy the rest!" By thus proving himself a "serious competitor" to the museum, Morgan had violated an implicit understanding of how acquisition and collection building should work. Fry was upset, but remained resigned for the time being. "I must go on doing my best in the hope that cultivated public opinion will have something to say before long." His patience presented no solution, and the hope of some response by the public was futile.

In the late spring of 1907, Morgan invited Fry to join him on his extended tour of European cities. With the Panic of 1907 starting to reverberate (in fact, the stock market crashed the day after he sailed from New York), Morgan meant to disentangle himself from the pressures of the country's financial industry to dedicate his efforts to spending a great deal of time and money in the pursuit of more art. He was on this occasion to spend and acquire at a rate far above his yearly average. Some have suggested that the Panic convinced Morgan that his days as a financier would slowly be given over to his pleasures as a collector.[10] The European tour could also be regarded as a second interview of Fry by Morgan, as the financier wanted to maintain access to Fry's expertise, enlisting him with the title of "European agent" for the museum. The tour began with Morgan celebrating his seventieth birthday in Aix-en-Provence. Morgan had brought his sister, Anne, along as a chaperone, for he was also entertaining and continuing his affair with Mrs. Adelaide Douglas. Adelaide's husband, William Proctor Douglas, was a very wealthy man, whose fortune was largely inherited from his father; the family memorialized their name by arranging to have a town on Long Island—Douglaston—named after them. Morgan and Adelaide had been intimate for a number of years, and Fry snidely referred to the couple's sleeping arrangements on the tour.[11]

All told, it was an odd tour. The relations between Fry and Morgan oscillated between a distant coolness and what seemed like genuine friendliness. Some of this mix was determined by Fry's odd position, since he presumably was facing up to the fact that he could not satisfy Morgan and the museum without spending more months a year in New York than he was willing to spare. Helen's illness was continuing to drain his resources, both monetary and psychological. But being in the European cities where the artworks were familiar to him, and where his expertise could shine, gave him an advantage that he hadn't enjoyed during his two trips to America. Watching up close as Morgan spent his money with unchecked insouciance must have sobered and distracted Fry at once. As for Morgan, the tour was taking place during one of the gravest stock market panics of his career. In fact, his status as a legendary figure, even an unmatched financial genius, would be certified by his response to this panic, and the consequent public admiration at the extent and force of his powers.

Meanwhile, there was more art to be bought. Morgan, having invited Fry to join him, along with his sister Anne and Adelaide, set the itinerary and the timetable. The travelers met up in Perugia in late May, then were driven to Assisi, making brief stops in Spello and Foligno, then went on to Florence, where the two men went their separate ways for a few days, then to Siena and San Gimignano together. Then it was on to the Mediterranean, where they boarded Morgan's yacht and sailed to Paris. By the middle of June, they were all back in London.

Their activities in Italy were various, and the sociability often rose to pleasant levels, as Fry wrote to Helen describing the events and the atmosphere. His state of mind was nevertheless agitated, and the traveling conditions probably only exacerbated the situation. Before he got to Perugia, he was able to tell Helen that Morgan "seems quite willing that I shall have my own terms with the Museum." He had also heard that back in New York things were "gradually turning in [his] favor," as some of the strife between him and other members of the Met staff was settling down. Presumably traveling with Morgan conferred on Fry a mark of approval. Since so much of Helen's situation depended indirectly on Fry's ability to work out his conditions of employment, he tried to strike the right note with her, not too optimistic but anticipating the best. "I hope the long period of unsettled anxiety about my position is gradually closing. I think I have been right not to precipitate things too much by being impatient of their odd ways, though it has been hard to hold oneself in. After all, it is the greatest opportunity I have ever had and I must not throw it away hastily."

Fry arrived in Perugia on May 25, having taken the train down from Milan; it was, he wrote to Helen, "a wonderful hot May morning and all the Umbrian hills the palest grey in the heat haze and the fields in stripes of pale olive green and pink sainfoin . . . It is like coming home in every way." He was there a day ahead of Morgan, so spent some of his time at an exhibit of Umbrian art. Fry, finding Morgan "affable," observed how he was treated. For example, when they attended the exhibit, and after they left the building "a little crowd of young men gathered to watch and . . . all the chief people come to offer their services." They had come to try to sell things in many cases, but also just to see Morgan. "It astounds me," wrote

Fry, "that here they should know and feel about him like that. Somehow he has touched the imagination of people as no other millionaire has." Obviously Morgan's earlier buying trips had carried all before them, and local artisans pursued him avidly. At such moments, noting that Morgan even looked at things that he couldn't buy (presumably altars, bell towers, and such), Fry said, "I've got on wonderfully with him in this mood." Absent the acquisitive mode, Fry could see Morgan differently.

The party left Perugia on May 29 and drove through pouring rain and fog, arriving in Assisi. Here the local populace, even the Franciscan monks, were "in a state of frenzied excitement." Fry quipped that "poor St. Francis's marriage with poverty seemed to have brought forth a strange offspring." However, Morgan's pleasure in viewing the lower of the two churches—he proclaimed Giotto's fresco of the *Raising of Lazarus* "the finest picture he had ever seen"—made the affair "not so crude after all." Further lightening of the mood came when they were joined by Berenson, who "watched the whole proceeding with a sense of humor of the whole thing. I dined with them afterwards and we laughed over my position as bearleader to the great man." On June 1, Fry went alone to Florence, where he stayed with Herbert Horne and joined Berenson and Mary for dinner. Berenson, whom Fry saw as "quite absurd," tried to catch his guest out by asking him about attributions of various canvases Berenson had collected, but Fry put him off; however, "he still tried to make my ignorance as apparent as he could with very little success," he told Helen.

From Paris, where he stayed for ten days in June and there bought "fine things for the Museum and some superb ones for Morgan," Fry reported to Helen on the 16th that Morgan was "more colossal than ever in his purchases but also much more intelligent. He's mighty pleased with me." Apparently Fry was convincing, to some extent, in his discussions with Morgan about attribution and esthetic values. Ironically, however, the problem of separating the "fine things for the Museum" from the "superb ones for Morgan" would be the difficulty upon which Fry's situation would founder. He left the next day to return home to his family, then residing in Hampstead.

WORKING AS AN AGENT FOR THE MUSEUM ALLOWED FRY
to draw on skills he had developed before his first association with
the institution. It looked as if the change in title—from curator to
European agent—would satisfy those concerns about the amount
of time in residence in New York and defuse the tensions that had
grown steadily. Because the amount of time required in New York
had never been spelled out while Fry held the title of curator, it
might have been assumed that acting as the European agent would
obviate any need for a close accounting of his time. But given Morgan's work habits, he may have felt all along that Fry's commitment
was less than strong. Others in the museum may have felt this way
too, or they might simply have sensed that Morgan's disapproval
wasn't likely to dissipate. The affair of the alleged damages to paintings didn't make matters any easier. In some sense Fry never settled in.

He also managed to sour some of his colleagues—especially the
then director, Robinson—when he bought a painting that did not
meet the approval of the trustees. Fry had approached Robinson and
secured permission to bid on a major painting by Pierre-Auguste
Renoir, *Madame Georges Charpentier and Her Children*. Since this was
one of the relatively early acquisitions by the Metropolitan of a painting by an Impressionist, its esthetic qualities were underappreciated,
to say the least, by many in the museum who were jealously protec-
tive of their influence. One can hear in the note about the Renoir
group portrait that Fry wrote for the museum's *Bulletin* an under-
tone of pedagogic and esthetic instruction. It might have put the
British art historian in an unfavorable light through its arch value
judgments.

*Indeed in the tardy recognition which the group of revolutionaries
who were working in the sixties and seventies has at last won from
the public, Renoir has as yet had no very conspicuous share. Not
only has he not yet obtained the fame of an older man like Manet
(now securely enshrined as one of the great old masters) but his work
is probably still barely human to many amateurs who have long been
familiar with his contemporaries Monet and Degas. Yet there are*

*good judges, especially among artists, who think that Renoir is destined ultimately to take a higher place . . .*[12]

Added to this somewhat high-handed estimate of the acquisition was the painting's steep price, for the time a relatively extravagant $20,000. Morgan's opinion on this score went unrecorded, but his tastes did not include an awareness of the then present and future enthusiasm that Renoir eventually attracted from American collectors and museums.

In early November 1907, Fry returned to New York after the summer and his tour with Morgan. He had managed to convince Morgan to keep him on as "European advisor" on painting, with no loss of compensation. By the end of the month he told Helen how the Panic of 1907 had kept people from "getting any money for ordinary purposes," though he himself used a "solid and safe" bank, and Morgan "by all accounts has saved the country from a terrible catastrophe." This referred to his marshaling his fellow bankers to persuade them to advance enough of their funds to restore liquidity to the financial markets. Popular opinion believed that a major depression had been averted by Morgan's powers of analysis and persuasion. More pointedly as far as Fry's personal interests went, Morgan had "stood absolutely to his word to me and arranged everything with the Trustees, only I must find the [replacement as curator], and that is what I am now trying for. If possible, I see, he should be an American." Six weeks later, Fry wrote to his mother and told her that in accepting the new title of European advisor he was resigning as curator, and Bryson Burroughs, the young assistant that Fry had hired to help him, had been made acting curator. Burroughs himself aspired to be a painter and had trained in part in Paris, where he developed an enthusiasm for Pierre Puvis de Chavannes; he favored a painting devoted to mythic and spiritual subjects.[13] He and Fry enjoyed a warm working relationship, and Fry was clearly pleased with the selection.[14] The situation looked temporarily resolved, but at the same time Fry wanted to "establish a reputation" in America for his lectures, which would pay well if he gave them to "a wider audience," and besides "one never knows what turn things at the Museum might

*Bryson Burroughs: A distinctive, but non-modern, painter in his own right,*
*Burroughs (1869–1934) was hired by Fry and eventually replaced him*
*as curator at the Metropolitan. He went on to manage and catalog the museum's*
*paintings for twenty-five years. Image copyright © The Metropolitan Museum*
*of Art. Image source: Art Resource, New York, NY.*

take." At this point Fry planned to ask for the museum to pay his steamship ticket back to England on a larger boat because he was "too wretched on the small ones to face it at this time of year." So his commitment was reaching a point of mutual understanding, but it still lacked the note of certainty.

What was certain, though known to none at the time, is that Fry's voyage home in late 1907 would be his last transatlantic crossing.

When he arrived in Hampstead in early January 1908, Berenson's latest book, *North Italian Painters of the Renaissance*, was waiting for him. He responded with a letter of praise, and probably felt that the book could well serve as a shopping guide. There was sad news to convey, however, as Helen's condition remained poor; "things begin to look very menacing for the future," he sadly confessed. The entire year of 1908 Fry spent scouring the European markets for paintings that the museum might acquire, and by the end of February he was also beginning to make visits to some of the collections in English estates and country houses. He worked diligently as the European agent for the museum, writing often to Burroughs, providing detailed descriptions, setting out the pluses and minuses of each canvas. John G. Johnson and Fry corresponded as well, and Fry continued to locate and suggest to his friend some pictures for possible purchase for his personal collection. Burroughs traveled to England, where he joined Fry in the late summer, and Fry generously introduced him to William Rothenstein, an old friend and an admired artist.

Work as an agent for the Metropolitan continued into 1909. In March of that year he helped the museum, through the expertise of the "indefatigable" Herbert Horne, acquire a "quite magnificent polyptych altarpiece by Taddeo Gaddi." Fry's attention to other matters was also energized. Most significant, perhaps, was his long letter to the *Burlington* in March 1908 concerning Monet and the Impressionists, in which he protested "against a tendency . . . to treat modern art in a less serious and sympathetic spirit than that which you adopt towards the work of the older masters." This interest in modern painting soon reached a crucial turning point, as the Impressionists and later French painters would become the focal point of Fry's criticism, which would begin to flower in the coming months. Fry's life as a critic for the next few decades was beginning to be reshaped.

In 1909 he even took a forward step in expanding his range of writing and studying about all periods by becoming the editor of the *Burlington*. The fact remains, however, that steady employment at the Metropolitan would have eased his situation considerably.

The fixed and underlying conflict in sensibilities between Morgan and Fry grew more untenable and finally reached a final rupture with an incident in June 1909, involving a Fra Angelico *Madonna* that Morgan had purchased from a London dealer.[15] In part the incident, which quickly became highly unpleasant and consequential, resulted from Fry and Morgan not being in contact with one another, as both assumed freedom of movement and choice applied fully to their arrangements with dealers. Because of the three-way miscommunications that occurred, the conflict mirrored those involving Fry's appointment and the cleaning scandal, though this time the consequences proved to be much more severe.

Fry had seen the Fra Angelico first, thought it most desirable, and wrote De Forest for permission to make an offer of £10,000 to the dealer.[16] De Forest agreed, but cautiously added that Laffan also had to agree. Meanwhile the picture had entered Morgan's ken, and he moved with his accustomed swiftness to have it. The dealer, F. Kleinberger, innocently believed that Morgan was merely making final the process that Fry had initiated and De Forest and Laffan were scrupulously and slowly approving. But the central fact remained: an important painting was being denied the museum, and being denied by the wealth and acquisitiveness of its main trustee. For Fry, with or without his Quaker sense of justice being invoked, this was clearly an unethical—and ungentlemanly—thing to have done. At no other time did the clash of esthetic, financial, and ethical concerns reverberate more deeply and at greater length than here.

What happened next did nothing to calm the situation. In June 1909, Fry wrote Morgan a letter detailing the events in their chronological order, explaining—it can be presumed—the facts about which he, Morgan, had not been aware. When Fry ended the letter saying that he was writing so that Morgan "should know the exact state of the case," the forensic and even prosecutorial tone showed through. Morgan, apparently thinking such an attitude and its attendant tone unthinkable, passed the missive to Belle da Costa Greene, writing on top of it a brief characterization and a sharp command, "The most remarkable letter I ever received. I do not propose to answer it until I see you. Bring it back." No record of any response exists. Whether Belle calmed Morgan, or Morgan calmed himself—thinking that no response at all would best serve his interests—Fry's feelings can only be guessed. But his feelings were to be drawn out in further conflict concerning his relation to Morgan and the museum, which came more and more to mean the same thing.

Given Morgan's character and temperament, such a letter as Fry had written inevitably further stirred the currents of feeling that would lead to his dismissal from the museum. The incident drew comments from several people Fry could hardly consider friends. In early 1910, after the dismissal was final, Belle da Costa Greene, for example, told Berenson that she didn't know exactly what had happened, and no one was "willing to tell just what was the last straw." Berenson, writing after the contretemps over the *Madonna* was known about, wrote a catty letter to Isabella Stewart Gardner in which he bragged that the *Madonna* had been offered to him for eight thousand pounds, and he was confident he could have had it for six. Fry, since he paid twelve, was to Berenson "a goose."[17] Berenson, always vain about his own ability to judge prices, in his letter to Gardner did not see fit to evaluate Morgan's role in what had happened.

The decisive break with Morgan, and the unchecked influence Morgan exercised at the museum, only made clear that Fry lacked control over the terms and conditions under which he worked. What Fry, caught in the torrent of misunderstandings, might not have realized is how unworkable the situation had become. While he was employed as an advisor to Morgan, and having no presence or shaping role in the museum, only part of Fry's expertise would be utilized. Morgan surely conveyed the details of the *Madonna* incident to the trustees—though the museum would not officially affirm that—and so from June until December of 1909 Fry was increasingly isolated and finally left altogether stranded. The process was to end much as it had begun.

Fry had sent a series of letters in the second half of 1909 trying to elicit some change or clarification in his position. Drawing again on his Quaker and British sensibility, Fry felt that the museum had waffled on the terms of his employment and was refusing either to honor its commitment to him or explain why it was not doing so. Robinson was outwardly sympathetic, but it became clear—in a way Fry could not swallow—that his advisory relation with the museum was at an end. With that relation vanished, any prospect of a curatorial or educational role was finished. In August 1909, Fry complained to Robinson that he had been badly treated, obviously relying on his belief, naïve as it proved to be, that the change in title had solved all the problems. Robinson responded in September with a two-page letter that outlined the situation in stark terms: that no meeting of the trustees had taken place, so no definite answer was forthcoming; that he, Robinson, had not raised the issue of the termination with Morgan (which Fry probably found hard to believe); that Fry should take a position elsewhere, such as the Slade Professorship; and if Fry should be offered and accept another position, then Fry would make things final and have the board officially terminate Fry. Burroughs, perhaps reluctantly but now carrying additional authority in his position as curator, joined Robinson in suggesting that Fry should resign. Their opinion had already hardened over the incident when Fry bought the Renoir.

Then on December 28, 1909, Robinson wrote to Fry with the final news: the board had voted to "terminate their present arrangement with you." This was further described as a board action "merely to discontinue your present office and salary." Robinson said the obvious, namely that he "felt for some time it was inevitable," and again he tried to evade acknowledging the real force at work when he added that the Fra Angelico incident had not entered into it. Fry responded three weeks later by saying that Robinson had not been straightforward and "so your letter becomes a little mysterious." Another letter from Fry followed, this one to De Forest, in which he said, "I note no explanation of this action is given." Once more a triangulation of forces—Fry, Morgan, and the Metropolitan's administration—produced a series of miscommunications, or cloudy evasions, or gentlemanly agreements. In effect, Fry persisted in requesting that the board say clearly that his services were no longer needed and would not be used in any way. To this implicit request Fry received no explicit answer.

On February 14, 1910, Fry had to summon his courage and inform his father about his employment situation. "Morgan could not forgive me for trying to get that picture for the Museum," he wrote, and added of one of the trustees he had been counting on for support, "[Joseph] Choate has proved a broken reed." He sent copies of the the Met/Fry correspondence to his father, but added that he felt "it is useless to make any fuss about it. I could get no satisfaction from these people, but they have behaved vilely." The Slade Lectureship at Oxford was vacant, and Fry had some hopes, eventually dashed, in that regard. Helen needed care of the kind only available in an asylum, and so the financial prospects were dimmer than ever. Five days later he would also inform Berenson as to Helen's precarious state, and thank him for being willing to write a letter of recommendation for the Slade, saying that it was of "vital importance, as America has failed me after treating me, well as anyone who knows those gents might expect." He told his father that he had his lecturing, and his chances for "a post as critic on the daily or weekly Press" were positive by any reckoning. He was doubtless physically and psychologically drained, but he ended the letter by asserting, "I am not at the end of my resources."

# CHAPTER V

# MORGAN AND
# THE BUILDING OF
# AN ENCYCLOPEDIC MUSEUM

ONCE J. P. MORGAN DECIDED THAT HE AND Roger Fry could not be compatible, and Fry's abilities as a European agent were dispensable, the two men had little reason to maintain any personal relationship. Morgan's secretiveness meant that only people in his closest circle of confidence would be consulted or rewarded. Fry, for his part, felt very ill served by Morgan and the administrators at the museum. In retrospect, both men might have seen their dealings as star-crossed at best, and thoroughly ungrounded in any lasting shared values. Morgan clearly knew what he wanted to achieve with the growth of the museum, and Fry's time there was beset with worries about his wife's illness, his shaky finances, and his conflicted estimation of how American culture was developing. Morgan, in the later years of the first decade of the new century, slowly turned his attention away from finance and toward his art collection, continuing to buy at a record pace and to donate artworks of all sorts to the Metropolitan. Indeed his philanthropy, unmatched in energy and willfulness, would remake the very idea of the museum into an encyclopedic institution. But it still had no place for Fry.

However, a threadbare relationship persisted between the two men, though largely based on commercial considerations. Fry hopefully sent a number of rather plaintive offers to Morgan, in July 1909, soon after the contretemps over the Fra Angelico, but to no avail. These included a detailed letter about some Aretine pottery, a favorite of Morgan, most of which was made in the first century by Romans using molds. The offer included an ingenious reproduction of an original Aretine mold that Fry had made, claiming it was "a special process of my own invention." Included as well was a fragment of the original pottery. Two days after Christmas Fry wrote again, this time with an important Persian astronomical treatise, at a price of 40,000 francs. Morgan rejected both offers. Fry meanwhile had at hand an offer of two volumes of the unpublished letters of Thomas Babington Macaulay, the famous English historian, mainly written to his family members, and for which the publication rights were already promised to someone else. This aroused little interest, though Morgan scribbled a note on the letter: "not now may see him in London."

However, Fry knew enough, and was desirous enough, to send some of his offers through Belle da Costa Greene. He may have recalled the earlier situation that required him to address any correspondence to Berenson through his wife. On October 15, 1910, he wrote Belle to offer Morgan a pair of bronze doors that he suggested would go well in Morgan's library. Included in this letter was the offer of a portrait of Elizabeth of France, the daughter of Henry V, though all he could vouch for was that it was done by an Italianizing Flemish painter. Belle, speaking for Morgan, declined, but graciously said that the sketch of the bronze doors Fry had sent her was now "very proudly hung in my best room." Two days before year's end in 1910 Fry asked Belle if there were any chance Morgan would be interested in a "marvelous little bronze from an old Russian family with Imperial connections"—an object that would surely have tempted Morgan decades earlier, and about which Fry could attest that "I firmly believe is by Benvenuto Cellini." With a wish that she enjoy a "Happy Christmas," Fry's correspondence with Belle—and with Morgan—ceased. It was only left to Belle three weeks later to convey Morgan's decision to pass on the Cellini, and to offer a bit of comfort by telling Fry that Morgan was on his way overseas, and "I dare say you will see him in London before long." There is no record that the two ever met again.[1]

Fry's disposition during the year or two after he left the museum was plainly driven by economic necessity. This was made especially burdensome by his decision to move into Durbins, the house he designed for himself and his family in Guilford. He fervently hoped this would make things somewhat easier for Helen. Morgan apparently was prepared to treat Fry at this time as just another agent, someone who had at a minimum the possibility of assisting in the acquisition of something of value. Morgan's failure—if that is what it was—to be interested in Fry's offers does not necessarily reflect his estimation of Fry's expertise. As for that expertise, Fry had only a few chances to describe what he was offering, but it is fairly clear that he angled for Morgan's taste, hoping that what he knew of the man's desires would give him an effective advantage. The coda of their relationship contained an irreducibly sad note, as Fry looked furtively for some sort of monetary gain (and a chance to maintain some contact with Morgan's wealth), while Morgan went on imperiously at the museum, and for his own collection, exercising the right of first refusal.

Morgan continued to buy and collect art, though his voracity began to diminish after this period. Several changes in his banking empire would make him rather a different figure, though he magisterially kept his position as president of the trustees at the Met until his death in 1913. However, his interest turned enthusiastically to Egyptian art, and his purchases of Italian Renaissance paintings tailed off considerably. Instead of the European buying tours, he spent more and more time traveling in Egypt, touring on a boat up the Nile. As with the *Corsair*, this vessel, a *dehabiyeh*, which Morgan named *Khargeh* (after an ancient town on a caravan route), was custom built for him, and usually carried parties of close friends and featured guided excursions and displays of various artifacts, most of which he donated to the museum.

His main advisor and close friend for many years in the area of Ancient and Egyptian art, as well as art matters in general, was William Laffan. Laffan's passing in late 1909 meant that Morgan had lost one of his most trusted advisors. With uncommon speed, especially considering Laffan's unexpected death, Morgan honored his friend with a generous endowment. This took the form, in January 1910, of a gift of $100,000 to Yale University to establish a chair in Assyriology and Babylonian literature in Laffan's name. Beyond a lasting friendship, this gift pointed to Morgan's growing interest in Ancient and Egyptian art and culture. The *New York Times* obituary for

Laffan made the connection explicit. Quoting the eulogy by Robert Weeks De Forest, the newspaper reported that "Mr. Laffan was as much at home in the field of Egyptian and classic art as in that of Oriental porcelains and primitive paintings. His expert knowledge was freely given to the Museum at all times and in all seasons." The praise reached the ears of those at Laffan's memorial ceremony, many of them leaders in finance and art collecting. De Forest further pointed out that, owing to Laffan's generosity and expertise, "the Museum [enjoyed] many recent opportunities to purchase advantageously." The burial ceremony itself was private, restricted to the Laffan family. Like John G. Johnson, Laffan valued his privacy in a way that not only emulated Morgan but probably had strengthened their friendship.

Still, Morgan did not altogether avoid the public eye. His position at the museum could hardly be considered a private activity. However, it seemed to suit his desire for discretion, combining as it did a chance to exercise his personal power on a large scale and still carry with it the aura of public service. Morgan left little by way of any personal writings, but his plans for the museum were clearly expressed in the way he reorganized and staffed the various activities according to his own lights. The episode with Fry was likely quickly put behind him. Whatever schemes for display and education Fry might have envisioned, Morgan's plans would virtually remake the museum in dimensions and directions far beyond the normal scope of a single expert.

## SHAPING THE MUSEUM'S DEPARTMENTS

The Metropolitan Museum's year-end report for 1905 first publicized the highly ambitious plan that Morgan and Sir Caspar Purdon Clarke had drawn up for the development of various departments to professionalize the institution and direct its educational mission. In this long-term context, of course, Morgan's influence continued to shape the Metropolitan Museum long after Fry had left its employ. This influence may have originated in Morgan's wealth and his strong will; the appointment of trustees, for example, became a personal prerogative for Morgan, and it directly shaped the museum's policies in countless ways. Most formative of all from an institutional point of view, however, were the addition of the museum's various departments and the determination of their future size and role. These departments were responsible for greatly expanding the number of visitors to the museum, as well as announcing the full range of its educational mission.

The three most popular and successful departments were the Department of Decorative Arts, headed by William Valentiner and established in 1907; the Department of Arms and Armor, officially formed in 1912 and first curated by Bashford Dean, who had joined the staff in 1906; and the Department of Egyptian Art, begun in 1906 and whose first curator was Albert M. Lythgoe. Morgan appointed each of these men, after his personal interview with them, a meeting that resembled the one that Fry and Clarke had undergone in 1905. If we set aside any final estimation of Fry's role in the development of the museum, the appointments of these three men—with the concomitant establishment of their respective departments—left the indelible mark of Morgan on the institution for generations.

By some measures, Valentiner was foremost among these three, if only for the variety of posts he would hold over a long career, the amount he would publish, and the forward-looking exhibits he would mount. His major distinction might best be summarized in the claim that he introduced German art history into America. The son of an astronomy professor at Heidelberg, he was born in 1880. He studied at Heidelberg, and then in the Netherlands with Cornelis Hofstede de Groot, a famous Rembrandt scholar. Through him Valentiner came to know Wilhelm von Bode, the legendary German connoisseur and curator at the Kaiser Friedrich Museum in Berlin, for whom he worked as an assistant. Bode's training of Valentiner meant seeing that he would be familiar with all the areas of a museum, so as to be a more effective administrator. Bode's prodigious reputation for rigorous learning led Morgan to ask him for a recommendation for someone who could manage the Metropolitan's collections of precious objects. Bode quickly suggested Valentiner, and Morgan hired him in 1907 to curate the newly established Department of Decorative Arts. It was an inspired choice.

*William Valentiner: Valentiner (1880–1958) was close to Morgan and became the first director of the Metropolitan's Decorative Arts Department. Later he would lead the Detroit Museum of Art, and eventually the North Carolina State Museum and the Getty Museum in Santa Monica. Photograph by Ben Williams, ca. 1956, courtesy of North Carolina Museum of Art.*

    Valentiner was the sort of expert that would become an ideal force in the remaking of the museum as an educational institution. Added to his many innovations in publicizing art throughout the country and professionalizing the post of museum director, in 1913 he founded the journal *Art in America*, aimed at a popular audience. He skillfully arranged displays of material from the extensive Hoentschel collection of medieval art, putting tapestries and sculptures together in prominent places in the museum. He and Morgan got along very well, and Valentiner believed Morgan's collecting impulse to be genuine, as he already lived among society's elite and didn't need to use art chiefly as a means to amass greater social prestige.[2] Valentiner's interview with Morgan followed a familiar script and took place in a familiar atmosphere. Edward Robinson, at the time the acting director since Clarke's illness had led to a year's leave of absence and eventual retirement, joined the two men and others at dinner. As with Fry's earlier experience, the interview was conducted around Morgan's dominant presence. However, Valentiner seemed not only unfazed by Morgan's forcefulness, he apparently relished it, though again an image of cryptic imperiousness attached to Morgan. Valentiner described the scene: "After shaking hands with me—he had very soft, big hands—in a very hearty way, he did not utter a single word, sitting like a big and powerful Buddha at the head of the table, saying at intervals a couple of unfinished sentences which I could not understand." Valentiner spoke relatively little English at this time, but even though Morgan's German was fluent, the conversation took place in German and English, and was typically tuned to Morgan's desires. Calling Morgan's silence "characteristic," Valentiner noticed that Morgan was able to "impose his will on those around him, who were numb with awe." With seeming inevitability, Valentiner won the appointment.

Again, as with Fry, however, a dispute eventually arose between Morgan and the new curator. Valentiner had occasion to describe a newly acquired sculpture as being by Andrea del Verrocchio, one of the great masters of the Italian Renaissance whose work was scarce in American museums. When Valentiner hailed it as one of the first Verrocchios to come to America, Morgan sternly demurred. According to his lights he already owned several, he informed the new curator. Valentiner would later reduce Morgan's holdings when he de-attributed a pair of Verrocchio andirons in Morgan's Library. Arguing instead that only a terra-cotta bust, also in the Library, was indeed authentic, Valentiner published his argument claiming so. No response or rebuttal by Morgan has survived. In contrast, Fry's way of approaching Morgan's ego had proved much less efficacious.

Despite the Verrocchio contretemps, comity between Valentiner and Morgan flourished. It was strengthened because of the Hudson-Fulton Celebration of 1909. That year, the states of New York and New Jersey, and particularly the City of New York celebrated the legacy of both Henry Hudson—the Dutch discoverer in 1609 of the river that flows into New York harbor—and the engineer and inventor Robert Fulton—whose steamboat company, founded in 1807, made its steamboat run from Albany to New York City in 1809. Valentiner contributed to the celebration by mounting an exhibit of seventeenth-century Dutch paintings at the museum in the city that used to be called New Amsterdam. Since part of the guidance for the celebration was in the hands of a general art and historical committee chaired by Morgan, which also included Andrew Carnegie, Joseph Choate, and Robert Weeks De Forest (soon to be the Met's new director), among others, Valentiner's work drew broad and positive attention. The curator allowed himself to sound a triumphal note in the catalog published by the museum: "Some little astonishment will no doubt be felt in European art circles that it was possible to assemble in New York one hundred and forty nine paintings of first importance, among them thirty-seven Rembrandts, twenty Franz Hals, and six Vermeers."[3] The flow of European masterpieces into America for the preceding three decades and more, a flow masterfully brought to a flood tide by Morgan and his peers, could now be publicly announced with a wry touch—"Some little astonishment" indeed. But Valentiner did not stop with a touch of light irony. The catalog, opening with an overview of the paintings of the period and followed by detailed notes on each work, presents a masterful example of how art history can be adapted for a popular audience.

When the First World War started, Valentiner returned to Germany, where he served in the army. (Franz Marc, the German expressionist painter and founder of Der Blaue Reiter, who was his company's sergeant, was killed in the war.) In Germany after the war Valentiner strenuously argued for opening museums to the general public, even though this offended his old mentor, Bode, and other more conservative art historians and curators. After the war he returned to America, where he would become a citizen in 1930. Meanwhile he wrote a catalog of the Widener Collection for the museum, where he worked for a few years before going on to important museum directorships at the Detroit Museum (where he commissioned a famous series of murals by Diego Rivera) and in Los Angeles and in Raleigh, North Carolina (the latter two for short terms). He mounted impressive and historically important exhibits on German Expressionism (the first in America), Leonardo da Vinci, and the German Expressionist Ernst Ludwig Kirchner, and was an early supporter of displaying African art in American museums. The culmination of his illustrious career came, just four years before his death, when, after a short stay at the North Carolina Museum, he served as the director of the new J. Paul Getty Museum in 1954.[4]

Valentiner's career was well served by his time at the Metropolitan. The use of objets d'art to create period rooms, and enhance—and be enhanced by—masterpieces of oil painting, became more sophisticated and historically coherent as a result of Valentiner's knowledge and skills. Operated institutionally as a museum within a museum, Valentiner's department at the Metropolitan became an important component of the museum's ability to proclaim itself as one of the great artistic showcases in the world. Equally important is the fact that the museum could do this, under the guidance of Valentiner and others, while deepening its educational resources as well as broadening its widespread popularity. Having been spurred by the master plan Morgan had formulated in the museum's *Bulletin* in 1905, the Metropolitan would also become both a great source of civic pride and an educational institution of openness and inspiration for all fields of design and esthetic improvement in American society.[5]

Another strikingly gifted curator, using skills similar to Valentiner's, helped Morgan exercise his will in another department, that of Arms and Armor, with commensurate impact. This individual was Bashford Dean.[6] After graduation from the City College of New York, he joined Columbia University as a professor in the field of zoology, where he further specialized in work on fish, becoming an expert on their evolution. Some have connected his focus on heavily scaled fish with his interest in arms and armor, which he had come to prize and collect as a young child. His major work was a three-volume *Bibliography of Fishes* (1916–1923), but he also traveled throughout Europe and in Japan searching for arms and armor, for which he had a childlike admiration; this led him to a full imaginative comprehension of the artisanal qualities of what he discovered. One of his commentators recalls a telling incident. During one of Dean's trips to Europe, he came across an ancient box in the corner of an attic in Dijon, France. The box had belonged to an armor maker some 600 years earlier and contained parts of unfinished gauntlets. Dean recalled the moment vividly: "It gave me a curious feeling to take in my hands these ancient objects which seemed only yesterday to have been put in the box by their maker. I had the strong impression that if I should go through the old door near by, I would by some 'Alice in Wonderland' wizardry, pass into the sixteenth century and find in the next room a veritable armorer at his table by the low window."[7]

Dean was also remembered for his practical ability in designing armor for the United States Army, as a recollection from *Time* magazine recorded that

> *almost as soon as War was declared, the War Department called for thin, small, dyspeptic Dr. Bashford Dean, made him a major, sent him to France to design body armor for U. S. troops. In France he slightly modified the saucer-shaped British trench helmet for U. S. use, then stood—a short, firm-jawed St. Sebastian in a suit of Dean's Body Armor, Light (9 lbs.)—while officers 10 ft. away fired automatic pistols at him. Dean's Body Armor, Heavy, withstood rifle fire at 50 yards, and though unwieldy was adopted by U. S. aviators.*[8]

Dean combined his imaginative appreciation of armor with a sound practicality, and he was especially adept at displaying the armor collection early on, even before adequate space and equipment were made available to him.

Morgan enthusiastically shared Dean's interest in arms and armor, and, through Morgan's auspices, the museum acquired an impressive collection that had belonged to the Duc de Dino, a once wealthy aristocrat in need of money. The divorced wife of Dino was a friend of Morgan's wife, and when Morgan heard the collection would be sold off, he asked a trustee, Rutherfurd Stuyvesant, to acquire it without delay. Stuyvesant offered Dino a flat fee for the entirety of the 800-piece collection. After Morgan drew on the trustees' bank accounts to reimburse Stuyvesant, the museum paid the sum back to the trustees and quite suddenly the Metropolitan had a world-class

*Bashford Dean: An expert in ichthyology, Dean (1867–1928) was a delightful addition to the Metropolitan's staff, becoming the first director of the Arms and Armor Department. He and Morgan oversaw impressive growth in the museum's armor collection. Image copyright © The Metropolitan Museum of Art. Image source: Art Resource, New York, NY.*

collection.⁹ Morgan's sway arose not only from his own wealth but also from the influence the amassment of it had on other wealthy supporters of the museum. Philanthropy was smoothly merged with peer pressure under Morgan's watchful eye.

Early on, Morgan realized he needed a group of independent-minded curators to manage things, in part by creating the various departments with their semi-autonomous standing. In 1904, when Morgan had just been chosen as the president of the museum, Dean was brought to his attention. At first Dean devoted his time and expertise to cataloging the museum's holding in arms and armor. But within two years the collection would more than double in size while maintaining its very high level of artisanship. Dean spearheaded a major expansion of the department when he helped acquire an extensive collection owned by William H. Riggs, which Morgan had set out to acquire in its entirety. Riggs had been a classmate of Morgan when they both attended a private school in Switzerland, and Riggs's father had been in business with George Peabody years earlier. What followed was an elaborate and tense courtship ritual of the kind that collectors tend to enjoy and curators strongly dislike. Again, the prime mover was Morgan.

Riggs was an unusual collector, having become an expatriate while still young, largely so that he might spend all his time looking for collections of arms and armor.[10] In 1913, after forty years of life overseas, he was accompanied by Bashford Dean when the two men sailed into New York Harbor, with the intention of donating Riggs's armor collection to the museum. But this was the end of a long journey in more than one sense.

The decades-long seduction of Riggs had begun with the founding of the Metropolitan, which chose him as a trustee in 1870, on the basis of his indication that he would leave his collection to the museum. But a few years later he resigned as trustee and the ambiguous courtship began. Three decades later his friend Morgan was elected president of the museum, and Riggs's interest was rekindled and redirected. Highly satisfied with Dean's installation of the Dino collection, Morgan assigned his young curator the task of securing Riggs's trust along with his collection. In late 1907, the museum elected Riggs an honorary trustee, which pleased him. Dean's first meeting with Riggs occurred around this time, and Dean was happily able to write to Morgan to report about the positive effect of the honorary trusteeship. Subsequently Dean forwarded Riggs's letter of gratitude to Morgan, and commented: "Please permit me to tell you how much Mr. Riggs has appreciated his talks with you and to assure you that your influence with him is very great, greater, I believe, than that of any of his other compatriots." Invoking patriotism would obviously enter into the negotiations that would follow.

Dean vividly sketched Riggs's appearance: "He was a man of sixty, clearly a scholar and a great personage—slightly built, shoulders stooping, nose aquiline, hands and feet surprisingly small, eyes clear and very bright. His face lighted up when he talked and he had charm of manner. . . . One could never forget his resonant voice which slurred no syllable, nor hurried, nor failed to choose a word which precisely 'fitted.'"[11]

The care he took with his speech obviously paralleled the care he took with his decision as to where he would donate his collection. He had earlier turned down an offer to give his collection to the nation, made directly by President William Howard Taft, because he feared that the display conditions would be inadequate. As was the case with the typical donor, the success in obtaining a collection involved constant adjustment as to the numerous terms and conditions of the gift, with the posthumous display often highest on the list.

Eventually, in the spring of 1912, Morgan took matters into his own hands and sailed to Paris where he could talk to Riggs in person. Soon, on May 12, he was able to wire Robinson that things were going very well: "Have had long and most satisfactory interview with Mr. Riggs His intention[s] in everything stand unchanged and as he says are irrevocable." After the arrangements were finally settled, Dean took charge of the transferral and sailed in 1913 with the collector and the collection—dispersed over a dozen ships—into New York Harbor, an event that occasioned considerable newspaper coverage. It was the sort of event that endeared Dean to all his colleagues. His encyclopedic knowledge—which was a close analog to the encyclopedic museum that he had helped build—was captured by the museum's announcement of his death. The board of trustees, in December 1928, passed a resolution that said,

> He seems to have known the location of every potentially purchasable piece of armor in existence and he never forgot it. He was indefatigable in pursuit. He never lost the trail. After years of effort he usually succeeded in obtaining the desired object, sometimes by purchase and not infrequently by gift. His recommendations to purchase were invariably approved. If the Museum itself did not have the needed money, he would persuade some of his friends to supply it. He was a generous donor himself, far beyond the amount of his salary. The Museum's collection of armor is really his monument.[12]

Morgan would not live to see the delivery of the armor, but he was probably never better served by any other of his employees.

The third, but by no means least, curator and department head chosen by Morgan was Albert M. Lythgoe. In February 1909 Morgan made his second visit to Egypt. He had first traveled there in 1877, but that visit had nothing like the consequences of the second. Lythgoe, who had become yet another of the experts who advised Morgan on matters of art, would render advice and information that would take Morgan far from the precincts of the museum in the final years of his life. The omnivorous nature of Morgan's collecting notably manifested itself in his taste for Egyptian art, a taste that from 1906 to 1912 would be intensely indulged, even as his taste had been handsomely expressed in the memorializing of his friend Laffan with the chair at Yale.

Morgan's connection with Lythgoe occurred in a somewhat roundabout way. In 1905, Lythgoe was on a field trip to Egypt, excavating for the Boston Museum of Fine Arts. Laffan had already become one of Morgan's most trusted advisors, and it was he who met Lythgoe and introduced him to Morgan. In typical fashion, Morgan was impressed to the extent that he soon decided to hire Lythgoe away from his current position as curator at the Museum of Fine Arts. Within a year Lythgoe had resigned from both his Harvard lectureship and the museum to become the first curator of Egyptian Art at the Metropolitan. Given a carte blanche similar to that enjoyed by Valentiner and Dean, Lythgoe began to build his own staff and to develop the scale and depth of the department devoted to Egyptian art. Lythgoe hired his former Harvard student, Herbert E. Winlock, who served as director for many of the museum's expeditions. He also added the expertise of the Oxford scholar Arthur C. Mace, Ambrose Lansing, and Charles Wilkinson, who later founded the Metropolitan's Department of Ancient Near Eastern Art. Meanwhile, for the next ten years after first joining the Museum, Lythgoe and his experts engaged in extended and important excavations in Egypt, most notably at Luxor (Thebes), in 1910. The professionalism of the Metropolitan's curators reached new heights, guided by Lythgoe's managerial skills.

The museum would sponsor excavations in Egypt in the years

*Albert Lythgoe: Morgan's enthusiasm for Egyptian art was aided by Lythgoe (1868–1934), who led archeological expeditions funded by the Metropolitan. He served as the first director of the Department of Egyptian Art. Image copyright © The Metropolitan Museum of Art. Image source: Art Resource, New York, NY.*

1905 to 1936, and so virtually half the museum's holdings today are from its own excavations. In 1910, Egyptian authorities granted the museum a concession in western Thebes, on the east bank of the Nile. Here was a great religious center and one of the richest archeological sites in the world. Other collectors, such as Henry Walters, who was operating out of the Walters Art Museum in Baltimore, were turning their attention from the masterpieces of the Italian Renaissance to the archaically rich and mysteriously spiritual works of an ancient civilization. Morgan became increasingly in thrall to the ancient feel of the Egyptian excavations, and began his habit of extended travels by boat up and down the Nile, often with Lythgoe and others in his company. He gave full bent to his practical needs as he had a boat especially built and equipped for his Nile excursions, one that could navigate narrow channels and still carry a large party of his friends.

During the first few decades of the twentieth century the science of archeology had been put on a more exacting and documented basis. This new scientific accuracy was spurred by a competition between various teams, often from different countries, and all eager to recover artifacts and put the history of the various Egyptian and Pharaonic dynasties on a firm basis. This enthusiasm would reach a peak in 1922 with the discovery by English archeologists of the tomb of Tutankhamen. Meanwhile Morgan grew increasingly reliant on Lythgoe and his team as his purchases came more often from his Egyptian than his European interests. While his interests as a collector were varied, he was drawn to the unconventional, as evident in his collection of ancient Near Eastern cylinder seals, numbering close to twelve hundred. There was also a group of cuneiform tablets, most of which are now in the Babylonian Collection at Yale University.[13] Between his fondness for mute objects and his love of ancient or historical manuscripts and books, Morgan's collecting appetite found full satisfaction in his enchantment by Egyptian matters. The museum came to achieve international acclaim in Egyptology, arms and armor, and decorative arts, due to three industrious and talented curators, all of whom reflected Morgan's tastes and enjoyed his gratitude.

With the appointments of Valentiner, Dean, and Lythgoe, Morgan shaped a museum that would change greatly over the next century, but in many ways it would be recognizable as his creation. He spent his furious energy on the museum in part because his life as a financier was drawing to a close. A pivotal date occurred with the Panic of 1907, when by force of will and immense leverage he called together the various bankers whose credit crisis was threatening everyone's fortune. The perhaps apocryphal story of Morgan locking them all in his study (while he went off to play one of his countless games of solitaire) until they could agree on the necessary fiscal and monetary arrangements contained enough truth to be widely accepted. It only added to his near mythic stature. In effect, Morgan himself was acting like a Federal Reserve Bank, controlling the loans and liens that occurred between banks as part of the country's economic system. No inner narrative exists that could definitively state whether the fabled events drained Morgan of his energy, or if he knew that regulation finally had to come on a national scale with a truly reform-minded government apparatus. (Interestingly, the Federal Reserve Act was signed into law by President Woodrow Wilson after Morgan's death in 1913.) In any case, he would soon turn more and more to the affairs of the museum. But the three new departments, gratifying as they were to Morgan personally, could not outweigh the burden that descended on him when, in 1912, he was called before the Congress to explain his role as the country's most powerful banker.

Though he had abhorred publicity and successfully avoided it for most of his career, near the end of his life Morgan became a much more public figure than he could have imagined. The House Committee on Banking and Currency—known as the Pujo committee, after its chairman, Arsène Pujo—was appointed by the 62nd Congress and would shed considerable light on Morgan's business methods and, by extension, his personal character. In a sense, the committee's report would serve as something like a summary judgment on Morgan's identity as a financier.

Morgan approached the event with full preparation and a care-

*Morgan berating a photographer, n.d. Morgan became well known for disliking publicity, and he was forthright in his antipathy to those who would violate his privacy. His choleric temperament shows up clearly here.*

fully modulated attitude of reserve and condescension. The preparation included salting the newspapers—control of several was one of the keys to Morgan's positive image—as he had done in the past, most recently as he successfully fought off the government's attempt in 1911 to break the trust of United States Steel, which he had formed, through various takeovers, into the country's first billion-dollar company. In that case Morgan had been called to Washington in October 1912 to answer whether or not his contribution to Theodore Roosevelt's 1904 presidential campaign had bought him any favorable treatment in the US Steel investigation. When one committee member asked if Morgan ever enjoyed the gratitude of the party's fund-raisers, he snapped, "No. Gratitude has been rather scarce in my opinion." The brittle humor added to the Morgan myth. Nevertheless, he was surrounded by partisans and they aided in managing his reputation, which was a source of pride to him that equaled the extent of his wealth. His daughter Louisa worried over the stress he was under; his son, Jack, supplied his associates with optimistic reports, claiming his father, referred to by the code-name Flitch, was in "splendid form" and "has never been better." He came to Washington for the Pujo committee appearance on a private train, with Louisa, several business partners, and fifteen lawyers in the retinue.[14] The congressional penchant for public spectacle approached a peak, and Morgan matched the theatrics.

The charge to the committee was to investigate the control and concentration of money and credit on the part of the nation's banks; this concentration was referred to as the "money trust." The committee met between May 16, 1912, and February 26, 1913. A representative from Louisiana, Arsène Pujo served as the chairman of the committee, and Samuel Untermyer served as the counsel. Spurred in part by the Panic of 1907, and the fiscal excesses of the Gilded Age with its monopolies and interlocking directorates, the men of the committee were stern and thorough, even though they would generate enormous publicity. Pujo's committee assembled in the summer of 1912 but delayed the hearings that involved Morgan, lest they unduly influence the upcoming presidential election.[15]

Roosevelt and Taft were the chief candidates, both proclaiming commitment to a progressive attitude toward the relations between industry and government. Known as "trust busters," Roosevelt and Taft introduced much of the legislation of the Progressive Era, including the income tax, the Pure Food and Drug Act, and the breakup of the Northern Securities, one of Morgan's companies, and one of the two richest corporations in the world. (The other was also run by Morgan: United States Steel, which produced one quarter of all the steel in the world.) Taft had a long career in public service, having served under Roosevelt as his secretary of war, and then succeeded him as president in 1908. Roosevelt had relied on Taft to a great extent, but would eventually split with him when he felt Taft failed to push hard enough for the continuation of Roosevelt's agenda. Thus the two became rivals in the 1912 election, and because they split the Republican Party vote, when Roosevelt bolted the party and formed his Bull Moose Party, the Democrat, Woodrow Wilson, emerged as the winner. Pujo and his committee opted for discretion, not wishing to appear favorably inclined to either Taft or Roosevelt.

However, during his first elected term, 1905 to 1909, Roosevelt had proved his progressive bona fides when he tempered railroad rates, creating the Interstate Commerce Commission. Taft, succeeding Roosevelt, busted the sugar trust and Standard Oil Company, ending their harmful sway over consumer prices and healthy competition. Neither president wanted to be seen as a footstool for a rapacious financier. Morgan, for his part, guarded the advantages his massive wealth brought him, and so he remained on cautiously good terms with Roosevelt, having contributed to his campaign in 1904, and he could expect support from Taft as well, should matters become too zealously reform-minded. Both presidents professed to know that banking and credit required transparency and rational justification. But public opinion had begun to run decisively against the big banks and corporations, moved in considerable measure by a press corps that energetically exposed the graft, self-dealing, and monopolistic tendencies of the country's major industries.

Now, however, came the search for the reality behind what was called the "money trust." Consisting of interlocking directorates, along with the arbitrary and restrictive policies of clearing houses, this trust dictated how banks loaned to, and borrowed from, one another. Like trusts in railroad, mining, and other enterprises, a money trust could exercise control over its members, dictating the flow of credit in ways that went far beyond that of any other entities. Character, contrary to Morgan's pious pronouncements about the need of individuals to measure one another's probity, apparently had little to do with it. Having gone from a basis of mercantile capitalism to one based on finance capital, the money trust had evolved slowly, but it functioned most effectively.

Near the end of 1912, on December 18 and 19, the seventy-five-year-old Morgan testified. Untermyer questioned him for several hours. Morgan's associates, James E. Stillman and George F. Baker, were also questioned.

According to one anonymous pamphleteer,[16] writing about Morgan's testimony, the financier began to take control of the proceedings by his nearly limitless knowledge of finance capitalism, which he had done much to shape. The anonymous author described the tight-lipped witness as "the money-king," a nearly fabled figure who "had early dealt in hundreds of millions of dollars and not even a handful of words," but because of the committee's thoroughness "now dis-

*Morgan arrives for the Pujo committee: This newspaper photo shows Morgan entering the Pujo committee hearings, flanked by his son, Jack, Jr., and his daughter, Louisa. He was also accompanied by a phalanx of lawyers.*

cussed freely and frankly the technique, the code, the ethics and the morals of [the] money market and stock market."

Treated by the Pujo committee as if he were an oracle of high finance, Morgan described the workings of "private vs. public banking, of interlocked directorates, of mergers, of voting trusts, of speculation, of credit and of money," and what he said "had behind it his own prestige and personality. His yes or no meant pages in themselves." With rather heavy irony, the anonymous commentator presented Morgan as explaining everything, though heretofore he had been nothing if not secretive. "Going further, Mr. Morgan laid down with the force of undisputed authority some of the basic tenets of finance. His definition of credit alone sufficed to lay the ghost of the 'money trust.' His observations on the functions and the faults of banker and broker set forth the essential service, while not blinking the incidental blemishes, of the country's apparatus for investment and speculation. He appraised and explained Wall Street."[17] But it was more than an explanation. The commentator, and many in the public, said of Morgan, that as far as his part in Wall Street went, "He did not have to defend it; he justified it." The not so gentle mockery in the tone of the commentator suggested that Morgan triumphed over the forces that would control or regulate his activities, let alone assess his culpability.

Opinion on all the practices and decisions revealed by Morgan would be divided, as were the assessments of his ethics and his politics. The committee, to some extent unintimdated by Morgan's reputation, produced an illuminating report.[18] Daunting and damning, its 258 pages contain careful explanations of the many obscure banking practices, such as the use of clearing houses and selling short, and it also offers supporting material to demonstrate how far speculation goes in the buying and selling of stocks and bonds. The assumed values of the committee members are evident in their approach to these conventions. Reporting on the necessity for banks to join the membership of clearing houses, for example, the committee pointed out that membership in such key organizations was very highly restricted, and clearly served consciously to restrain trade and limit competition. The same was true of the New York Stock Exchange as well. The committee's belief that "membership in such an institution should be an office of distinction and public usefulness"[19] may have guided their expectations, but such a pronouncement was seldom met with clear compliance. The committee's report quoted the report of an earlier committee, the Hughes Committee of 1909: "It is unquestionable that only a small part of the transactions upon the exchange (NYSE) is of an investment character; a substantial part may be characterized as virtually gambling." The Pujo committee went a step further. "Such excessive and indiscriminate speculation in stocks as is shown to be conducted on the New York Stock Exchange is not only hurtful in the way that all public gambling is hurtful, but in addition it withdraws from productive industry vast quantities of capital."

The committee concluded that the concentration of credit and currency resulted from a number of factors, such as the consolidation of competing banks, banks acting as controlling stockholders in various industries, the control of industrial policies resulting from such stock ownership, and partnerships and joint accounts between big financial

*Cartoon of "The Helping Hand": This cartoon parodies a famous sentimental painting by Emil Renouf, showing an old man and a young girl handling the oar of a small skiff. The scene here expresses how the government's reliance on Morgan's wealth reverses the usual scale of power.*

houses.[20] Of course, Morgan was a master at each of these practices. Since he had refused to supply the committee with his personal business records, Morgan was subjected to a detailed listing of the public enterprises in which his role and office were public knowledge. This led the committee to concentrate on two institutions, Guaranty Trust and Bankers Trust, which it identified as the first and second largest trust companies in the United States. Their combined resources came to $437 million. However, the committee went further and totaled all the assets of the seven trusts that Morgan controlled, which came to $1.389 billion. This amassing of financial assets also included, as the committee detailed, ownership through stock holdings of railroads, producing and trading companies, and public utilities. All told, the entire cadre of the officers of Morgan & Co. and the five trusts they controlled were involved in 341 directorships and 112 corporations with aggregate resources of $22,245,000,000.

Spelling out the existence of such large sums of money resting in the hands of a few men would seem to be sufficient evidence for the committee to conclude there was a "money trust." But they proceeded to gather more evidence, turning to the single most powerful banker in the country. The committee questioning Morgan was more than a little exasperated by the way he answered questions regarding the monopoly control of credit. Surely one could try to gain such monopoly control, but no, not according to Morgan. The questioner asked, "If you owned all the banks in New York, with all their resources, would you not come pretty near having a control of credit?" Morgan's denial was steadfast: "No, sir; not at all." A moment later he strengthened this claim, denying the possibility of such unlimited control: "All the money in Christendom and all the banks in Christendom can not control it." Credit for Morgan had, from the days of his ascendance, been based not on any material substance or system of accounting but on the character of both the borrower and lender, each acting as an individual, and as a judge of the other man's character. The committee considered this view as virtually unique, as they found no other witness to agree with it. The report would make Morgan's near solipsism explicit.

Pointing to the fact that Morgan's view meant that group control of credit was impossible, the committee clearly saw that his claim "rests upon the theory that credit is not based on money or resources, but wholly on character." This was true to such an extent that it applied as well to loans on the stock exchange. "This is an obvious economic fallacy," the incredulous committee insisted, "as the every-day transactions of business demonstrates [sic]." As Morgan would persist in believing that the role of character outstrips the force of financial power, the report encapsulated Morgan's sense of his own power by quoting this exchange:

Q. Your power in any direction is entirely unconscious to you, is it not?

A. It is sir. . . .

Q. You do not think you have any power in any department of industry in this country, do you?

A. I do not.

Q. Not the slightest?

A. Not the slightest.

The committee concluded that Morgan's self-serving remarks were untenable. "This again illustrates that Mr. Morgan's conception of what constitutes power and control in the financial world is so peculiar as to invalidate all his conclusions based upon it."[21] If Morgan in his own eyes had no power, then he could not have been responsible for any concentration of such. Peculiar though his views on power and control might have sounded to the committee, the legislators were intent on drawing out their conclusions.

They turned at one point to a specific example, involving the takeover of an insurance company. After trying to ascertain why a Mr. Ryan, one of Morgan's business associates, was willing to sell Morgan certain stocks at a low price simply because he desired them—it being clear that the committee knew Ryan to be intimidated, and that the sale to Morgan would give him, Morgan, control of the company—the committee's language in its report was unequivocal. Of Morgan they said that "among other things his testimony as to the circumstances under which he obtained control of the Equitable Life Assurances Co. from Mr. Ryan demonstrates his possession of power in the fullest sense, and also that he knows how to exercise it."[22] The complexity of the deals that Morgan constructed, which enabled him to control not only numerous companies but virtually entire industries, was hard for anyone but a finance capitalist to comprehend or explain. In many ways, this complexity was key to Morgan's power. The complexity made some of his actions appear irrational on the surface, which obviously added to his aura, at once suggesting and concealing the fact that he made the rules to suit his own advantages.

The knowing use of full power was the chief desideratum of Morgan's life as a banker. It extended as well to his role as a collector of fine art, and to his various offices directing the nation's cultural institutions. Perhaps the most impressive achievement that Morgan's power brought his way was his ability to maintain a reputation of integrity. Samuel Untermyer referred to this reputation when he spoke of how the findings of the Pujo committee would be forged into federal law. As for the "money trust," the committee "will say that its further growth would be a menace to the welfare of the country."[23] To prevent such further growth, the committee would recommend regulation of both the New York Stock Exchange and the Clearing House—this eventually took the form of the creation of the Federal Reserve Bank—because this was "the psychological time," since the banking laws were about to be revised. Then Untermyer added another reason: "because Messrs. Morgan, Baker and Stillman—the three dominant figures in the concentrated money power—are regarded as having such high character that their advice will be of value in connection with such remedial legislation as may be recommended."

Whether Untermyer took his cue about Morgan's "high character" from Morgan's testimony or whether Morgan's sense of his own high character was conveyed by his self-presentation is a nice question. In any case, Morgan was in many ways, and to many supporters, vindicated by the Pujo committee. Though according to the committee, a hurtful concentration of power over the credit and currency in the nation had been amassed, Untermyer had gone on record that it was not the result of any illegal activities.[24] Morgan died in March 1913 and did not live to see the creation of the Federal Reserve Bank in December of that year, and it remains a piece of historical irony that that institution can be seen as either a tribute or a rebuke to Morgan's character and his skills at consolidation.

In January 1913 Morgan left, along with a large party including Louisa and Lythgoe, to visit Egypt and again sail up the Nile. Senator Nelson W. Aldrich of Rhode Island traveled with the financier, having been a great help to Morgan by eliminating the tariff on works of art, and also planning the Federal Reserve System, which was approved under President Woodrow Wilson later that year. Upon reaching Cairo, Morgan and his party stayed in the Shepheard's Hotel. Within a few days, Morgan had a stroke. From then on his health deteriorated slowly but steadily. Beset by insomnia and nightmares, he suffered from increasing dementia, intermittently imagining plots against him and contemplating suicide.

Lythgoe and the others worked hard at turning away the press, now a group swollen with reporters from around the world. Despite all the efforts of his inner circle, rumors leaked out, and the stock market plunged. In mid-February Morgan read the Pujo committee's report and wired his associate Henry Pomeroy Davison: "Perfectly splendid. I am deeply grateful to you myself for all you have done. Love to you and Mrs. Davison. I feel quite seedy myself, but Doctor says I am improving."[25] As it happened, Morgan was more accurate than the doctors, and not even his "victory" over the committee could lift his spirits for long. He decided—or those around him decided for him—to curtail the Egyptian trip, and they set out for Rome on March 13. There he briefly recovered, long enough to visit the impressive neoclassical building underway at the American Academy atop the Janiculum hill, a last trip to see one of the more distinctive cultural institutions made possible by his philanthropy. Now, however, he couldn't shake the life-long depression that had afflicted him in regular bouts. His son-in-law ministered to him, and he would take no food or medicine from anyone but Louisa.

Plans to visit Dover House, near Wimbledon just seven miles from London, were considered, and preliminary arrangements had begun. Though Morgan was able to attend church on Easter Sunday, the aftermath was another collapse. Heavy sedation had become the rule, as counteracting the depression and panic appeared to be the most urgent need. Louisa cabled her brother—Jack had been managing all the banking business for some time at this point—to say that their father was "unconscious and does not suffer." On the last day of March, his temperature soared and his pulse raced dangerously high. Just after noon Louisa cabled Jack that "Charcoal died today twelve five." It would be the last time a code name was necessary.

Morgan's most imposing achievements survive to this day, now called JPMorgan Chase & Co. and the Morgan Library and Museum, representing his financial acuity and his artistic interests respectively. The latter represent, at least, an outgrowth, and symbolic display, of the former. His many philanthropic activities, stretching back to his days as a young man making donations to a lying-in hospital, were also possible because of his wealth, and so his philanthropic power easily extended to his art collection when it came time to plan his final gifts. However, his gift giving to the Metropolitan, and by extension to the public, did not occur as many expected.

Notably included on a list of his gifts to the public would be his many donations to the Metropolitan, such as the Hoentschel collection in 1907, the wide-ranging assortment of medieval art along with eighteenth-century gilt-bronze mounts that started the Department of Decorative Arts. However, what might have been his most notable legacy, the collection of European paintings and drawings that he gathered at great expense and with expert guidance, was scattered after his death. This was a collateral effect of Morgan having decided before he died not to give the entire collection to the Metropolitan Museum, despite the widespread assumption that he would do so. He did include in his will the proviso that his art collection be made "permanently available for the instruction and pleasure of the American people." For this purpose it was generally assumed that he had pledged $1 million toward a new wing of the Metropolitan, which would then house his collection. But approval by the city of construction of the new wing was delayed. Morgan drew up the final terms of his will with this problem in mind, and left it to his son to determine the final destination of the thousands of artworks in the collection.

Between 1914 and 1916, the museum, hoping to sway Jack's decision as to the disposition of the collection, staged several impressive exhibits of many of his works of art in various media and from various countries and periods, but this curatorial bid for consideration was unavailing. Jack served as executor of his father's will, and he decided to sell off many of the paintings in order to pay for the tax on the estate. However, portions of the collection that were not offered for sale were donated to the Metropolitan Museum and to the Wadsworth Atheneum in Hartford. Most notably, Jack also gave the Raphael masterpiece *Madonna and Child Enthroned with Saints*, also known as the *Colonna Altarpiece*, to the museum in 1916. This was followed by a gift of his father's objets d'art a year later. These were then installed in the wing of Decorative Arts the following year, and the wing was named the Pierpont Morgan Wing in 1918.

Of course his invaluable rare books, drawings, manuscripts, and incunabula still reside at the Morgan Library and Museum, along with his formidable collection of cylinder seals. The latter now occupy a room of their own, near the office where some of the more cherished items remain on display in the spots where Morgan placed them. A stunning collection of drawings—again from various hands and widely various places and times—appears from time to time in small but exquisite exhibitions. As with the museums that house the collections of people like Isabella Stewart Gardner and Henry Clay Frick, Morgan's taste and acquisitive powers are fully on display. It remains difficult to determine if his reputation rests more on his art collecting or his financial dealings; it is likely that he felt both activities manifested his skills and determination equally.

What resides in the Metropolitan from Morgan's collection of paintings is enumerated by the catalog that the museum published in 1931.

> *At all stages in the history of the collection valuable aid has been given by those who have generously lent their pictures. Mr. Morgan, besides his gifts of* Columbus *by Sebastiano del Piombo, the* Assumption of the Virgin *by Benvenuto di Giovanni, the* Argonauts *by Pesellino, and many more, helped continually by lending works from his collection. With but few exceptions the pictures that he acquired after 1906 were shown in the Museum and many of them have never left its walls since their purchase by him. In 1916, his son, J. Pierpont Morgan, presented to the Museum the* Virgin and Child Enthroned with Saints *by Raphael, the so-called* Colonna Madonna, *which had been on exhibition in the Museum since his father lent it in 1912.*[26]

The *Madonna and Child Enthroned with Saints* represents the height of Morgan's largesse, and it far outstrips the other paintings mentioned here in terms of fame and popularity. The catalog goes on to note that the following year—1913—Morgan made a gift of other unnamed paintings. The catalog, however, implies that some other collections formed on a personal basis but subsequently incorporated into the museum's holdings—such as those of H. O. Havemeyer, Benjamin Altman, and William K. Vanderbilt—have constituted the most striking enrichment of the museum's paintings.

The museum gathered many of the paintings and the plentiful items—including reliquaries, enamels, ivories, bronzes, jewels, and porcelain—that Morgan had for years held in the house at Prince's Gate and other overseas residences. They were put into a dedicated exhibition, and the catalog the museum published to mark the occasion runs to over 270 pages.[27] Making clear that the artifacts brought back to America did not constitute the whole of Morgan's collections, the catalog clarified in general terms just what was included: "To form an idea of the extent of his collections in their entirety, it should be remembered that in addition to what is now placed on view, there is in the Museum a vast amount of material belonging to them, distributed through its various departments." Specifically named were the Chinese porcelains, the Hoentschel collection of medieval art, and individual objects from the Egyptian and classical holdings. Praising Morgan's "feverish zeal" as a collector, the museum claimed of the "assemblage," that since it was "formed as it was by one man, and during a comparatively short period of his life, it is probably without parallel in the history of collecting." Not only was he "willingly pursued by dealers wherever he went," he was a "prince of collectors . . . in more ways than one." No one, not even Morgan, had seen all his collections in one place at one time. In a real sense, the catalog celebrates Morgan's idea of an encyclopedic museum, where all the several individual collections and their myriad objects represent the will and desire of a single person.

Museum curators and scholars especially value a collection formed by—and hence significantly expressing the taste of—a single person. Frick and Gardner and Morgan, in institutionalizing their personal museum collections, contributed chiefly to their own prestige. Still, the idea of an all-encompassing public institution exists in a museological category different from a "personal" collection. The dimensions of Morgan's collection can be reconstituted on paper, testimony to his singular taste. It remains, nevertheless, a loss for the general public that a considerable number of its works were dispersed, and so were not integrated into the other holdings of the Metropolitan. If they had been, the ideal of an encyclopedic museum would exist beyond dispute in the Metropolitan's holdings. By the end of the century in which Morgan died, the Metropolitan had become the second most visited museum in the world (after the Louvre), and its holdings in masterpieces of painting and objets d'art in dozens of areas outstrip the comprehension of any individual. Morgan no doubt rested in knowing that he played his part in the life of the institution.

# CHAPTER VI

# GROWTH OF AN ART EXPERT

## *Fry's Radical Vision*

ONCE FINISHED WITH HIS EFFORTS AT THE MET-
ropolitan Museum of Art, Fry turned his attention fully to the art
world in London. Mainly this meant taking up a position in 1911 as
a lecturer at the Slade School of Fine Art and continuing to write
essays and reviews, while keeping faith with his own painting. As
an institution set up to challenge the hegemony of the Royal Academy, the Slade gained recognition as one of London's more advanced
institutions in terms of the ethos and esthetics of early twentieth-
century British painting. Fry's appointment there was desirable to
the extent that it alleviated his financial straits, which were decidedly
narrowed by his having to commit Helen to an asylum in 1910, where
she would remain for the rest of her life. Still, his willingness to approach a generation of artists younger than himself signaled that his
ideas about art were leading him into a more contemporary frame of
mind. Though he never completely abandoned his interest in Italian
Renaissance painting, his focus more and more seized on the present and future worlds of art and artists. Settled into London and willing to put the bitterness of his American experience behind him, Fry
rather quickly created a role for himself in the vanguard of British
art. This would eventually culminate in his entwinement with the
promotion and defining of Post-Impressionism.

Britain itself, however, hardly represented the vanguard of modern art, especially when compared to the styles and schools developing in France and Germany, while American artists would soon
be an important part of the avant-garde as well. Nevertheless, at the

Slade a generation of young British artists began to experiment with breakthroughs first spotted elsewhere, and they were eagerly trying out the new lifestyles of bohemianism and anti-bourgeois aggression. Chief among the newer artists that attended the Slade in the second decade of the century were Stanley Spencer, Christopher R. W. Nevinson, Paul Nash, Mark Gertler, and Dora Carrington. They were taught by Frederick Brown and Henry Tonks, men with conservative tastes who were more than content to teach the older approaches that valued accurate drawing over esthetic experimentation. The more successful Slade artists would eventually build spotty and embittered careers that were gravely affected by the horrendous disruption of the Great War. Further bitterness came about as the fate of their reputations was bound up with being offered government positions as official war artists—a plan that was part of Britain's efforts to maintain morale. In the midst of this shattered culture, some of the artists felt that it was Fry and his keen mind and bold theories that helped moved the Slade and its attendees closer to modernism.[1]

But more than his work as a teacher of contemporary painters at the Slade, Fry's contribution to the theory and development of modernism became most historically significant when he mounted an exhibition in 1910, followed up by a sequel two years later. This first show prompted Fry to give to art history a new term—Post-Impressionism—that, despite the various disputes that its delineation occasioned, became an importantly fixed marker for a chapter of modernist art and culture. Behind the furor about Post-Impressionism lay a rapidly enlarging sense of art, where an esthetic based on modernist sensibility would, over the next half century and more, develop several branches of the new painting, each of which caused consternation equal to that stirred up by Fry's forward-looking exhibition. Though Fry had lost his position at the Metropolitan Museum, and the influence that would have come with it, he soon found himself becoming a major force in modern art.

So much of Fry's reputation as a leading art critic and historian involves the impact of this famous Post-Impressionists exhibition. Without that event, his would likely be a fairly average contribution to the questions that help to define modern—and modernist—art. But by providing what would be understood as the key term to classify the generation of Paul Cézanne, Vincent van Gogh, and Paul Gauguin, Fry's public identity joined with that of the Post-Impressionists to frame the narrative for what is regarded as one of the main lines of influence and development in modern painting. Two major forces shaped the narrative for Fry: the importance of Cézanne as a key innovator, and the stylistic and esthetic values that separated the Post-Impressionists from their immediate predecessors. Working out the ideas behind both of these forces took Fry deep into his own future as a critic and theorist. It also coincided with his links to the artists, writers, and thinkers who came to be known as the Bloomsbury Group, from whom he gathered important support and to whom he gave intimate friendship and intellectual stimulus.[2]

The Bloomsbury Group originated at Cambridge and was formed around friendships between and among Thoby Stephen (the brother of Vanessa Bell and Virginia Woolf, both women eventually playing major roles), Lytton Strachey, John Maynard Keynes, Clive Bell (Vanessa's husband), Duncan Grant, and others. Most of the earliest members were heavily influenced by the philosophy of G. E. Moore, known as ethical intuitionism. This laid great stress on a person's sensibility and was to a marked extent formed as a counterweight to logical positivism and scientism, both of which emphasized an unrelenting reliance on empirical data and demonstrable facts. The role of sensibility and subjectivity in Moore's philosophy led many of those who shaped the Bloomsbury circle to stress the esthetic dimensions of experience, which were garnered most frequently from works of art and questions of taste. Fry's participation in the circle drew on his thoughtful commitment to these matters and his efforts to make them readily available to definition and contention, as well as to social application.

The members met for aggressively frank discussions at the Stephen's London home, where Thoby and his sisters, Vanessa and Virginia, reshaped the model of the literary salon at their address in Gordon Square. Many of the Bloomsbury Group would go on to build variously successful careers in different areas—Keynes, for example, becoming one of the greatest economists of the century. Fry's deep knowledge of esthetics not only played a major part in the group's debates, it drove the extensive dialogue he had with certain members, especially Clive Bell. He had met Bell during a train ride between London and Cambridge (they had introduced themselves while waiting on the train platform), and Bell shared Fry with the others right away. Virginia Woolf summed up the effect his arrival generated: "It must have been in 1910 I suppose that Clive one evening rushed upstairs in a state of the highest excitement. He had just had one of the most interesting conversations of his life. It was with Roger Fry. They had been discussing the theory of art for hours. He thought Roger Fry the most interesting person he had met since Cambridge days."

Then Woolf turned from Bell's impressions to record her own: "So Roger appeared. He appeared, I seem to think, in a large ulster coat, every pocket of which was stuffed with a book, a paint box or something intriguing; special tips which he had bought from a little man in a back street; he had canvases under his arms; his hair flew; his eyes glowed."

Woolf's novelistic eye, in recording the assemblage of objects in his pockets, captured one of the features many of Fry's admirers pointed to, namely his wide-ranging interests and eager curiosity to take up and test all manner of objects and inquiries. (The repetition of the word "appeared" also lends Fry a certain numinous quality.) Bloomsbury provided Fry with friendships that brought to his ideas wide reception and intelligent amplification. At least one historian has claimed that he was "decisive in the making of the group." In any case, the influences were strong and reciprocal.

Fry's mounting of the famous 1910 exhibit—known officially as "Manet and the Post-Impressionists"—coincided with his induction into the Bloomsbury circle. The exhibit was shown at the Grafton Gallery in London from early November 1910 to early January 1911. Starting with Manet, the show included numerous works by Cézanne, van Gogh, and Gauguin, followed by other painters less well known at the time, such as Georges Rouault, Odilon Redon, André Derain, Félix Vallotton, Maurice Denis, and Maurice de Vlaminck, with a few canvases by Picasso and Matisse. The final separate gallery room contained an extensive collection of drawings, many of them untitled, but all demonstrating the change in assumptions about representational, or "illusionistic," accuracy that the entire exhibit

*Fry's portrait of Virginia Woolf: Drawn to Fry's spirit and wit, Woolf (1882–1941) would write the first biography of him. From the time they met in 1910 until Fry's death, they were two of the brightest lights in the Bloomsbury circle.*

embodied. The catalog listed over 200 drawings and paintings, and twenty-two pieces of pottery and sculpture, by slightly more than two dozen different artists. Ambitious in its scale and its readiness to declare firm opinions on style and historical continuity, the exhibition commanded attention from many in the art world, and even more among the general public. As many as four hundred visitors came on a single day.

It remained the challenge for the catalog's relatively short essay to find the esthetic center of all of this work by many hands.[3] More than a single generation was on display. Cézanne had passed away five years earlier, but some of the artists were in the relatively early parts of their careers, especially Matisse and Picasso. Their birth dates spanned almost five decades, ranging from 1832 (Manet) to 1881 (Picasso). The large majority were French, and Manet and Cézanne had well-established reputations and even were represented in a few progressive English private collections. However, few if any top London galleries were known for handling the painters whose work Fry assembled. There was no doubt that the exhibit was forward-looking enough, and posed enough of an aggressive challenge to the orthodoxy of London society to create a tempest that had all the force of a national scandal. Fry enlisted several English notables to sponsor the event, but as the catalog pointed out—in two separate places—"The ladies and gentlemen on the Honorary Committee, though they are not responsible for the choice of the pictures, by lending their names have been kind enough to give this project their general support."[4]

The British popular press, with little hesitation, responded viciously, often flaunting their philistinism, and giving rise to many anecdotes.[5] Perhaps the most widespread one told how Claude Phillips, then the lead critic for the *Daily Telegraph*, upon leaving the galleries, threw the catalog on the ground and stomped it with his foot. Journalists bruited the usual reactions against avant-garde art, claiming to see it as a sign of stunted emotions, mental disorder, and social decay. Two years later a similar event—to some extent influenced by Fry's exhibition, and showing some of the same paintings—took place in New York City in the form of the Armory Show of international art that left a similar crowd of disapproving journalists and shocked social arbiters in its wake.

As violent and aggrieved as the reaction in the English popular press sounded, the din rather quickly abated.[6] Where the exhibit held sway most effectively was the coinage of the term "Post-Impressionism," which entered into countless historical explanations of modernist art and its eventual entry into the canon. Fry's role in all this, which went far beyond questions of vocabulary, cannot be overestimated, at least in an English-speaking context. On a personal level, Fry's own acceptance of modernism—as exemplified in his critical response to Cézanne—had begun to change around 1908–1910, two dates which mark his early public analysis of Post-Impressionist esthetics.[7] The first salvo was a letter to the editor in the March 1908 issue of the *Burlington* commenting on negative criticism in the previous issue directed at an exhibition of contemporary French paintings. The letter, under the title "The Last Phase of Impressionism," carved out the beginnings of a historical account that featured Cézanne's break with his Impressionist peers. Contrasting Cézanne's work with that of Monet—generally considered the chief Impressionist—Fry argued that "In the placing of objects, in the relation of one form to another, in the values of color which indicate mass, and in the purely decorative elements of design, Cézanne's work seems to me to betray a finer, more scrupulous artistic sense." The break with Monet's Impressionism, and the newly evident stylistic attributes, would form the core of Fry's sense of Cézanne and modernism in general. Fry had already begun to think about the "post" in Post-Impressionism.

The historical account and the esthetic theory of his formalism were perhaps the major intellectual work by Fry in the first decade of the twentieth century.[8] Put briefly, Fry claimed that Cézanne's work, far from being a decadent extension of Impressionism, instead formed a historical reversion to the principles of classical painting, as shown most forcibly in the work of the Italian painters of the Renaissance. This reversion was the sign of great energy, even the test of genius. By attending chiefly to questions of form, while using his "finer, more scrupulous artistic sense," Cézanne joined the tradition inaugurated by Giotto and continuing chiefly with Nicolas Poussin. Modernism, by drawing on and allying with this long and rigorous tradition, came to mean much more than a passing shock to the sensibilities of journalists.

Fry's historicizing scheme introduced modernism and its innovations in a way that looked to a dedicated tradition for a universalized sense of form, and thus allowed Fry's conceptions of esthetic emotion and significant form to determine a crucial supporting role for his theorizing, and to stand at the apex of his artistic values. In achieving all this, of course, his public role became pre-eminent, for he was listed as the lead member of the exhibition's executive committee. Moreover, he provided the notes and the general argument for the catalog essay, an extended version of which would later be more widely disseminated by Clive Bell. Desmond MacCarthy was assigned credit for the introductory essay in his role as the "secretary" of the exhibition, but it was common knowledge that Fry was the main source of the ideas and much of their formulation. MacCarthy was an aspiring freelance reporter who would soon land a position as drama critic for the *New Statesman*, and would go on to an illustrious career as editor and literary critic. Various friendships brought him into the Bloomsbury circle, and he had met Fry in 1910, at the same time Fry began to form his Bloomsbury friendships.[9] In the company of Fry and Bell, MacCarthy had gone to galleries in Paris for the task of selecting, from collectors and dealers, the paintings that illustrated the Post-Impressionist style. Along with Mac-Carthy, Lady Ottoline Morrell, a wealthy and free-thinking patron of the Bloomsbury Group and a member of the honorary committee of the exhibition, aided in the selection process. She knew several Paris dealers and was keen to make connections and to ingratiate herself with Fry, who had already come to know important French dealers.

All the selecting of pictures took place, however, under the self-conscious guidance of Fry's careful and well-informed eye. Still, he was quick to reveal to his friend Goldie Lowes Dickinson the help he had received, telling him in a letter that "Lady Ottoline was with us in Paris. She is quite splendid. . . . The show will be a great affair. I am preparing for a huge campaign of outraged British Philistinism." The preparation was needed. Fry was willing to share the credit, however, and he testified in a letter to Morrell, "I can't tell you how it helped me to have you at such a difficult time, to help and advise. I don't think I could have done it without you." Relying on the sponsoring and idiosyncratic bohemianism of Morrell, Fry once again tilted at the upper classes even as he drew on their resources.

The 1910 exhibition brought Fry into the very core of the Bloomsbury Group, an association he valued and maintained until the end of his life, placing him near the center of the progressive art world in London. There a *succès d'estime* counted for a lot, even, or especially, if accompanied by more than a hint of scandal. Fry also came to enjoy two new positions, as it were, after the exhibition opened: he knew that he could flourish, albeit in a different key, as a force for public taste and education in the field of modern art after his unpleasant time at the Metropolitan Museum, and he also knew that he had a new platform where he could gain access to the commercial side of the London art world, even as he continued his pedagogic activities. Most of the paintings that were in the Post-Impressionists show were

*Poster of Post-Impressionists exhibition: The scandal, and the art history theory, connected to this exhibition mounted by Fry remain important parts of his legacy.*

from French artists and, equally important, from French dealers.[10] Chief among the dealers who loaned works was Ambroise Vollard, whose renown was fostered by his representing Cézanne. And it was a painting by Cézanne that was the only picture from the exhibition that was sold. But representatives of London galleries were on the honorary committee that "certified"—socially, if not esthetically— the art on display. Fry thus again used his social skills to mediate and navigate among dealers, patrons, artists, and critics in order to make the exhibition a success. Obviously, he also took pleasure in forwarding the idea of an international art world, which among other features, freed him from the English insularity he often censured.

The success of the exhibition could be accounted for by various measures. Prominent among these was the fact it spawned a second exhibit, held a year later, in which some of the less represented artists from the first show—Picasso and Matisse, notably—figured more prominently. The Paris dealers, such as Vollard, Daniel-Henry Kahnweiler, and Josse and Gaston Bernheim-Jeune, operated with the same commercial savvy as their London counterparts, whose network linking sellers and buyers, critics and connoisseurs had grown in complex interrelatedness for several preceding decades. The most imposing demonstration of importance operated over the long term as Fry's coining of the term Post-Impressionism served to monumentalize the esthetic he had come to favor. From 1910 onward, Fry's eye and historical knowledge remained in demand by gallerists and academic institutions. Though Fry didn't realize it at the time, the newly coined term not only helped the painters achieve canonical status, it remained a label for a historically shaped group in a manner that cemented Fry's reputation as an art historian, connoisseur, and critic.

So it became chiefly Fry's possibility, as well as his burden, to make the argument that a broad public should appreciate the exhibit, not only for its formal properties and stylistic innovations, but for its historical continuity, and its break, with the work of the Impressionists. By 1910, these artists were on their way to being accepted into the canon of Western European oil painting. By conceiving the exhibit and justifying its scope and content, Fry fully displayed his pedagogic skills. His framework of ideas forms the shape of the catalog essay, but MacCarthy's wit comes through when the initial question—that of vocabulary—arises. At first the term "synthesists" was proposed as the general category for the painters. MacCarthy demurred: "it is the principal business of this introduction to expand the meaning of that word, which sounds too like the hiss of an angry gander to be a happy appellation." "Synthesists" had the advantage, however, of standing ready to encompass all kinds of artists and their myriad strategies, but it was too general, as all artists synthesize. By shifting to "Post-Impressionists" as the master term, Fry invited the scrutiny of a historicizing point of view. At this point in the essay, Fry's knowledge as an art historian takes over, and the reader is presented with the hallowed trope of historical writing—"and then, but still"—that will allow for both rupture and continuity.

The lineaments of the immediate task emerged clearly. Fry had to create a context by characterizing Impressionism so that it could be seen as coherent, yet serve as the foil for the work at hand: "the main current of Impressionism lay along the line of recording hitherto unrecognized aspects of objects; they were interested in analyzing the play of light and shadow into a multiplicity of distinct colors; they refined upon what was already illusive in nature."[11] The newer artists were fully aware of their predecessors and their struggles. "They were interested in the discoveries of the Impressionists only so far as these discoveries helped them to express emotions which the objects themselves evoked[;] their attitude towards nature was far more independent, not to say rebellious." From the start Fry regarded the central esthetic question to be concerned with the emotions. This concern would never be far from his main point. The problem remained, however, as to just what the shaping acts of selection and arrangement did with and for the emotions of the artist and the viewer. The defense of the Post-Impressionists rested on their attitude toward the representation of nature, but not in a merely "naturalistic" or literal sense. "[I]t is the boast of those who believe in this school [Post-Impressionism], that its methods enable the individuality of the artist to find completer self-expression in his work than is possible to those who have committed themselves to representing objects more literally." For Fry the distinction was crucial: "This, indeed, is the first source of their quarrel with the Impressionists: the Post-Impressionists consider the Impressionists too naturalistic." The Impressionists' insistence on recording the momentary optic sensations that make up all vision had grown restrictive and was making it difficult, if not impossible, to represent the values—at once visual, esthetic, plastic, and emotional—that lay at the heart of easel painting. Fry always felt, and did so more strongly from this point on, that the mere recording of aspects of the visual world was of limited purpose, and for a painter, a limiting effort. This claim, though often modified and contested, formed one of the main tenets of modernist art.

As far back as his Cambridge days, Fry had generally shied away from philosophical analysis, relying instead on the more directly causal explanations favored by scientists. But his commitment to his own painting, and his dedication to explain the principles—and practical consequences—of various painterly strategies led him to something like a phenomenological interest in what the artist tries to capture. (He had written an extended essay on phenomenology while at Cambridge.) He knew that the Impressionists somehow stopped short; he wagered that the Post-Impressionists had taken the next step, one that reverted to a certain simplicity, yet still moved forward to a more direct emotion, and finally deeper to an essence, however ineffable. He insisted that "The 'treeness' of the tree was not rendered at all [by the Impressionists]; all the emotion and associations such as trees may be made to convey in poetry were omitted." Impressionism effectively "hindered artists from exploring and expressing that emotional significance which lies in things, and is the most important subject matter of art." By qualifying, even minimizing, the success of the leading French Impressionists, Fry was able to reformulate his esthetic standpoint—and that of others—in a way that defined an important phase in art history. This bold historicizing move stirred him as much as it stirred many others.

The consequences of the aftermath of the Post-Impressionists show for Fry on a personal level were that he gained new friends and animated old enemies. As for his life situation, that, too, took on both positive and negative aspects. He finished building the home, called Durbins, he had designed for himself, near the town of Guildford in county Surrey. There his sister kept house for him and helped raise his two children. Helen had finally reached a point where her changing moods and conditions did not respond to treatment or show any improvement. In early 1910, Fry committed her to a home where she stayed for the rest of her life. His own painting, meanwhile, absorbed more and more of his interest and energy. As for his standing as a critic, the old guard of English painting—represented by Sir William Rothenstein, Henry Tonks, and Charles Ricketts, among others—were vituperative and unforgiving. Fry stayed calm, by and large, in the face of this enmity, but he also deeply resented what he felt was a betrayal by the cultured class. Woolf reports in her biography that "For so many years he had helped to educate the taste of the public," and they eagerly attended his lectures on the Old Masters and "respectfully" accepted his views. But the Post-Impressionists exhibition changed their view of him; Woolf chose Fry's bête noire to set out what was at stake: "Now, when he asked them to look also at the work of living artists whom he admired, they turned upon him and denounced him. It seemed to him that the cultivated classes were of the same kidney as Pierpont Morgan. . . . Their interest in his lectures had been a pose."[12] Fry remained stoic and resolute—his planning for the second Post-Impressionists exhibition began in early 1911—and the exposure of the old guard helped cement his influence with the younger generation. He became, according to a grudging Rothenstein, "the central figure round whom the more advanced of the young English painters grouped themselves."[13] Fry would need to formulate a deeper and broader rationale for his campaign.

The experimentalism of the exhibitions, more than bold enough to show the way forward, also continued to provoke some painters, as well as critics, to a strongly negative reaction. The catalog essay had said of its argument that such principles "may even appear ridiculous to those who do not recall the fact that a good rocking-horse often has more of the true horse about it than an instantaneous photograph of a Derby winner." Running the risk of appearing ridiculous became one of the hallmarks of Fry's critical writing. Here he offers a strong alternative to the purely empirical and naturalistic, and his argument suggests that merely recording details won't suffice to display the dynamics of their relationship to the essence of a thing. Loosely related to the intuitionism that centered Moore's ethics and philosophy, Fry's invocation of an essence that would serve as the goal of the painterly eye led him to a new vocabulary that he would try often to clarify and apply to works of art in general. The chief need for every artist remains a rendering of structure, or form. Much of what followed in Fry's subsequent writings becomes a search for what he came to call "significant form" and "esthetic emotion"; he needed a strongly supportive vocabulary that would render justice to the complexity of art.

Over the course of the next two decades Fry attempted to define the indefinable, and so his vocabulary occasionally shifted. Some took this as the basis for praising his flexibility and pragmatism as a critic, while others pointed to inconsistencies and a lack of clarity. Some saw him in the first decade of the twentieth century as reliant on Berenson's notions of plastic values and ideated sensations. Where Berenson sought an unchallengeable certitude, however, Fry remained interested in the emotional reactions that were irreducibly involved in looking at art. After the success—and scandal—of the Post-Impressionism show, Fry delved into the use of purely visual experiences to analyze paintings. This meant he needed to shift the frame of examination from the content to the form and formal qualities present in the individual work of art. Working with Clive Bell and others in the Bloomsbury circle, he raised the term "significant form" to a prominent place in his writing. For a long while, this stood in as the master term in what came to be called, rather exaggeratedly, Fry's "formalism." However, he wanted to do more with the explanation of the experience of esthetic values than a single term could permit. In addition, he needed examples that would keep the viewer fixed on certain aspects of specific artists that couldn't be ignored.

A CONSIDERABLE PART OF FRY'S CRITICAL IMAGINATION came from his engagement with the painting of Cézanne, and it was lodged, somewhat oddly, in a book by his friend Clive Bell. Though *Art* (1914) was published as a work authored by Clive Bell, it owes much to Fry's sensibilities. From the beginning and for several subsequent decades it stood as a noteworthy contribution to a formalist approach to art. As such it had several features that set it apart, while also making it a target for some critics. Bell and Fry were thinking alike when the book was written, and their early and intensive conversations are more or less summarized and canonized by Bell in his introduction. The major pivot in the thought of both men occurred when they settled on the notion of "aesthetic emotion," which, however, they could never define in great detail or at great length. But they agreed that the centering features of "aesthetic emotion" stood apart from the more common workaday emotions of life. "Aesthetic emotion" sprang from the perception of "significant form," and, in a circular way, "significant form" was cognitively available only to those who could perceive it through the experience of an "aesthetic emotion." The realm of the esthetic, conceived and understood as a specific mode of experience, was built on the thought of late-eighteenth-century philosophers and the Romanticism they spawned. As with Moore's intuitionism, the force of esthetic emotion created an integrity that had to be thought of as shaping a world.

*Fry's portrait of Clive Bell: Bell (1881–1964) wrote a book,* Art *(1914), that helped put Fry's theories into circulation, though the book also missed some of the nuances of Fry's approach to "aesthetic emotion" and "form."*

Such world-generative thought and emotion had to be rigorous, self-sustaining, and unmistakably distinct from the rest of life. A point of summary by Bell put the matter directly: "What I have to say is this: the rapt philosopher, and he who contemplates a work of art, inhabit a world with an intense and peculiar significance of its own; that significance is unrelated to the significance of life. In this world the emotions of life find no place. It is a world with emotions of its own."[14] The dichotomy of art and life—at least in reference to the emotions experienced in and through each—structured the argument that followed, but without resolving all the questions it raised.

Although an elitist esthetician and committed defender of formalism, Bell willingly conceded a number of points. For example, he intends "significant form," his master term, to refer to and include not only lines and shapes but colors—he never meant, as some superficial readings had it, to suggest that only black and white, or the outlines of shapes, could be used in the making of works of art. He extends the same level of adaptability concerning the use of color to the relations between forms, as well as to forms themselves; this relationality he calls "rhythm." But in some instances he labors at defining his key term by saying what it isn't, quite. "Beauty," for instance, might be substituted for "significant form," but Bell feels that it has too many habitual connections with the beautiful aspects of nature or of human beings as bodied agents. In short, beauty has too many associations that are not strictly esthetic. As with much esthetic theorizing, the adjustment of vocabulary takes up much space.

All these modifications form part of Bell's somewhat pragmatic approach to his argument, but they never allow or induce him to abandon his key notion. He comes close to his purest stance when he introduces the supreme negative example, William Powell Frith's *The Railway Station*, a massive Victorian favorite from 1862. This painting was greatly beloved because of its use of anecdote and sharp detail to represent a scene in London's Paddington Train Station, where a large crowd is engaged in a myriad of activities, all rendered with photographic accuracy and charming narrative flavor. Bell's testimony against the work's merit as a work of art is absolute. Though it's certain many viewers have whiled away their time, Bell snapped, seeking out and appreciating the life-likeness of the many scenes recorded by Frith, "it is not less certain that no one has experienced before it one half-second of aesthetic rapture—and this although the picture contains several pretty passages of colour, and is by no means badly painted, 'Paddington Station' is not a work of art." Such a claim would never endear Bell or Fry to their contemporaries who acted as the established authorities, nor would it wear very well in the long run in a middle-class culture that eschewed elitism or rigor. Nevertheless, Bell—and in this regard Fry as well—felt so strongly about the absolute necessity and priority of "aesthetic emotion" that he conferred a nearly spiritual quality on it: "provided that there be some fraction of pure aesthetic emotion, even a mixed and minor appreciation of art is, I am sure, one of the most valuable things in the world—so valuable, indeed, that in my giddier moments I have been tempted to believe that art might prove the world's salvation."

Setting up a bright line to separate works of art widely acknowledged as such from others that answer to a stricter standard has long been one of the main activities of those who argue about esthetics. This strict categorization follows from the equally strict separation between the two realms of art and everyday life. Again, Bell is firm: "to appreciate a work of art we need bring with us nothing from life, no knowledge of its ideas and affairs, no familiarity with its emotions. Art transports us from the world of man's activity to a world of aesthetic exaltation." Though the separation of the two realms, as well as the means of "transport" between them, demotes or throws out a number of contested qualities and categories, the stark duality of art and life is inescapable. Fry takes it up at the very beginning of his early collection of essays, *Vision and Design* (1920). Calling the opening essay—one of the cornerstones of his esthetic—by its fundamental dichotomy, "Art and Life," Fry tries to spell out his version of art and what it entails.[15]

Fry begins by recounting his experience with "an old gentleman" who collected art from past epochs. The gentleman used these works to prop up his imaginary time travel, "a dream of himself as an exquisite and refined intellectual dandy living in a society of elegant frivolity." This, of course, represents everything Fry opposed as a critic and historian of art. It was imperative that art be seen as more than, and radically different from, "crystalized history." His deep distaste breaks through as he insists that, "For this old gentleman, as for how many an American millionaire, art was merely a help to an imagined dream life." Though likely an allusion to J. P. Morgan and others of his ilk, Fry means to erase any chance that the history of art would be regarded as no more than a catalog of various sites where the "dream life" of the wealthy class might be pursued.

Instead he wants to confront the thousands of years of European art as having a complex relation to thousands of years of different social forms, values, and changes. In a sweeping historical overview, Fry sets out the several places where the life of society developed in one direction and art in another. For example, the change from classical Roman to Christian values was counterposed by art continuing to use the same systems and images of representation. Only with the Renaissance did social change and artistic development substantially mirror each other. However, in his own era Fry suggests that art—in its pursuit of a thorough examination of sense experience such as the Impressionists pursued—may more fully mirror the turn in the mid-nineteenth century to a society driven by science and technology. But this social and historical turn involves forces that make art "more and more remote from the ordinary man." So the modern era sees that "as in so many cases in past history, the revolution in art seems to be out of all proportion to any corresponding change in life as a whole." The duality of the two areas of experience stands reaffirmed. (However, it should be noted here that Fry's arguments about art history serve to refute those who see his criticism as narrowly restricted to a pure formalism.)

In Fry's estimation, art and life frequently developed in two different directions, if only because they rested on different principles. He supported this claim in part by arguing that the common way of looking at art—especially that of a new and experimental sort—was severely handicapped by pursuing the wrong standards. The chief example in this regard was judging art by how clearly it represented its naturalistic subject and how clearly it made its moral point. Here he and Bell thought alike.[16] Representation of "real life" or recognizable subjects (even if drawn from myth and the Bible) could only be a false criterion. Art was meant not to show us how the world appeared to our senses but to induce in us emotional reactions by presenting the many aspects of form and design—he lists line, mass, space, light and shade, color, and planes—that have their own order and variety. Bell drove this point hard, claiming that, though it was true that artists often represented objects from "real life," form trumped whatever recognition a represented object might offer: "if a representative form has value, it is as form, not as representation." For many viewers of art, the notion of representation itself was problematic and contested. The contestation grew more tangled when Fry would sometimes deplore what he saw as an overemphasis on skill (when its main purpose was to create an exact likeness), and he often used words, such as illustration and representation, that were at least loosely cognate, to mean quite different things. Bell was willing to make at least one exception to the dictate against representation when he conceded, "If the representation of three-dimensional space is to be called 'representation,' then I agree that there is one kind of representation which is not irrelevant." Otherwise a painting should not be looked at for any sort of recorded fact or information. Through the esthetic principles they advocated, Bell and Fry stood as two of the more single-minded announcers of the modernist spirit in the visual arts.[17]

CÉZANNE INCREASINGLY PLAYED THE PART OF FRY'S leading example of the painter who most successfully advanced the art of painting in the late nineteenth and early twentieth centuries. In 1927 Fry published the first English-language monograph of Cézanne, and so contributed to the Frenchman's reputation as the father of modern painting. This use of Cézanne as a strong instance of what he valued in the art of his own time originated prior to the Post-Impressionists exhibition. The embryonic ideas were set out with a number of brief articles, which served to set the art-historical framework for Cézanne's signal importance, which is fully articulated in the 1927 monograph. Two appeared in the *Nation*, the weekly newspaper published in London, and two in the *Burlington*.[18] In the second of these two early pieces in the *Burlington*, Fry spoke with conviction, having decided to bring Cézanne to a wider public by translating and publishing an analytical article on the painter by the French critic Maurice Denis. In his introduction to the essay, Fry wrote that "it is generally admitted that the great and original genius—for recent criticism has the courage to acclaim him as such—who really started this movement [Post-Impressionism], the most promising and fruitful of modern times, was Cézanne."[19]

In the 1910 catalog essay, Fry chose to expound upon the term "design" as a way of extending his efforts to canonize Cézanne's work. Cézanne's technique enabled him to build up the density of objects and the tactility of the space they occupied, all of which was accomplished by his sense of design, which was more than a graphic or linear element. Fry focused on what Cézanne learned from Manet, and how this lesson led to a certain understanding of simplicity. In the Post-Impressionists catalog, Fry focused on a major pivot, a historical turning point, that showed how art had developed beyond Impressionism. "Cézanne, however, seized upon precisely that side of Manet which Monet and the other Impressionists ignored," Fry claimed. With a firm objective in mind, Cézanne "aimed first at a design which should produce the coherent, architectural effect of the masterpieces of primitive art. Because Cézanne thus showed how it was possible to pass from the complexity of the appearance of things to the geometrical simplicity which design demands, his art has appealed enormously to later designers." Fry here touches on his newly acquired interest in so-called primitive art, an interest that had begun to gather momentum in some of the same Paris galleries where Fry had collected his Post-Impressionist oils. This interest was soon reflected in the publication of essays on African art and other subjects such as Chinese and ancient American art, all of which resulted from Fry's eagerness to expand the range of valuable esthetic experience and to test his own ability to explain their significance.[20]

As happens with many enthusiasts, Fry erected a more general theory from what he felt and saw to be the singular contribution of Cézanne, hoping thereby to bolster his arguments for a skeptical public. In Cézanne's case, Fry began—as early as the Post-Impressionists exhibition—to universalize the pattern of cultural renewal and stylistic innovation generated by a feeling on the part of the artist—an omnipresent "he"—who feels the need to revitalize all the traditional principles he has been taught and was busily practicing, until the moment of reckoning arrives and the imperatives are re-formed. Melding the techniques of Cézanne and so-called primitive artists would eventually fall into disfavor among art historians and critics of modernism. But Cézanne proceeded with confidence. Here is part of the argument, drawn from the catalog for the Post-Impressionists show:

> He [the "primitive" artist, and by extension Cézanne] begins to try to unload, to simplify the drawing and painting, by which natural objects are evoked, in order to recover the lost expressiveness and life. He aims at synthesis in design; that is to say, he is prepared to subordinate consciously his power of representing the parts of his picture as plausibly as possible, to the expressiveness of his whole design. But in this retrogressive movement he has the public, who have become accustomed to extremely plausible imitations of nature, against him at every step; and what is more, his own self-consciousness hampers him as well.

What Fry offers here is a description of the modernist avant-garde artist as a transcendent type.

This argument, which has a clear autobiographical resonance for Fry's own paintings, provided the eventually rejected term "synthesists." Shifting to a historical term such as Post-Impressionism invokes art historical models and keeps the emphasis on stylistic features. The phrase "the expressiveness of his whole design" (a key point from the Post-Impressionists catalog), however, makes clear how Fry thinks of painting as a process of combining and fusing elements so as to make the emotional urgency of the singular artist manifest. Public reception must always lag behind, wedded as it is to standards of "plausible imitation." In his earlier study of the Italian Renaissance painters, Fry had no specific need to spell out how the individual artist worked with and against public standards of reception, since obviously wealthy patrons and the church eventually provided sufficient acceptance. With twentieth-century painters, however, and largely as a result of his experience with the Post-Impressionists exhibition, Fry in his writings would be more and more involved in how and why the general public should be taught to turn to painting for a kind of truth and "emotional significance" difficult to find elsewhere in the crush of a mercantile culture. Fry's criticism, always innovative yet trusting in a corrigible audience, here becomes nevertheless open to the charge of being conservative, as modern art moved further away from his values.[21]

Fry nevertheless found a strong measure of comfort in the social role of Bloomsbury, since it functioned as an artistic avant-garde in a country that lacked the desire for innovation. Fry's affiliation with it—including his often agonized affair with Vanessa Bell, his championing of Duncan Grant's painting, and his sometimes conflicted collaboration with Clive Bell in developing a theory of art—rested on deep friendship and the understanding of a common ethos. These intertwined relations culminate, of course, in Virginia Woolf's very affectionate and admiring biography of Fry. On a daily level, Fry enjoyed the heady conversation about art and social matters, and those who drove Bloomsbury's various agendas saw him in highly positive terms. In a way, the Bloomsbury circle gave him the grounding sense of an artistic and intellectual community that was so sorely lacking during his time at the Metropolitan Museum of Art. But Bloomsbury was certainly no utopian scheme, let alone a realized redoubt of excellence and comity. The group suffered constant alienation from the surrounding society and faced constant criticism, which Fry rather easily ignored or blithely contested. A later commentator, writing in the *Burlington* in 2000, cites the reasons behind the main tensions, which resulted in the "condemnation of Bloomsbury in general and its art in particular by England's critical establishment." Of the several causes for such condemnation, most prominent were the critics who loudly protested their "anxiety over England's relation to a strong French modernist tradition," which "animated almost every review, with Bloomsbury paradoxically blamed for importing French influences and for failing to live up to the standard set by Picasso and Matisse." (The commentator seems especially to have Fry in mind.) In addition to this anxiety, "critics, themselves claiming the authority to guide public taste, complain of the success Bloomsbury's writers achieved in guiding the taste of their day."[22] Fry was perhaps more than anyone else responsible for introducing "French influences" to the art world of London just before and after the Great War. He also appreciated the paradox that resulted from a critical establishment's arbitration of taste which all too often substituted presumed propriety for engaged insights.

Fry carried his struggle against the establishment to a new front when, in 1912, he created the Omega Workshop. Expending impressively substantial amounts of time and energy—much of it in raising funds from a range of backers—Fry plunged into the project as he had done with the founding of the *Burlington*. Both projects had a didactic impulse at their core, but each made its own specific demands. On December 11, 1912, Fry wrote a fund-raising letter to George Bernard Shaw.[23] He chose Shaw in part because of the older man's socialist sentiment, the influence of which Fry had felt back when he was at Cambridge, two decades earlier. Beginning with his desire to "start a workshop for decorative and applied art," Fry went on to claim that the Post-Impressionist movement was "as definitely decorative as was the Pre-Raphaelite."[24] Invoking the then rather diminished Arts and Crafts movement founded by William Morris,

*Vanessa Bell: Virginia's sister and Clive Bell's wife, Vanessa (1879–1961), had an intense affair with Fry in 1911–1912. Subsequently Fry wrote her impassioned letters for a number of years and tried in several ways to praise and influence her painting.*

Fry looked to "develop a definitely English tradition." This meant, among other things, that there were artists who "have already formed the habit of working together with mutual assistance instead of insisting on the singularity of their personal gifts. This spirit is of the utmost value in such decorative work as I propose, where co-operation is a first necessity." In addition to working on a coopera-tive basis, Fry aimed at a "profit sharing scheme," and added that "In the business details I have the promise of assistance from Mr. Leon-ard Woolf." Leonard, Virginia's husband, was a former civil servant, a writer, and a fellow Fabian socialist. Fry ended his appeal by telling Shaw that he recognized "the speculative nature of such an attempt," and there was "no guarantee of success, other than my own convic-

*Poster for Omega Workshop: Fry's commitment to beautiful handicrafts lay behind this effort at making and selling useful domestic objects. But the workshop never managed to be successfully profitable, and it foundered in part because of the Great War.*

tion and determination." Shaw responded with a gift of £500. Even so, the Workshop began with less funding than Fry felt was needed, and, much like the early days of the *Burlington*, the economics of the enterprise would never provide clear sailing.

Actively begun in 1913, the workshop sought to counteract the dominance of mass-produced items intended for everyday use, to foster a sense of communal effort, and to expand the boundaries of form and design in handicraft and the domestic arts. A disparate group of artists, recruited by Fry, offered handmade and decorated products, including painted furniture, painted murals, mosaics, stained glass, and textiles. Some were created on commission, while others were based on designs submitted by the individual artists. Never broadly supported by middle-class Londoners, the enterprise managed to continue for six years, gradually expanding the kinds of work it turned out. Using the skills of well-known artists, but anonymously, Omega presented its products identified only by the workshop's logo. Fry worked hard, often called upon to mediate disputes as he had done with the *Burlington*, handling the finances for the overall operation and soothing the egos of those involved. He undertook a commission to decorate a room for the 1913 Ideal Home Exhibition, and a year later assembled an illustrated catalog, to which he added an introductory text.

Contradictions and internal strife unfortunately plagued the workshop throughout its existence. One of the better-known participating artists, Wyndham Lewis, angrily left early on, denouncing Fry in the wake of a dispute over a commission. Always dyspeptic and combative, Lewis took several fellow participants with him and with great fanfare inaugurated a rival workshop, known as the Rebel Art Centre, before going on to launch the Vorticist movement. Other contributors to Omega found fault with Fry's business practices, and the ideals of an artists' cooperative—set against the model of a profit-making corporation—soon became abraded as sales suffered during the war. Whatever strokes of fortune were necessary to keep the Omega project alive, they never struck.

Still, Fry possessed an abiding interest in artisanship and the craft sensibility, going back decades, to Helen's work on clavichords with Arnold Dolmetsch and to his own fashioning of a gift of a painted platter in the Renaissance style to celebrate the wedding of the Berensons. Clearly indebted to William Morris and the ethos of the Arts and Crafts movement of an earlier generation, the Omega Workshop gave Fry an important outlet for his belief that art is governed by general principles that apply to all forms of facture. In a sense the workshop was a place where Fry could continue to introduce the emphasis on form as a universal element in art, and thus extend the insights he had come to through his study of Cézanne.

JUST AS FRY, LIKELY ALLUDING TO MORGAN, HAD SHOWN little sympathy for the "old gentleman" who used his ownership of art as a prop for his "imagined dream life," so he also used in his writings characters from a social stratum and historical era to delineate his views on art and commerce. He first set these views out in detail in an essay titled "Art and Socialism." Fry included it in his book *Vision and Design* (1920).

Fry's tone in the essay largely manages to be relaxed while making broad arguments, the relaxation springing in part from his opening disavowal of any commitment to defining socialism once and for all. "I am not a Socialist, as I understand that word," he writes, "nor can I pretend to have worked out those complex estimates of economic possibility," which Fry notes are routinely offered by political scientists or theorists. What he offers instead is a negative discussion of "plutocracy," and its effect "upon one of the things which I should like to imagine continuing upon our planet—namely, art." Here the note of a possible near-apocalyptic elimination of the esthetic realm balances the tones in the essay between wry and drear. Though he was fifty-six when the essay was published, he still had little or no prospect for regular full-time employment, as his financial worries persisted.

Buttressing this complexly dark tone, Fry introduces the fixed element in most socialist denunciations of the deleterious effect of commerce on art, namely the notion of exploitation, especially as it works throughout the realm, and in the products, of human labor. He uses a strict formulation of this well-known notion: "the man who works at some uncreative and uncongenial toil merely to earn enough food to enable him to continue to work has not, properly speaking, a human life at all." Between the extremes of the specter of wage slavery and the promise of leisure as providing the basis of culture there exists a spectrum of images by which historians and theorists have often placed the working class in a position that moves between despair and sublimation. Fry's view had little redemptive force at this moment, since to work without a chance to be creative is to be dehumanized. Because "nature demands with no uncertain voice that the physical needs of the body should be satisfied first," Fry says, invoking his materialist and scientific roots, humans are condemned to la-

*Roger Fry, lounging in chair, n.d.: This shows Fry in a rare moment of relaxation. The chair is upholstered with a fabric made from an Omega Workshop design.*

bor. How to organize this necessary activity, in its economic and social dimensions, Fry fails to mention. But he points to at least one redemptive horizon, art.

If the Post-Impressionists exhibition allowed Fry his greatest success, then the failure of the Omega Workshop at the end of the Great

War marks the lowest ebb of his energy. Less than a decade separated the two events, and this gloomy change of prospect serves to explain why Fry probably felt that his attempts to revolutionize the understanding of art had fallen short. Though he had another fifteen or so years left, he never conceived of a scheme—artistic, pedagogic, or commercial—that would match his opportunities at the Metropolitan Museum, the Grafton Gallery, or the Omega Workshop. He went on painting, with dedication and occasional flashes of self-fulfillment, many of the works focused on his friends in France and his frequent visits there. His writings and teachings on art became increasingly catholic in taste and broader in reach, going back as far as the ancient Egyptians. His lecturing skills were continually welcomed in a variety of venues. Between numerous visits to France, he organized a number of gallery exhibits, showing many different artists, mostly in group shows held at the Grafton Gallery, the Mansard Gallery, and the Alpine Art Gallery, all in London. His appointment as the Slade Professor at Cambridge in 1933, the year before he died, surely gave considerable, but brutally short-lived, gratification, and showed that his reputation had continued to grow. As for his posthumous reputation, though most often thought of as the "formalist" art critic, he managed to write tellingly about the relations between art and commerce, attempting to show how the social and historical dimensions of art need our understanding as much as its formal qualities. He embodied a paradox throughout his working life, possessing breadth of vision and knowledge, and a strongly concentrated devotion to his main purposes. Un-self-consciously, he became that truly rare thing, a broad-minded expert.

# FRY AND MODERN THEORIES

*Taste, Teaching, and Social Values*

ROGER FRY'S REPUTATION AS AN EXPERT HISTO-
rian and critic of art originated with his essay on Giotto, but he solidified it with the appearance of his study of Giovanni Bellini. This latter monograph shared a format with Herbert Horne's study of Botticelli and Berenson's monograph on Lorenzo Lotto. The format,
grounded in rigorous connoisseurship, featured a chronology of the
artist's life, his historical context, a focus on attributions, and a consideration of his distinctive stylistic features and habits. These three
monographs together served incidentally to suggest the lineaments of
their triadic friendship—and to some extent the rivalry—among the
three men. All of them began as amateurs, not exactly self-taught,
but building up their expertise through an emotional commitment
and long hours of study on their own terms. Imposing scholars stood
in the background, to be sure, and men like Wilhelm von Bode and
Giovanni Morelli and Giovanni Cavalcaselle erected guidelines and
standards that held firm for years.[1] What set Fry apart, however,
from Horne and Berenson, as well as the more senior figures, were
his experiences as a lecturer, a museum curator, a practicing artist,
and the founder and editor of and major contributor to a scholarly
journal.

Though neither Berenson, Horne, nor Fry invented the scholarly
monograph, they each added to its prestige. Eventually the writing
of monographs would be one of the standard measures of achievement and merit in what would become academic art history, a field
that flourished in many countries but especially in American uni-

versities. The three men set high standards for themselves, by dint of efforts that were largely self-affirming and self-taught. By using a perspicuous sense of history and a deep esthetic feeling, each man was able to turn what previously had been rather superficial learning into a structured and rigorous knowledge. The place this knowledge occupied, outside the rather circumscribed world of the amateur-turned-expert, was between a general readership (largely but not totally made up of tourists) and the established dealers whose main clients were millionaires primarily interested in prestigious acquisitions. Thus the twin limits these monographs faced were superficiality on the one hand and a co-optation by commercial interests on the other.

Most immediately obvious as a surrounding historical development, and with less and less genteel amateurism, the institutionalization of art history arose with the concomitant rise of an educated public, formed through exposure to museum esthetics and other forms of art appreciation. This academic discipline of art history, along with the related disciplines of art theory and art criticism, itself rested on a social commitment to preserving, through convincing narratives, the artistic genius of great art from all periods and countries. With the sometime aid of art history, the major museums in America's largest cities, and the personal collections that served as their originating or supporting base, would achieve, directly and indirectly, a level of art and culture that remains stunningly impressive. The Mellon, Widener, and Kress collections in the National Gallery, the Morgan, Havemeyer, and Lehman in the Metropolitan, the Johnson and McIlhenny in Philadelphia—to name only the older museums—together formed a national resource that remains matchless. Collections of paintings such as these did much to anchor in distinctive, some would say critical, ways the nature and scope of the encyclopedic museum. The identification and validation of artistic genius that was at once the rationale of all such museums mainly relied on an intensified academic study and the securing of very large sums of disposable wealth.

Fry's contributions to this historic transformation of art history and art knowledge proved formidable, mainly because of his intellectual strength, his wide geographic and historical range of interests, and his many different ways of sharing his expertise. Though his experience at the Metropolitan ended badly, Fry continued to expand his thinking on the subject of art by outlining an argument for a fundamental understanding of the relations between art and commerce. He knew that it was inevitably through the mechanism of commercial interests and vast wealth that education in the arts would be advanced, given how the encyclopedic museum was financed and sustained. From his post-Metropolitan days until the end of his life, Fry continued to paint, act as a curator, write voluminously on art from all over the world, and address an ever growing audience on the nature and value of esthetic experience. But he chose not to turn a blind eye to the commercial values that both served, and were served by, the modern museum.

AFTER HE ENJOYED SOME MEASURE OF THE *SUCCÈS d'estime* of the Post-Impressionists exhibition, and its follow-up show two years later, Fry went on to set in motion the Omega Workshop, beginning in 1913. This later project would last—with only fitful success, however—until after the end of the Great War, but the depressing experience of that war and its aftermath did not deter Fry from his labors in some of the most important aspects of the arts. He always considered the fine arts in a continuum with the beauties of handicrafts, all of which served noble ends by their use of artistic forms and their satisfaction of sensory desires as well as practical uses in everyday life. Determined to understand and explain the social role and function of art, Fry broadened his focus far beyond that of the Italian Renaissance masters whom he first encountered as a beginning expert, eventually including the general study of esthetics and the particular analysis of several national and ethnic art forms. In a sense, his own capacious expertise paralleled the development of the encyclopedic museum.

As a thinker, critic, and public intellectual, Fry focused his considerable energies and talent on three important projects: defining esthetic form, investigating psychology and the arts, and spelling out the relationship between commerce and the world of the visual arts.

Esthetic form remained in many ways the central intellectual topic

in Fry's career, from his first studies of the Italian Renaissance painters, to his commitment to Cézanne and beyond, and to various areas of non-European art. But up until his monograph on Cézanne in
1927, form and esthetic emotion remained his key terms.[2] Though his
work on the Post-Impressionists show by no means exhausted Fry's
attempt to examine all the nuances of esthetic emotion and its relation to form, his writing in connection with the Post-Impressionists
exhibition and "An Essay in Aesthetics" (1909) (which would be reprinted in 1920 as one of the key essays in *Vision and Design*) spelled
out the main lineaments of his formalism. The second of his preoccu-
pations, his thoughts on the relations between art and the psychology
of esthetic activity and experience, culminated in a paper, "The Artist and Psychoanalysis," given to the British Psychological Society
and published as a pamphlet by Leonard and Virginia Woolf's Hogarth Press in 1924. This paper clearly manifests Fry's willingness to
add the then much-discussed aspects of Sigmund Freud's thought to
the long history of esthetics, a further indication that he felt art to be
at the center of human learning and values, no matter the era or the
ideology under consideration.

HIS DRIVE, HOWEVER, TO SAY SOMETHING OF DEPTH
and importance on the third topic, the entanglements and inter-
connections between commerce and art, directed his major intellectual commitments and efforts in the immediate wake of the period
devoted to the Post-Impressionists exhibition and the Omega Workshop. His ambition and focus in these matters may have been driven
by his experience at the Metropolitan Museum. He was not, however,
trained in economics, so when he came to discuss economic issues
he relied mainly on his professional knowledge of the art world, especially his work on the *Burlington* and with the Omega Workshop,
and an intelligent person's understanding of how art and commerce
intersect.

Fry's concern with the issues that constellate around commerce
and art, however, reaches back to the early issues of the *Burlington*. As was the situation with the first editorial comment in the journal,[3] the column, titled "Criticism and Commerce," appeared anon-

ymously in 1904. But it is safe to assume that Fry fashioned the argument.[4] In fact, there are two arguments at stake, both of which may appear to be based on fine points, but both contain Fry's serious thoughts and strong arguments. In the first argument, the issue is whether or not artworks owned and offered for sale by dealers could be discussed or represented in the journal, since this could be construed as the *Burlington* acting as a trade publication. The second argument—in an issue that appeared several months later—because of the change in the ownership of the magazine, reconsidered and refined the first argument. Both versions came out in favor of reproducing works of art that were "on the market," but they did so only with certain qualifications, qualifications reflective of Fry's esthetics and meant to diminish or eliminate any suggestion of purely economic concerns. Fry made clear that his views on esthetics were in important ways ineluctably connected to his thinking about the relations between art and commerce.

At first "it was decided that works of art worthy to be reproduced in the magazine should not be excluded merely because they belonged to dealers." This decision, Fry explained, "evoked some unfavorable criticism, [and] the reasons for it were set out at length . . . in an editorial article expressly devoted to the subject," referring to the "Criticism and Commerce" piece. The issue then seemed settled, as "the great majority of those interested in the magazine considered that the policy had been amply justified," Fry confidently claimed. But the problem did not vanish, and the *Burlington* had to try again to clarify its position in terms of its stance on commerce and its commitment to objective or disinterested criticism. Could the two varied activities be reconciled?

The reconsideration of the issues in the second editorial focused on the question of how the nexus of commerce changed the monetary values of an artwork simply by displaying it in a reputable journal. Here the core of the problem became inescapable. There existed no clear way to keep questions of buying and selling completely off limits. "The publication of a work of art, to whomsoever it may belong, in any periodical of standing and repute tends to enhance its commercial value, and who can tell that it will not be put up for sale at Christie's within three months of its publication?" Fry here acknowledges the *Burlington*'s participation in the economic consequences of what later came to be called "the art world," that congeries of museums, critics, dealers, artists, and collectors that collectively serve to determine the monetary value of paintings and other works of art. He goes on to confess that many people are unsettled by the magazine's policy, since it is admitted that publishing a representation of a painting will drive the price up, seemingly in an arbitrary way. In order to address these concerns, he spells out three precautions and policies that will, he hopes, lead to a more disinterested or ethically proper approach. The first two were by this time already in practice at the *Burlington*, and the third was to be immediately added. These new policies indicate how scrupulous Fry meant to be, while dealing with how ambiguous were the relations between prices and artistic quality.

First, any work reproduced in the *Burlington* had in important ways to merit publication on its own terms. For the second regulation, "no dealer nor anyone connected with the trade" would be allowed to write an article about any work they owned, and all descriptions of an illustrated work would be written and signed by a certified expert. This was spelled out and pointedly directed mainly to the question of connoisseurship: "It will be a condition of publication that the writer is perfectly free to express his own opinion as to attribution and all other matters." The values of the market and those of experts were seen as potentially capable of becoming muddled, even mutually contaminating. The third rule, added in an attempt to remove any further shadow of a doubt, specified that all works owned by a dealer and currently for sale "will be published under this general title in a particular section of the magazine expressly devoted to that purpose." A *cordon sanitaire* would thus separate, emphatically in terms of the physical layout, the artistic and commercial sections of the journal.

For these editorial comments and arguments, Fry drew upon his experience as a part-time dealer, as well as his knowledge of the activities of Berenson and others. Among the things he knew all too well was the recent rise in the prices paid for Italian masters, and others, by the likes of Morgan and Gardner, and the ways in which attribution by experts carried with it not only a scholarly patina but a cash value. The editorial went on to speak in stern terms. "Some years ago a mistake about the authenticity of a work of art had much smaller consequences, from the commercial point of view, than is the case now when large sums of money are often involved. It is now more necessary than ever that the utmost care should be exercised." The world of dealers and collectors—and its "cash nexus" —had greatly expanded in Fry's lifetime, and today such ethical questions have putatively been more openly developed (though hardly resolved). Fry's invocation of a situation that was "now more necessary than ever" to be addressed with transparency and consistency reflects how seriously he took the issues.

But it was not only connoisseurship that could cause a fluctuation in prices, it was also the relatively new phenomenon of advertising; not only did advertising influence prices, but the revenue from its sales helped support the journal itself. On this score, of how to deal with advertising, Fry seemed to adopt a double tone, of stern self-justification on the one hand, and on the other of condescension toward the effects of this instrument of social valuation: "the very fact that they [the dealers] are potential advertisers makes it essential that every precaution should be taken to avoid the slightest suspicion that there is any connection between the advertisement and the editorial columns. This is really as much to the interest of dealers of repute as to that of the magazine, for praise inspired by an advertisement counts for nothing with any intelligent reader." This last claim seemed optative rather than convincing.

Fry also spent time in his editorializing to spell out just what makes a dealer a dealer. Again he would draw on his own experience. Careful not to imply that dealers were purely mercenary, he argued that the term "dealer" would be used only for those whose main source of income was generated by buying low and selling high. Collectors were the other class, so to speak, occasionally operating with mercantile interests in the foreground, but importantly different from dealers. Fry was content to distinguish the two groups, and to say unequivocally that "it may be taken as certain that when collectors wish to sell they sell at a profit if they can. But they do not thereby become dealers, and here there is really no difficulty in drawing the line." Presumably dealers are always commercially minded, while collectors are only so on occasion. At this time in his life, Fry would make every effort to be clear-headed about the entanglements between commerce and art. Having in his past (though with less and less frequency) been involved not only in attributions and working for a commission in the buying and selling of masterpieces, he meant to spell out in detail how the system worked. He still had, however, to more clearly define what was at once a meshing of, and a contradiction in, the formation of values.

THIS CONCERN WITH THE ECONOMIC FUNCTIONS IN THE art world lay behind the essay "Art in a Socialism," which appeared in the *Burlington* in April 1916. He subsequently exposed his thinking to a specialized audience, delivering the essay as a lecture to the Fabian Society, writing to Vanessa Bell in August 1917 that the talk would be "on the relations of movements in art to movements in life." The argument here extended some of the reflections from "Criticism and Commerce," but enlarged the field of consideration to include the main features of political economy and not just the rules and conventions of the art world. Yet Fry—perhaps drawing on his close friendship with John Maynard Keynes, whom he had come to know through his association with the Bloomsbury Group—began early on to carve out an inchoate field, generally referred to as cultural economics, which would flourish only several generations later. "Art in a Socialism" displays Fry's typical rhetoric and reasoning, as he begins with broad categories and attempts throughout to mediate between sharp observations (occasionally indulging in satirical views of the plutocracy) and general formulations (whose mild tone is one of a melioristic socialism).

Fry initiated his argument by both singularizing the category of artist and linking it to others, whom he called "anarchists" and "intransigents." (It would be the latter term that most interested him.) Fry insisted that "The artist in the widest sense of the word represents the crucial difficulty of all socialisms," because his nature intersects with that of others in distinctive ways. "He is an anarchist by nature . . . one of the anarchists that socialism must either crush or make room for. The other anarchists are the insane, the religious and the philosophers; all of these on different grounds deny the supremacy of the ethical dogma on which societies are founded—on which socialisms as the completest conceptions of society are bound most to insist."

The intransigents are such because they claim to have a value that is more important than that of the merely ethical; for them, ethics is "only of the nature of mechanism, not an end in itself." Fry forces the issue because he values the independent thinking (though less so the behavior) of the artists more than that of the other intransigents. But just because artists rely on a higher sense of ethics or social values does not mean their métier is cleansed of all difficulties. Indeed, that higher sense remains a constant, though often unsuccessful, challenge to social values.

Much of Fry's emphasis throughout the essay falls on the intransigence of the artist-as-maker, unbound by social norms of productivity and order. Yet the artist sees his work being valued by the rest of society for reasons that are not consonant with esthetic values as such. In fact, the general public, with its economic and social arrangements, sees to it that art's true worth is dis-valued since works of art are bought mainly to establish their owner's prestige. The artist's intransigence has little sway, given such a situation. There is no comfort for artists in realizing that "a million works of art are produced and sold and bought with the object of securing prestige or advertisement to the happy ones who are rich enough to buy them." Fry here draws heavily on the notions of Thorstein Veblen's *The Theory of the Leisure Class* (1899), whose key term, "conspicuous consumption," would enjoy widespread usage. Fry's preoccupation with prestige indicates that he focuses on the circulation as well as the production of art. Both the artist and the public must account for their behavior, while often at odds with one another.

Fry turns his hand to satirical portraiture when it becomes necessary to say what the social forces are that make the consumers of art—especially those in the plutocratic class—behave the way they do and hence become important structuring forces in society. He introduces a Mr. Bounder, an allegorical figure drawn it would seem from English music-hall comedy but resting on American stereotypes.

*Mr. Hiram S. Bounder, having made his pile in the Middle West, has done with mere advertisement, and now turns his attention to prestige, a slightly more difficult matter. He begins, perhaps, by buying up the greater part of some company's stock and carrying the quotations to an unheard-of point; but he is little better off. In Wall Street he may be reckoned a new force, but the flutter will not reach to the drawing-rooms of the great, and there are hundreds of his compeers who can do the same stunt.*

Faced with the possibility of his social status being leveled, Mr. Bounder responds with another form of circulation. "Then, if he is a clever man, he may try to become a public benefactor, but in America a gift is looked upon as a weapon—a weapon which only those who are authorized to carry arms (who are in effect knights) must be allowed to use. . . ." It is easy to hear at this point some of the muffled resentment Fry felt for the values and behavior of Morgan and others of his class. There is also a glimpse here of how the encyclopedic museum controls its economic balance sheet. The grotesque transformation of a gift into a weapon can be overlooked as a piece of ready wit, but Fry carried a memory of just how effective the weapons of a rich man could be.

The tensions in Fry's argument reach a peak when he tries to focus directly on how the artist stands in social terms and what happens to what he produces. On the one hand, Fry must preserve the artist's solitary and intransigent nature even if it entails seeing him as a parasite. On the other hand, the artist's work, normally thought to be the source of his redemptive values, comes into full profitability, so to speak, only after his death. Only a "minute" group of art lovers stands between the artist and total frustration, caught as he is between the values of self-sacrifice and an elite audience: "The real artist depends for his very precarious existence upon two things: (1) the chance of having enough to live upon—being a parasite upon society, or (2) the enthusiasm of that minute group of people who actually love art." This dilemma only intensifies when the question of money comes into it. The results are mediated only by the most contingent of historical forces.

"The amount of money at the disposal of this small group (usually none of them are rich) is so limited that what we may call the pure art value of modern works of art is very low compared to the prestige value they tend to acquire later." By pointing to "modern works of art" as enjoying only in the long run a measurable prestige value, Fry conjures up his own failure to sustain himself as a painter, as well as the failure of the general public to embrace the advanced art of the Post-Impressionists.

However, socialism would present the possibility of some relief. A more equitable distribution of wealth offers a major change in the prospect of the system driven and sustained by prestige. Artists who were thoroughly mercenary would be driven from the market, leaving the field to "real" artists and thus worthy artisans would enjoy a healthier relationship with their supporters. "In our socialism, then, we should see a great fall in the prestige value of real art and a great restriction in the production of art for prestige. This would surely be a gain from the point of view of real art. The ground would be cleared, a deal of confusion would be done away with." The problem of certification and distribution remains, of course: "how to give a livelihood to the real artist; and admitting that our socialist state is willing to do this, how it can distinguish the real artist, since it would not wish, under the heading artists, to support in idleness or useless activity a vast body of shirkers." Not only is such a utopian system of governmental support highly unlikely to gain wide acceptance, it would require a system of validation and accreditation of a sort that Fry generally opposed. The strain in the argument remained something Fry could not ameliorate.

Here, drawing to a close, Fry admits that he is "rather by way of asking for suggestions than laying down any prescriptions." His final turn, typical of his style throughout much of his writing, sounds a transcendent note: "all I can hope to have done is to clear the way of some of the misunderstanding which our colossal indifference to spiritual values, our slipshod habits of thought and the resulting poverty and confusion of our language, in all that appertains to art, have brought about." This presents Fry the modernist, hoping to keep some buoyancy of spiritual transcendence in the secular world of mass man and industrial society. Seven years or so later he would try to spell out in more detail, and with more rigor and nuance, just how society—now having rather drifted further away from the socialist ideal—could still find a way to show how the values of art were pursued, but not conquered, by the forces of commerce.

FRY'S CULMINATING EFFORT TO SPELL OUT THE COMplex relations between art and commerce shapes the fundamental arguments in an essay titled with just those terms. Called "Art and Commerce," and printed as a pamphlet by the Woolfs' Hogarth Press in 1926, the essay reveals that Fry had prepared himself to offer an extended set of reflections directly on the issue of these two large forces of social structure and social valuation.[5] Fry's life was full at this time, as his monograph on Cézanne was soon to be published, and he had moved in with Helen Anrep, whom he had met only the year before, and with whom he would live happily for the remainder of his life.[6] His collection of essays *Transformations* also appeared in 1926, and except for those included in his posthumous *Last Lectures* (1936), most of his major writings were completed. In "Art and Commerce" he found an occasion to make some of his most sweeping claims about the social function of art, concentrating on a society to whose values he could not finally lend full credence.

"Art and Commerce," which began as a lecture at an exhibition of advertising posters at Oxford, is Fry's fullest analysis of these intersecting subjects. It is longer than "Art in a Socialism," as well as his two *Burlington* editorials, and presents Fry at his most speculative. The analysis here sets out a vocabulary and a scope that obviously demonstrate Fry's ambition to build a definitive account of issues that had been occupying his mind for several decades, at least since his early days as an advisor on the purchase of fine art and the role of connoisseurship in the art world.[7] It would not be enough for him to parrot the first key terms of economics—supply and demand—and their interrelationship as determined by the shrinking supply of masterpieces and the increasing demand of wealthy collectors. Instead, Fry would try in the space of a single essay to define just how esthetic and monetary values were generated, and how each became the shadowy force and reflected desire of the other.

Complicating the task of exploring the nexus of commerce and art,

*Fry at his easel, n.d.: This was probably taken during one of his trips to the south of France. Fry's unwavering lifelong commitment to his own painting influenced his ideas about the role of art in modern society.*

Fry's continuing commitment to art persisted, even as his political views continued to be at least mildly socialist (though he never advocated revolution or anything remotely like a Leninist party). This complication advances to the level of a paradox, even to some a contradiction. For Fry retains a clear distinction between what many call "journeymen" artists and those possessed of real genius sufficient enough to produce groundbreaking styles; his identity and training as a critic drove the making of such distinctions, of course. In "Art in a Socialism," the distinction worked out into three classes: the bad artist, the mercenary artist, and the true artist. He would bring this categorizing over into "Art and Commerce" by creating a new term for the second group (the largest in terms of numbers), namely the mercenary makers who design and produce only for commercial and prestige value. For this group Fry coins two (admittedly rather ungainly) terms, "opificers" and "opifacts," deriving them from *ops*, the Latin word for wealth. The first term refers to those who produce, and the second names the objects produced. (Behind both terms lies the cognate "opulence," which for Fry was clearly a disvalue.) The compendious category of opificers contains all those who produce objects "for other purposes than the necessities of life." But Fry goes on "to pick out from the large class of opificers those workmen" who make opifacts in which "we can trace a particular quality, the quality of expressing a particular emotion which we call the esthetic emotion." The men who make such things as these he calls artists, and the things themselves, works of art. Fry's first use for this distinction, between artist and works of art and opificers and opifacts, is to spell out his major claim: human beings "always require a great many opificers to produce a great variety of opifacts," but "society can get along quite comfortably and for an indefinitely long time without the existence of artists or works of art." Here Fry, unable or unwilling to shed his connoisseurship, conjoins several features: mediocre artworks are abundant, unnecessary, and lacking in true esthetic emotion, while those that contain such emotion are always (comparatively) few in number.

Fry apparently realizes these terms, opifacts and opificers, are crude, if not a little barbarous, for he points out in a footnote than he would have used "artifact" and "artificer" instead, but their meanings had recently been preempted by archeologists. In other words, he was willing to coin a set of clumsy terms just to maintain the persistent category of indifferent and mediocre artists who are neither simply bad nor worthy of the title of genius or groundbreaker. (His Quaker dislike of indifference and passivity may be evident here.) Of opificers there are many, but true artists, we find, are few in number. The true artists are thus relegated to an implicit axiological subcategory, where they maintain some of the features of the opificers, but distinguish themselves by involvement with "aesthetic emotion," the term that Fry had employed in a privileged way since the first Post-Impressionists exhibition. Separating true artists from mere opificers was for Fry not an idle judgment of value; rather, he wanted to assert a fundamental difference of kind and worth between the two sorts of makers. It might be said that distinguishing between them was either a task he left for another day, or that his whole life was dedicated to realizing such a distinction.

The lecture, ironically enough, was occasioned by an exhibit of advertising posters. Fry was motivated by the need, and the invitation, to say something about advertising (to which he would give a special meaning) and the role that art played in this socially influential activity. His friend Edward McKnight Kauffer was well established as a designer of advertising posters, adapting his keen graphic sense to commercial ends. Kauffer was an American-born graphic artist who immigrated to England just before the start of the Great War, having already studied in Paris and Munich. Along the way he witnessed the Armory Show in New York and enjoyed a one-man show at the Omega Workshop. His reputation blossomed because of his skill and friendship with the Bloomsbury Group and the Hogarth Press, for which he did a number of illustrations for book jackets. Considerable financial success followed as he did commercial work for the London Underground and large companies such as Standard Oil. In 1918 Fry tried to entice him to be an assistant editor for the *Burlington*, but Kauffer's graphic work kept him too busy to take on such a task. In May 1925 Fry published a laudatory piece in the *Nation*, called "Poster Designs and the Art of Mr. McKnight Kauffer." This was followed by another laudatory article, "The Author and the Artist," in the *Burlington*, in July 1926. Kauffer had illustrated Robert Burton's *Anatomy of Melancholy*, and Fry saw in the work a very modern approach to line and form, crediting Kauffer with using both Cubist and Futurist styles.

*He has drawn from Cubism a new and quite unforeseen possibility.*
*We are so little accustomed to rest contented in the contemplation*
*of abstract visible forms . . . that Cubism, which set out to discover*

*purely formal relations, has always tended to suggest some acciden-*
*tal significance. People have insisted on reading into [Cubism] sym-*
*bolical or expressionist meanings, and many artists, such as the Fu-*
*turists, have exploited it in that direction. Nothing could be more*
*delightfully witty and apposite, therefore, than the peculiar and*
*quite distinct use which Mr. Kauffer has found for it.*[8]

"The Author and the Artist" not only testifies to Fry's high regard
for his friend but demonstrates how Fry's critical eye—focused here
on the purity of formal relations in Cubism—had stayed fresh and
pertinent as he looked at work beyond the first two decades of the
twentieth century.

In any case Fry spent much of the bulk of "Art and Commerce"
trying to link various social values and formations with the out-
comes that would affect esthetic experience. His friendship with
Kauffer produced another shift in his vocabulary in the lecture, since
he equated advertising with the display and ostentation that prestige
utilized in asserting itself. At one point he even argued that religious
and political rituals can best be seen as forms of advertisement, going on to give special meaning to the term by claiming that "advertisement in one form or another has been one of the greatest of social
forces throughout human history." By using a word like "advertising" instead of more direct terms such as "ostentation" or "display,"
Fry had already begun, as he told Vanessa Bell, to relate "the relations of movements in art to movements in life."

Fry would use the last page or so of his lecture to spell out how
what he calls "trade advertising" functions in modern society. He
was, after all, addressing people who had come to see an exhibition
devoted to prize examples of good graphic art in the service of advertising posters. Here he presciently mentions some of the features that
many people now take as commonplaces: advertising creates false
or superfluous demand; advertising has become such a fixture that
manufacturers build it into the cost of production; advertising merely
shifts the fixed expenditures of the public from one brand to another,
and so forth. But he strikes a more positive note when he refers directly to the exhibition of advertising posters that is the occasion for
his lecture. Fry sees in the advertising poster a possible advantage for

good art in that its traditions have not yet been subject to "mummi-fication," which he considers the bane of all good art; here he clearly has in mind his earlier praise for Kauffer's work.

However, before he reaches this coda about advertising posters, Fry refers a number of times to his two main postulates. The first postulate states that fine art is strictly speaking unnecessary for human beings, as it answers no pressing practical needs. The second says that the distinction between opifacts and opificers, and, respectively, works of art and artists (with the latter being a much smaller group than the former), explains most of the complex and shifting relationships that obtain between art and commerce. The first postulate means that changes in art—regarding matters of style, the social position of the artist, and so forth—are random, and implicitly subject to large social and historical shifts. In brief, Fry offers a weak version of historical determinism that accounts for the specific state of culture and art at any one time, in any one society. The second postulate offers a somewhat more particularized description of how the art world and society commingle, since the cultural authority, so to speak, is often passed back and forth between opificers and artists.

His postulates lead Fry to a very sketchy history of art of the sort that he would rely on for his lectures. On this occasion, Fry says that a highly organized civilization like that of Egypt required a profusion of opifacts, because the "ruler who symbolizes in himself the whole social organism" needs to have his ostentation support his "pre-eminence . . . and ambition and power." However, "in the reign of Akn-aten, a spiritual upheaval . . . allowed a free play of sensibility"⁹ to create new forms, which eventually also led to stylization and repetition. During the Renaissance, Florence and Siena, on the other hand, "had likewise an essentially commercial civilization," which nevertheless produced great artists. Fry must be content to record this as "an extremely rare phenomenon of people who actually preferred the artist to the pure opificer." Almost more rare is the case of nineteenth-century England and France, where "the sense of individual worth and independence had been highly developed in the middle classes." This meant that the artist refused to be suppressed and hence withstood social ostracism, even "in the face of the organized body of opificers."¹⁰ But, as a summary of this skeletal history of art, Fry concludes: "it is almost the rule of civilized life to pro-duce a great many opifacts and to be quite indifferent to works of art." The "almost" is Fry's saving note in what the Italian communist philosopher Antonio Gramsci called the tension between "the pessi-mism of the intellect and the optimism of the will."

This negative note is sounded here and there in "Art and Com-merce." Fry appears to keep it at bay, but it surfaces most severely when he introduces the idea that society has a certain interest—and a certain skill—in "inoculating" people against art. The satiric sting shows itself in this passage, as Fry directly addresses his audience.

> *You are many of you already inoculated by this feverish interest in spiritual things, but it is probable that society will help you to get over it and forget it ultimately altogether. You may be now in doubt whether Matisse or the winner of the Derby is the more important person; when once you have settled down, merely to put such a ques-tion will appear the mark of an unbalanced character and a rather scandalous reputation.*[11]

The knot of allusions here brings together the great innovative artist, the commercial frivolity of a horse race, and the public's question-able judgment as to what makes for good sense and a sound moral character. A paragraph later, Fry opens with the mocking announce-ment that "The École des Beaux Arts is one of the most admirably equipped of those laboratories for inoculation against art." Though his views were elitist, they were views of a distinct kind.

Fry's anti-establishment views became more explicit and more in-tense as the century drew on. The conflict with Morgan, the dispute over the Chantrey Bequest, the relatively short life of the Omega Workshop, the scandal in the wake of the Post-Impressionists show—all of this was enough to turn Fry's view of the plutocracy, and its role in shaping the art world, in decidedly negative direc-tions. The same would apply to his view of the "establishment." Yet he ended his career as the Slade Professor of Art at Cambridge, an il-lustrious post he was given just a year before his death. Praised by many of his contemporaries as pragmatic in his approach to art, he paradoxically had his greatest influence in the art world as the formulator and defender of the formal elements in art. He never stopped thinking of himself as primarily a practicing artist, and yet he spent countless hours in all the ancillary activities—writing, curating, organizing, reviewing, appraising, editing, lecturing—that constitute the complex formation of the art world.

Fry lived for the same number of years in the nineteenth century as in the twentieth. He never consciously described himself as a Victorian who became a Modernist, since he never fully adopted the personal self-assurance of the former or the radical experimentalism of the latter. In this sense, his life, thought and work are illumined by his willingness to challenge and redefine the reigning tastes and values of his time. Virginia Woolf summed up his character, in part by her own words, and then by quoting from E. M. Forster's obituary of Fry:

> He was a difficult man, it is easy to believe, on committees. He gave his opinion uncompromisingly; he gave it wittily and pungently, or sometimes he gave it sufficiently with one deep groan. He had no respect for authority. "If you said to him, 'This must be right, all the experts say so, Hitler says so, Marx says so, Christ says so, The Times says so', he would reply in effect, 'Well, I wonder. Let's see. . . .' You would come away realizing that an opinion may be influentially backed and yet be tripe."[12]

Fry's final value resides in his ability as an expert and a critic, but one who questions all merely official influence, all comfortably invalid expertise.

# NOTES

1. For an engaging account of this rather eccentric man, see the biography of Cesnola by Beth McFadden, *The Glitter and the Gold* (New York: Dial Press, 1971).

2. Jeffrey Trask, *Things American: Art Museums and Civic Culture in the Progressive Era* (Philadelphia: University of Pennsylvania Press, 2012), 4.

3. Blake Gopnik, *Daily Beast*, April 10, 2013.

4. Marco Grassi, "Reflections on Taste," *New Criterion* (December 2004), 27.

## CHAPTER I: THE BIRTH OF DYNASTIC FINANCES

1. Louis Auchincloss, *J. P. Morgan: The Financier as Collector* (New York: Harry Abrams, 1990), 74.

2. Biographical details are taken largely from the account given on the Morgan Library and Museum website: www.themorgan.org/research/FindingAids /archives/ARC1196-MorganPierpont.pdf.

3. Jeremy Byman, *J. P. Morgan: Banker to a Growing Nation* (Greensboro, NC: Morgan Reynolds Publishers, 2001), 8–27.

4. Leslie Hannah, "J. P. Morgan in London and New York Before 1914," *Business History Review*, Vol. 85 (Spring 2011), 113. However, it would not be until several years after Morgan's death that the New York Stock Exchange (NYSE) surpassed the London Stock Exchange (LSE) in size; but the rate of growth of the NYSE was outstripping that of the LSE even by the end of the nineteenth century. See Hannah, 114.

5. "Finance capitalism is characterized by a predominance of the pursuit of profit from the purchase and sale of, or investment in, currencies and financial products such as bonds, stocks, futures and other derivatives." This definition is

from Wikipedia. In 1857 the Panic was triggered by a failure in production of a natural resource (grain), followed by a chain of negative consequences; this is known as merchant capitalism. In finance capitalism, it is the actions and events in the banking system—among the financiers and their "financial products"—that trigger the sort of panic that Morgan later experiences (in 1907 especially). Morgan began as a merchant capitalist, and ended as a finance capitalist.

6. Ron Chernow, *The House of Morgan: An American Banking Dynasty and the Rise of Modern Finance* (New York: Grove Press, 1990), 20.

7. Ibid., 22.

8. Ibid., 23.

9. Ibid., 24.

10. The story is told in many studies of Morgan.

11. Leverage comes from the metaphor of using a force to create a larger force. In finance, this means using borrowed money to increase one's gains. Leverage is sometimes meant to convey the ratio of debt to a company's cash or market value. The greater the leverage a company "holds," the more "exposed" it is, which is to say, in simpler language, the larger is the amount of its debt.

12. Leslie Hannah, "J. P. Morgan in London and New York before 1914," 113–150.

13. Some of the details in what follows are drawn from the lecture by Jennifer Tonkovich, "Panic and Purchases: Pierpont Morgan in 1907," given at a symposium on collecting at the Frick Library, March 2, 2013.

14. Details about the architecture of the Library are found at www.themorgan.org/about/historyArchitecture.asp.

15. The story of Morgan's blocking Berenson as director is discussed in Heidi Ardizzone, *An Illuminated Life: Bella da Costa Greene's Journey from Prejudice to Privilege* (New York: Norton, 2007), 116–117.

16. For a full account of the Berenson-Duveen relationship, including their eventual estrangement, see Rachel Cohen, "Priceless: When Art Became Commerce," *New Yorker*, October 8, 2012, 64–71.

17. The interview where Greene tells the story of the Lord Amherst auction is in the April 7, 1912, edition of the *New York Times*, entitled "Spending J. P. Morgan's Money for Rare Books."

18. This and the following remarks by Greene about Morgan are drawn from the excellent article by Jean Strouse, "The Unknown J. P. Morgan: A Biographer Uncovers the Private Life of the Famous Banker," *New Yorker*, March 29, 1999, 66–79. Greene's defense of Morgan against Berenson's negative attitude is also discussed by Ardizzone, *An Illuminated Life*, 146–149.

19. Cited in Jean Strouse, *Morgan: American Financier* (New York: Harper Collins, 1999), 486.

20. The letter from Gaspard Farrer is quoted in ibid., 490, as is the anecdote about the Hercules, 486.

21. Satterlee's biography of his father-in-law is *J. Pierpont Morgan: An Intimate Portrait* (New York: Macmillan, 1939), 382–383.

## CHAPTER II: THE ESTHETIC EDUCATION
## OF AN ART CRITIC

1. See *Letters of Roger Fry*, ed. Denys Sutton (London: Chatto & Windus, 1972), I, #15. The letters are in two volumes and are numbered consecutively. All further references to Fry's correspondence cite volume number and letter number, as above.

2. Virginia Woolf, *Roger Fry: A Biography* (London: Hogarth Press, 1940), 44.

3. Sutton, *Letters of Roger Fry*, I, #9.

4. For a discussion of McTaggart and his role in forming the thoughts of Dickinson and Fry, see the illuminating article by Christopher Green, "Into the Twentieth Century: Roger Fry's Project Seen from the 20th Century," in Christopher Green, ed., *Art Made Modern: Fry's Vision of Art* (London: Merrell Holberton, 1999), 13–30. The collection of essays is of great interest.

5. See *The Autobiography of G. Lowes Dickinson and Other Unpublished Writings*, ed. Daniel Proctor (London: Duckworth, 1973). The book has several interesting aspects, especially Dickinson's frankness about his foot fetish, which he treats with striking objectivity.

6. Ibid., 79.

7. Frances Partridge, *Memories* (London: Phoenix, 1999; reprint of 1981 Gollancz edition).

8. From Woolf, *Roger Fry: A Biography*, 262–263.

9. For a full account see the excellently detailed article, "Impudence and Iconoclasm: The Early GRANTA and an Unknown Roger Fry Essay," by Panthea Reid Broughton, in *English Literature in Transition, 1880–1920*, Vol. 30, No. 1, 68–79. I have relied on this article for many details.

10. The entire essay itself is inserted into Broughton's article, ibid., 75–76.

11. Fry's work as an art critic took place against a background that saw the development of a complex part of the late Victorian art world. For a full and engaging description of this new form of writing, with its styles, theories, and special interests, see Pamela Fletcher and Anne Helmreich, "The Periodical and the Art Market: Investigating the Dealer-Critic System in Victorian England," *Victorian Periodicals Review*, Vol. 41, No. 4 (Winter 2008), 323–351. The secondary material on this subject is vast; Fletcher and Helmreich cite much of it.

12. Sutton, *Letters of Roger Fry*, I, #122.

13. See the introduction by Werner in Roger Fry, *Cézanne: A Study of His Development* (New York: Macmillan, 1958), a reprint of the original 1927 edition by Leonard and Virginia Woolf.

14. Sutton, *Letters of Roger Fry*, I, #79.

15. This description appeared in a review of Fletcher and Helmreich; see Rebecca Scragg, *Victorian Studies*, Vol. 56, No. 2 (Winter 2014), 334–337.

16. Fry wrote his father about Sickert's change of mind on March 25, 1894 (Sutton, *Letters of Roger Fry*, I, #157), and then repeated the news in a letter two days later to his sister Margery (#158).

17. Ibid., #157.

18. Ibid., #156.

19. A distinctive reading of the portrait is offered in Michael Neve, "Sexual Politics," in *London Review of Books*, Vol. 3, No. 2 (February 5, 1981), 21–22. "This is Carpenter in 1895, as Bloomsbury [in this case, Roger Fry] captured him. He seems downcast, serious-minded, isolated in a world of glass that reflects him at an odd angle. An awful thought crosses the mind, that Carpenter in fact represents a fastidiousness, an aloofness, a Cambridge donnishness, which, allied to sexual indeterminacy, has left him marooned."

20. The chore of Fry's biography did not come easily for Woolf. One scholar, Georgia Johnston, has traced her difficulties: "Woolf undertook the writing of Fry's biography at the request of his family. Despite 'a long debate about the book on Roger' with his sister Margery, and Woolf's concerns about whether she 'could be free' with the subject . . . she began to gather material in April 1938. . . . As she worked on the text, she described *Roger Fry* [the mss.] as 'donkey work' and 'drudgery' . . . Even when she 'set the last word to the first sketch of Roger' on March 10, 1939, she anticipated the revisions would be a 'terrible grind' . . . She sent the manuscript to Margery in February 1940, but continued to work on proofs and index through June. *Roger Fry* is published in July [1940]." See Georgia Johnston, "Virginia Woolf Revising Roger Fry into the Frames of 'A Sketch of the Past,'" *Biography*, Vol. 20, No. 3 (Summer 1997), 284–301. That Virginia's sister, Vanessa, had an affair with Fry, while still married to Clive Bell, and that Virginia was slow at first to appreciate Fry's esthetic theories, may well have added to the psychological burdens Virginia carried into the writing of the biography.

21. See the article by Laing in the *Virginia Woolf Miscellany*, Spring 1980, 2. His research was published as Donald Laing, *Roger Fry: An Annotated Bibliography of the Published Writings* (Ann Arbor: Garland Publishing, 1979).

22. The correction is offered by Elizabeth Prettejohn, "Out of the Nineteenth Century: Roger Fry's Early Art Criticism, 1900–1906," in Green, ed., *Art Made Modern*. I have borrowed several details from this carefully researched article.

23. Roger Fry, "Art and Religion," *Monthly Review* (May 1902), 126–139.

24. See *The Letters of Bernard Berenson and Isabella Stewart Gardner*, ed. Rollin Van N. Hadley (Boston: Northeastern University Press, 1982), 147. In July 1898 Berenson was the guest of Sir George Trevelyan in Cambridge, and told Isabella Gardner that Trevelyan's son "Bobbie" was "a very dear friend of mine and my pleasant traveling companion." Though a Harvard graduate, Berenson was a devout Anglophile: "I love to go to English universities," he told Gardner,

"and to be with men who are in great earnest about problems as remote as possible from the hot pressing ones of the day." My thanks to Susan Dackerman for this reference.

25. For basic facts about Morelli, see www.dictionaryofarthistorians.org/morellig.htm.

26. For a sense of Morelli's rigor, see Hayden B. J. Macginnis, "The Role of Perceptual Learning in Connoisseurship: Morelli, Berenson, and Beyond," *Art History*, Vol. 13, No. 1 (March 1990), 104–117. Macginnis points out, however, the three more up-to-date charges against connoisseurship: it relies on something like an initiated priesthood, it suffers from methodological individualism (and thus leaves out any sociological framework), and many of its claims have been proven false. The three charges could readily be set at Berenson's door.

27. See Jenny Graham, "A Note on the Early Reputation of Roger Fry," *Burlington Magazine*, Vol. 143, No. 1181 (August 2001), 493–499. The detailed article (which includes the Fry letter cited) is of great interest in showing how he handled controversy.

28. Sutton, *Letters of Roger Fry*, I, #183. As for Professor Hoppin, he was trained as a minister and taught in the Theological Seminary at Yale for more than two decades. He apparently lacked any academic training in art history, and his book was the sort of amateur effort that connoisseurs would utterly reject.

29. The literature on Berenson is formidably extensive. But for a good account of his career from the standpoint of his relations with Joseph Duveen, the dealer who signed him to a secret contract, see Rachel Cohen, "Priceless," *New Yorker*, October 8, 2012, 63–71. Duveen himself is profiled by S. N. Behrman, "The Days of Duveen," *New Yorker*, September 29, 1951, 33–61.

30. Sutton, *Letters of Roger Fry*, I, #80. In the same letter Fry laments that Walter Pater had made "so many mistakes" about paintings, but defended the esthete by saying "the strange . . . thing is that the net result is so very just." As for Berenson, his theories were extremely complex, built upon a notion of an "artistic personality." This concept has been discussed by many; an especially astute analysis is by Jeremy Melius, "Connoisseurship, Painting, and Personhood," *Art History*, Vol. 34, No. 2 (April 2011), 288–309, where we find this passage: "The text [*Florentine Painters of the Renaissance*, 1897] held a special, stressed position in Berenson's process of self-explanation. It was meant to be a placeholder for a more ambitious work on the psycho-physiology of viewing art that would never be written. The unfixed, yet hyper-sensate body at its core recurs in all he would write afterwards. In *Florentine Painters*, the nebulous outlines of the connoisseur's own embodiment prefigure the instabilities inherent in Berenson's later imaginary artistic personalities . . . Painting 'lends a higher coefficient of reality to the object represented', and we experience an 'exhilarating sense of increased capacity' in which the viewer's 'whole personality is enhanced'." (302–303) These "instabilities" are used by Melius to explore how great painters both consolidate and disperse their genius, not only in their paintings but in their followers, and in their

viewers. On the other hand, Fry's theory of painting also never totally integrated a deep or scientific psychology into its exposition.

31. There is a modern reprint, on which I have relied: Roger Fry, *Giovanni Bellini*, with an introduction by David Alan Brown and an afterword by Hilton Kramer (New York: Ursus Press, 1995).

32. Hilton Kramer, in his afterword, helpfully argues that this sort of detail resulted from Fry's own experience as a highly trained painter (64).

33. This contretemps, which she correctly refers to as an "absurd storm in a tea-cup," is well sorted out by Caroline Elam, "Roger Fry and Early Italian Painting," in Green, ed., *Art Made Modern*, 87–106. I have relied on this article for several details.

34. See note 49, on page 98 in ibid., where Elam mentions Berenson's comments in his late diaries on Fry's "perceived perfidy and disloyalty," which induced in Berenson a "bitterness that only grew in time."

35. Details are in Sutton, *Letters of Roger Fry*, I, #119.

36. Ernest Samuels, *Bernard Berenson: The Making of a Legend* (Cambridge, MA: The Belknap Press, 1987), 21.

37. Roger Fry, "The Painters of North Italy," *Burlington Magazine*, Vol. 12, No. 60 (March, 1908), 347–349.

38. Sutton, *Letters of Roger Fry*, I, #209.

39. For more on the different ideas about art between Fry and Berenson, again see Elam, "Roger Fry and Early Italian Painting."

40. Roger Fry, "The Berensonian Method," a review of *Three Essays in Method* by Bernard Berenson, *Burlington Magazine*, Vol. 52, No. 298 (January 1928), 47–48.

41. Donald A. Laing, *Roger Fry: An Annotated Bibliography of the Published Writings* (New York: Garland, 1979).

42. See the informative survey in Elizabeth Prettejohn, "Out of the Nineteenth Century: Roger Fry's Early Art Criticism," in Green, ed., *Art Made Modern*, 31–44. I have borrowed a number of details from this essay.

43. Caroline Elam, "'A More and More Important Work': Roger Fry and *The Burlington Magazine*," in *Burlington Magazine*, Vol. 145, No. 1200, Centenary Issue (March 2003), 142–152.

44. Sir Charles Holmes, "Roger Fry and the Burlington Magazine," *Burlington Magazine*, Vol. 65, No. 379 (October 1934), 145–146. Holmes (1868–1936) was Fry's nearly exact contemporary. A model of English probity and considerable talent, he served as director of the National Portrait Gallery (1903–1909) and then of the National Gallery (1916–1928). When the *Burlington* announced the awarding of his knighthood, he was described in these terms: "His vision and his energy won for the Magazine the pre-eminence and the trust which it now enjoys throughout the civilized world, and gave to English art-learning and art-criticism a channel of expression, for lack of which they had previously been too little recognized either at home or abroad. As painter, as author, as Slade Professor of Fine

Arts at Oxford, as officer in the Anti-Aircraft Corps, as Director of the National Portrait Gallery and of the National Gallery, he has served art and his country well; but by no means the least of his services to both was achieved as Editor and Managing Director of THE BURLINGTON MAGAZINE." In *Burlington Magazine*, Vol. 39, No. 220 (July 1921), 49. A painter and etcher, he and Fry were friends and showed their work together at the New English Art Club.

45. "Editorial Article" in *Burlington Magazine*, Vol. 1, No. 1 (March 1903), 3–5.

46. See Elam, "'A More and More Important Work,'" 149.

47. From the Tate Britain website: "The sculptor Sir Francis Chantrey (1781–1841) bequeathed a fortune, and asked that the income on the money be used to buy paintings and sculpture made in Britain with a view to encouraging the establishment of a 'public national collection of British fine art'. The fund is administered by the Royal Academy, and the first work was bought for the collection in 1877, after the death of Lady Chantrey. After the founding of the Tate Gallery in 1897 the Bequest was allocated to support Tate acquisitions. Until the 1920s this was the main purchase grant for the Tate Gallery."

48. Sutton, *Letters of Roger Fry*, I, #140.

49. All three pieces are reprinted in *A Roger Fry Reader*, ed. Christopher Reed (Chicago: University of Chicago Press, 1996), 251–258.

50. The condition is known as hyperostosis frontalis interna, and involves accretion of bone tissue on the inside of the skull. Often the condition is not serious, but when it is, the chief symptom is depression.

51. As reported by Woolf, *Roger Fry: A Biography*, 101.

52. Ibid., 103.

53. Sutton, *Letters of Roger Fry*, I, #172.

54. See the brief monograph by Caroline Elam, *Roger Fry and the Re-Evaluation of Piero della Francesca* (New York: The Council of the Frick Collection, 2004.)

55. Elam, "'A More and More Important Work,'" 148. The others mentioned besides Morgan—Johnson, Walters, and Frick—were all American collectors who relied heavily on people like Fry and Berenson. Johnson—John G.(raver) Johnson—was a Philadelphia lawyer who would soon become fast friends with Fry during the time Fry was being considered for the post at the Metropolitan Museum of Art.


CHAPTER III: THE METROPOLITAN MUSEUM

1. Calvin Tomkins, *Merchants and Masterpieces: The Story of the Metropolitan Museum of Art* (New York: Henry Holt, 1970; I use the revised and expanded edition of 1989).

2. Henry James, *The American Scene* (New York: The Library of America, 1993), 513–514. This is a reprint of the original 1907 edition.

3. For some details and an overarching argument, I have relied on Daniel M. Fox, *Engines of Culture: Philanthropy and Art Museums*. The sense of a public trust in American museums, especially in their philanthropic origins, differs in important ways of legitimation from those in Europe (which were typically founded by the state), a point made by James N. Wood in "The Authorities of the American Art Museum," in *Whose Muse? Art Museums and the Public Trust*, ed. James Cuno (Princeton: Princeton University Press, 2004), 103–127.

4. The charter for the museum was approved in 1870, and the main portion identified its mission as being "for the purpose of establishing and maintaining a museum and library of art, of encouraging and developing the study of the fine arts, and the application of arts to manufacture and practical life, of advancing the knowledge of kindred subjects, and to that end, of furnishing popular instruction and recreation." It was quoted in *The Metropolitan Museum of Art: A Review of Fifty Years' Development Printed on the Occasion of the Fiftieth Anniversary of the Founding of the Museum* (New York: Metropolitan Museum of Art, 1920).

5. The role of director in many instances became the focal point for the tensions between the philanthropists and the professionalized staff. Morgan, according to one account, described the necessary qualifications of the director as "executive capacity and gentlemanly qualities," which he said were "essential." As for expertise, "museum experience can be acquired," he claimed, suggesting that elaborate professionalized training was not necessary. Quoted in Fox, *Engines of Culture*, 85.

6. Sutton, *Letters of Roger Fry*, I, #122.

7. Ibid., I, #125.

8. Ibid., I, #116.

9. Horne has left an excellent account, the subject of an informative article by Edward Chaney and Jane Hall, "Herbert Horne's 1889 Diary of His First Trip to Italy," *The Volume of the Walpole Society*, Vol. 64 (2002), 69–125. The diary is transcribed.

10. Lee Sorensen, "Horne, Herbert P[ercy]," *Dictionary of Art Historians*, www.dictionaryofarthistorians.org/horne.htm.

11. The book appeared in a limited edition of 225 copies: *Sandro Botticelli* (London: Chiswick Press, 1908). A reprint is available from Princeton University Press and also at http://archive.org/details/alessandrofilipeOOhorn.

12. The letters have been edited and very usefully annotated by Denys Sutton in *Apollo: The International Magazine for Collectors*, Vol. 122 (August 1985), 130–159.

13. In sensibility more a collector that a merchant, while still deeply involved in authentication and the buying and selling of old masters, Horne filled his residence in Florence, the Palazzo Corsi, with paintings and objets d'art, almost all of which were from Italian artists and craftsmen from the twelfth to the sixteenth

centuries. The palazzo, bequeathed to the city of Florence by Horne, acting at the urging of Mary Berenson even as Horne was virtually on his deathbed, is now known as the Museo Horne.

14. Sutton, *Letters of Roger Fry*, I, #117.

15. Mary was a caretaker in all matters relating to her husband. Nicholas Penny, director of the National Gallery, reviewing the second volume of Ernest Samuels's biography of Berenson, remarks on a letter Mary wrote to Fry: "The sharpest observations on Berenson in this book came from Mrs Berenson—above all from a letter in which she warned Roger Fry about the difficulties of resuming good relations with her husband. It begins by sounding like the sort of explanation we have to endure from the owners of vicious dogs or the mothers of beastly children. 'At the bottom of everything is a curious lonely wish to be loved. It acts just the wrong way, often, making him suspicious of not being loved.' This, of course, as Fry well knew, was likely to be rather more often a problem with men than with women. 'Another thing,' Mary Berenson observed in a more patronising tone, 'which imposes on ladies and drives men to thoughts of murder is his occasional manner of seeming to think himself omniscient.'" In "Bonking with Berenson," *London Review of Books*, Vol. 9 No. 16 (September 17, 1987), 6–7. I refrain from quoting other passages from Penny's review, which mocks to the point of nearly complete dismissal Berenson's pretensions to possess a genuine scientific or esthetic expertise. Near the end of his exposé, however, he allows Berenson a small measure of justice: "Berenson's attributions were probably little affected by commercial interests, but his arrogant over-confidence may have been stimulated by them."

16. William MacKay Laffan (1848–1909) had a longtime interest in art. Besides being Mark Twain's publisher, he wrote the catalog for the Metropolitan's collection of Chinese porcelain, most of which was a gift from Morgan. He was a trustee of the museum.

17. There is a detailed list of those present, along with other details, some of which I have borrowed, in the definitive biography by Jean Strouse, *Morgan: American Financier* (New York: Harper Collins, 1999), 497–501.

18. From *Miscellaneous Addresses by Elihu Root*, Robert Bacon and James Brown Scott, eds. (Cambridge, MA: Harvard University Press, 1917), 189–196, as cited by Strouse.

19. The following account draws heavily on the informative article by Colin B. Bailey, "Henry Clay Frick, Roger Eliot Fry and Rembrandt's *Polish Rider*," *Frick Members' Magazine*, Spring/Summer, 2002, 10–12. I am indebted to Martha Hackley for graciously making this article available to me.

20. Sutton, *Letters of Roger Fry*, I, #280.

21. Louis Ehrich (1849–1911) collected and dealt in Flemish and Italian paintings; a prize named after him is to this day offered by the Art History department at Yale University.

22. Sutton, *Letters of Roger Fry*, I, #203.

23. The shift of interlocutors, from Clarke to Laffan, probably meant the question of compensation had become the central focus.

24. One standard text in this area is *The Art of Art History: A Critical Anthology*, Donald Preziosi, ed. (Oxford and New York: Oxford University Press, 1998).

## CHAPTER IV: THE METROPOLITAN
## AND THE CONFLICTS OF A NEW VISION

1. The report is in the Metropolitan Museum of Art archive.

2. The bequest is described in the *Metropolitan Museum of Art Bulletin*, Vol. VI, No. 7 (July 1911).

3. The obituary is dated April 15, 1917, and contains an account of Johnson's art collection.

4. The obituary is reprinted in Reed, ed., *A Roger Fry Reader*, 264–265. It originally appeared in *Burlington Magazine*, May 1917.

5. Sutton, *Letters of Roger Fry*, I, #200.

6. Ibid., I, #217; the earlier remark about Morgan is in #214.

7. See Strouse, *Morgan: American Financier*, 562.

8. For Duveen, see Meryle Secrest, *Duveen: A Life in Art* (New York: Alfred A. Knopf, 2005). Secrest had access to Duveen's archive, which makes her biography fuller than that of the earlier one by S. N. Behram in 1952.

9. See Strouse, *Morgan: American Financier*, 568. As for the Rembrandt, it was purchased by the Metropolitan in 1961 for $2.3 million. At the time this was the highest amount ever paid for any picture at public or private sale.

10. Morgan's reputed ability to stop the disastrous consequences of the Panic of 1907 solidified his reputation as the country's leading, indeed indispensable, banker. At the same time some historians trace his growing disengagement with banking to this storied event.

11. Fry passed on this remark to Woolf for insertion into her biography: "I always wondered that his Mistresses in New York got such substantial subsidies as they did." I borrow this detail, and a number of others, from Strouse, *Morgan: American Financier*, 571. Strouse convincingly notes that Fry's attitude toward Morgan, and his estimation of Morgan's character, fluctuated from quite high to very low, often depending on how Morgan treated him.

12. Fry's note appeared as "The Charpentier Family," *Metropolitan Museum of Art Bulletin*, Vol. 2, No. 6 (June 1907), 102–104.

13. The first paragraph of an article about a posthumous exhibit gives a good overview of Burroughs's career: "Born in 1869, Bryson Burroughs lived 65 years, working for the last 28 of them at the Metropolitan Museum of Art. There, he began as assistant to Roger Fry and, when the British scholar and critic left in 1909, assumed his position as curator of paintings, doing much to further the museum's

collection. Calvin Tomkins, in his 'Merchants and Princes,' reports that Burroughs's coups included the first Cezanne to enter a public collection, 'La Colline des Pauvres,' Bruegel's 'Harvesters' and Van Eyck's 'Crucifixion and Last Judgment.' The curator didn't neglect native talent either, organizing shows by Albert Pinkham Ryder and Thomas Eakins, as well as buying their works." Vivian Raynor, "Art by Byson Burroughs, Inspired by Myth," *New York Times*, March 2, 1984.

14. See Frances Spalding, *Roger Fry: Art and Life* (Norfolk: Black Dog Books, 1999), 86.

15. The incident has been recounted by several writers, perhaps most notably by Tomkins, *Merchants and Masterpieces*, 103–110. Tomkins is harsh in his remarks about Fry, calling him "an intellectual snob of the most prickly sort." Morgan, on the other hand, is given a wide ethical berth when Tomkins says, "it is quite conceivable in making a major acquisition he did not always distinguish clearly in his own mind between the museum and his private collection." Of course, Morgan's use of "his own mind" as the sole venue where such judgments are made remains the central issue.

16. As to the painting itself, opinions varied as to its originality and value. After the incident put Fry in Morgan's bad graces, Herbert Horne wrote to Fry with a negative assessment: "The motive of the picture is really a vulgar one: and [Fra] Angelico was never that. . . . In short, Providence evidently designed it from the beginning as a snare and a lure to Morgan. I am very glad that your Museum has missed it; tho I am very sorry you have had so much vexation of spirit over it. What Morgan buys will soon be forgotten: but what the Museum buys will remain." See Horne's letters in Denys Sutton, "Herbert Horne: A Pioneer Historian of Early Italian Painters," *Apollo: The International Magazine for Collectors*, Vol. 122 (August 1985), 130–159.

17. Strouse, *Morgan: American Financier*, 570. Perhaps the final irony is that the painting is now attributed to a follower of Fra Angelico, rather than the master, and is now in the Baron Thyssen Collection in Madrid.

CHAPTER V: MORGAN AND THE BUILDING
OF AN ENCYCLOPEDIC MUSEUM

1. The letters from which these excerpts were taken are in the archive at the Morgan Library.

2. Details are taken from the biographical account at www.dictionaryofarthistorians.org/valentinerw.htm.

3. The Hudson-Fulton Celebration: W. R. Valentiner et al., *Catalogue of a Collection of Paintings of Dutch Masters of the Seventeenth Century* (New York: Metropolitan Museum of Art, 1909), ix.

4. Valentiner was also successful in choosing his assistants. When he first

joined the museum, he chose Joseph Breck to work under him as assistant curator, in 1909. Breck was a Harvard graduate who had studied at the Fogg Museum there, and would in 1917 replace Valentiner when the latter returned to Germany during the war. During two periods (the second being after Edward Robinson's death), Breck served as acting director of the museum, and in 1952 became the director of the Met's uptown center of medieval art, the Cloisters. He was also in charge of installing Morgan's collection at the Metropolitan, just after Morgan's death. See Timothy B. Husband, "Creating the Cloisters," *Metropolitan Museum of Art Bulletin*, Spring 2013.

5. See the important study by Jeffrey Trask, *Things American: Art Museums and Civic Culture in the Progressive Era.*

6. Details of Dean's life and career are drawn from Strouse, *Morgan: American Financier*, 494–495, and from his obituary in the *Metropolitan Museum of Art Bulletin*. The museum celebrated his career, and the centennial of the founding of the department, with a special months-long exhibit in the Arms and Armor hall, now named in Dean's honor, in late 2012 to late 2013. A review by Charles McGrath is in the *New York Times*, October 4, 2012. An excellent video accompanying the show is available at www.metmuseum.org/metmedia/video/collections/aa/bashford-dean.

7. See Enrico Coen, "The Making of a Blossom: A Flower's Evolutionary Past May Be Read in the Genes That Influence Its Development," *Natural History*, Vol. 111, No. 4 (May 2002), 48.

8. In a biographical sketch in *Time*, Vol. 15, No. 17 (April 28, 1930), 40.

9. Other details about the Dino collection are from Tomkins, *Merchants and Masterpieces*, 152–153.

10. See the account by Aleksandr Gelfand, a Metropolitan Museum intern, "The Devoted Collector: William H. Riggs and the Department of Arms and Armor," available at www.metmuseum.org/about-the-museum/now-at-the-met/features/2013/the-devoted-collector.

11. Cited in ibid.

12. "At a meeting of the Board of Trustees, held on December 17, 1928, the following memorial resolution upon the late Bashford Dean was adopted." See "In Memory of Bashford Dean," *Metropolitan Museum of Art Bulletin*, vol. 24, no. 1 (1929), 5. The museum also held a centennial celebration of Dean's service as curator, a video of which can be viewed at www.metmuseum.org/metmedia/video/collections/aa/bashford-dean.

13. This information is drawn from the Morgan Library and Museum website.

14. I have drawn several details from Strouse, *Morgan: American Financier.*

15. At one point the committee decided to delay its hearings until December so as not to appear to influence the November election, in which Wilson, Taft, and Roosevelt were candidates. Roosevelt and Taft were running in part on their reputations as "trust busters." Wilson won, of course, since Roosevelt's Progres-

sive Party (nicknamed the Bull Moose Party) took away votes from Taft, who came in third. Eugene Debs, running on the Socialist ticket, came in fourth.

16. The commentator appeared to have been an eyewitness to the testimony, and perhaps drew from the extensive coverage in the *New York Times* and other newspapers. See the following note.

17. A transcript of Morgan's testimony, in which he was questioned by Untermyer while being counseled by Mr. Richard V. Lindabury, was published as an anonymous fifty-five-page pamphlet, "The Justification of Wall Street." It is available at http://memory.loc.gov/service/gdc/scd0001/2006/2006051700Ite /2006051700Ite.pdf. The anonymous commentator supplies an introduction to the testimony.

18. Pujo Committee Report: The entire report can be downloaded from www .scribd.com/doc/34121180/Pujo-Committee-Report-Report-of-the-Committee -Appointed-Pursuant-to-House-Resolutions-429-and-504-1912-1913-Pujo -Committee-Report.

19. Ibid., p. 33.

20. Ibid., p. 56.

21. Ibid., pp. 136–137.

22. Ibid., p. 137.

23. This is part of the report summarized in the *New York Times*, January 12, 1913.

24. Untermyer, even before the committee's report appeared, had said that he felt the "inner group" of bankers who had amassed the "money trust" had broken no laws.

25. As quoted in Strouse, *Morgan: American Financier*, 675. I have also taken details from her account of Morgan's last days.

26. This is from Bryson Burroughs's catalog of the paintings in the Metropolitan, ninth edition, 1931, xiii. An excellent article about the bequest of Benjamin Altman to the Metropolitan offers an enlightening set of implicit contrasts and comparisons between Morgan's procedure as a donor and Altman's. See Francis Haskell, "The Benjamin Altman Bequest," *Metropolitan Museum of Art Bulletin*, Vol. 3, 1970, 259–280.

27. The items are listed in *The Metropolitan Museum of Art: Guide to the Loan Exhibition of the J. Pierpont Morgan Collection* (New York: The Gilliss Press, 1914).


CHAPTER VI: GROWTH OF AN ART EXPERT

1. See David Boyd Haycock, *A Crisis of Brilliance: Five Young British Artists and the Great War* (London: Old Street Publishing, 2009) for a detailed account, which relies largely on memoirs of the various artists and stresses the social rather than the artistic issues.

2. Peter Stansky, *On or About December 1910: Early Bloomsbury and Its Intimate World* (Cambridge, MA: Harvard University Press, 1996), 70. This book contains detailed accounts of the many different and often tangled relationships that characterized the group's ethos.

3. The original catalog essay is available in Reed, *A Roger Fry Reader*, 81–85. The extensive commentary on the exhibit is virtually mountainous. The centennial issue of the *Burlington* made this point, and added some others that the tide of history has left stranded: "It might be thought that there was little more to discover about *Manet and the Post-Impressionists*, shown at the Grafton Galleries, London, in the winter of 1910–11. So celebrated an exhibition has been written about and chewed over by art historians and cultural commentators for several decades. But, as is evident from the articles in this special issue to mark the centenary of the show, there was still a good deal to find out. . . . It should be remembered that progressive art from abroad was comparatively rarely seen in Britain at that time and although several of the artists shown at the Grafton Galleries had had work in exhibitions in London and elsewhere (notably in *Modern French Artists* at Brighton in June 1910), the examples were not always of the best. There were few dealers who risked showing European Impressionism and Symbolism, let alone anything more advanced. Even Durand-Ruel's great exhibition of the Impressionists at the Grafton Galleries in 1905, although critically acclaimed, sold nothing. Five years later and the situation was almost reversed: Manet and the Post-Impressionists opened to a hailstorm of critical abuse and over 25,000 paying visitors made their way to the West End gallery, in the plush centre of the art establishment, to discover what it was all about. The show made healthy sales. It was well publicized with posters and press advertisements (in three consecutive months in this Magazine, for example). One visitor, who thought most of the pictures were 'abortions', found the galleries 'uncomfortably crowded with a horde of giggling and laughing women'." Available online as "The Shock of the Old: 'Manet and the Post-Impressionists'" www.burlington.org.uk/magazine/back-issues/2010/201012/editorial/.

4. As pointed out by David Boyd Haycock in *A Crisis of Brilliance*, "Although some of these paintings were already twenty or even thirty years old—and four of the five major artists represented were dead—they were new to most Londoners." The scene was set for cultural strife.

5. The critic for the *Pall Mall Gazette* described the paintings as "the output of a lunatic asylum." Robert Ross of the *Morning Post* agreed, claiming the "emotions of these painters . . . are of no interest except to the student of pathology and the specialist in abnormality." These comments were especially hurtful to Fry as his wife had recently been committed to a mental institution. See the biographical entry for MacCarthy, on www.spartacus.schoolnet.co.uk/ARTmacCarthyD.htm. For the full record of the contemporary reception, see J. B. Bullen, *Post-Impressionists in England* (London: Routledge Kegan & Paul, 1989).

6. In his introduction to his *Post-Impressionists in England*, 1–38, Bul-

len makes it clear that a more reasoned and even appreciative reaction followed within months. The book contains over a hundred responses (mostly excerpts from newspapers and magazines) to the exhibit. I have borrowed details from several, as well as from Bullen's introduction.

7. The first salvo was a letter to the March 1908 issue of the *Burlington*, titled "The Last Phase of Impressionism." The second was a two-part article in the *Nation*, "The Grafton Gallery" (November 19, 1910) and "A Postscript on Post Impressionism" (December 21, 1910). All three are reprinted in Bullen.

8. In his essay "Art and the State" (1924), reprinted in Roger Fry, *Transformations: Critical and Speculative Essays on Art* (London: Chatto & Windus, 1926), Fry suggested that "the intelligent understanding of the artistic products of mankind is a quiet serious profession." Citing the German term *Kunstforscher* and the absence of any translation in English, Fry showed his commitment to what might be called the role of the "art researcher" or scholar, a role that he had exemplified for several decades. Such skillful research ability would combine both a historical and a theoretical mastery of the arts.

9. MacCarthy (1877–1952), eleven years younger than Fry, attended Cambridge, where he joined the Apostles and absorbed many of the same influences, such as G. E. Moore and Bernard Shaw, that shaped Fry's outlook. Their friendship and their roles in the Bloomsbury Group varied as time went on, but their early work together meant a great deal to both.

10. For a carefully researched view on this subject, from which I have borrowed several details, see Anna Gruetzner Robins, "Marketing Post-Impressionism: Roger Fry's commercial exhibitions," in Pamela Fletcher and Anne Helmreich, eds., *The Rise of the Modern Art Market in London, 1850–1939* (Manchester: Manchester University Press, 2011), 85–97. One way to think about this period is to see it as the time when the distinct but overlapping meanings of two terms, dealer and gallerist, were at their most convoluted.

11. The quotations in this paragraph are taken from Desmond MacCarthy, "The Post-Impressionists," Introduction to the catalogue of the exhibition "Manet and the Post-Impressionists," reprinted in J. B. Bullen, *Post-Impressionists in England: The Critical Reception* (London: Routledge, 1988), 94–99.

12. Woolf, *Roger Fry: A Biography*, 158.

13. As quoted in ibid., 159, from Sir William Rothenstein's *Memoirs*.

14. *Art*, by Clive Bell, The Project Gutenberg eBook, # 16917, is most readily accessible at www.gutenberg.net. Quotations from *Art* are taken from this eBook; the title is in the public domain. This format is un-paginated, but all my citations are from the first section, called "The Aesthetic Hypothesis," unless otherwise noted.

15. The essay "Art and Life" is based on a lecture given to the Fabian Society in 1917. It expands on some of the principles set out in "An Essay on Aesthetics" from the *New Quarterly* of 1909. This may be viewed as the central statement of Fry's esthetic. However, Michael Fried gives that distinction to "A Retrospect."

16. The two men differed on some points, however. Fry reviewed Bell's *Art* and attempted to distance himself from his friend's rasher formulations. No less an observer than George Bernard Shaw saw Bell in these terms: "My friend Clive Bell is a fathead and a voluptuary. This is a very comfortable sort of person to be, and very friendly and easy and pleasant to talk to. Bell is a brainy man out of training. So much the better for his friends; for men in training are irritable, dangerous, and apt to hit harder than they know. No fear of that from Clive. The layer of fat on his brain makes him incapable of following up his own meaning; but it makes him good company." *New Republic*, February 21, 1922. Bell, at least distantly, admitted to such flaws, as when he said this about the relation between his writing and Fry's: "it is clear that should one affect the judgments of another, he may affect, indirectly, some of his theories; and it is certain that some of my historical generalisations have been modified, and even demolished, by Mr. Fry. His task was not arduous: he had merely to confront me with some work over which he was sure that I should go into ecstasies, and then to prove by the most odious and irrefragable evidence that it belonged to a period which I had concluded, on the highest a priori grounds, to be utterly barren." Clive Bell, *Art* (New York: Frederick A. Stokes, 1914).

17. Bell used his sense of esthetics to confirm his notions of art history (and vice versa) with deterministic conclusions. As he rather stridently puts it in "Aesthetics and Post-Impressionism," the second section of *Art*: "The fact that significant form was the only common quality in the works that moved me, and that in the works that moved me most and seemed most to move the most sensitive people—in primitive art, that is to say—it was almost the only quality, had led me to my hypothesis before ever I became familiar with the works of Cézanne and his followers. Cézanne carried me off my feet before ever I noticed that his strongest characteristic was an insistence on the supremacy of significant form. When I noticed this, my admiration for Cézanne and some of his followers confirmed me in my aesthetic theories. Naturally I had found no difficulty in liking them since I found in them exactly what I liked in everything else that moved me." Fry was more cautious when it came to such claims.

18. See above, note 7. In addition to the two-part article in the *Nation*, Fry contributed to the *Burlington* a translation of an article by his friend the French painter Maurice Denis. See "Introductory Note to Maurice Denis' 'Cézanne,'" *Burlington Magazine* (January 1910), 207–208. The latter piece is reprinted in Reed, *A Roger Fry Reader*.

19. Reprinted in Reed, *A Roger Fry Reader*, 76–79.

20. It is ambiguous here whether Fry means "primitive" to refer to what were known as the Italian primitives (Giotto et al.) or the African art which Fry would later write and lecture about.

21. See, for example, Frances Spalding, "Roger Fry and His Critics in a Post-Modernist Age," *Burlington Magazine*, Vol. 128, No. 1000 (July 1986), 489: "Roger Fry's significance, as a painter, critic, exhibition organizer and arbiter of

taste has in recent years been reassessed. The recognition awarded him in his own lifetime and up until the 1970's has been questioned; his influence, formerly acknowledged to have been generally innovative and advantageous to the growth of modern art in Britain, is now considered, by some, to have been restrictive, elitist and, in the long term, pernicious. . . . [Some] question whether this man, who did much to introduce modernism into British art, can still be regarded as a source of insight and direction in a post-modernist age." This context doesn't take into account Fry's diverse tastes and his openness to art in different media, epochs, and countries.

22. Christopher Reed, "Roger Fry; The Art of Bloomsbury. San Marino and London," *Burlington Magazine*, Vol. 142, No. 1165 (April 2000), 262.

23. The letter is reproduced in Reed, *A Roger Fry Reader*, 196–197.

24. Fry here uses "decorative" as a term of positive value, though in later years many critics used it to mean superficial, lacking integration at a deep level, as especially in the phrase, "merely decorative."


## CODA

1. It should be pointed out, however, that in his preface to his study of Lotto, Berenson, almost in passing, rejects attributions to Lotto made by Morelli and Cavalcaselle. The air of competition among experts never fully dissipates.

2. One leading art historian, Michael Fried, holds little faith in the ability of Fry to be wholly convincing on the issue of what are meant by "form" and "aesthetic emotion." "Fry's position on these matters seems dated, to say the least: it would surely be impossible to find anyone today who shares his belief that the task of an artist is essentially to communicate esthetic emotion, or that what he means by pure form or relations of pure form actually exist. Let me quickly say that I have no wish to challenge this negative consensus, though perhaps I ought to add that despite the prima facie unpersuasiveness of Fry's esthetic theories I consider him a writer on art of immense subtlety and interest (I assume that this too is a widely shared opinion)." This astringent formulation is from Fried's Tanner Lecture of 2001, which is available online: http://tannerlectures.utah.edu /_documents/a-to-z/f/fried_2001.pdf. The lecture is richly detailed and powerfully argued. Fried's estimation of Fry as an esthetician rests on how Fried reads "Some Questions in Esthetics," where Fry is trying to win over I. A. Richards, whose main claim is that the esthetic response has no special epistemological status. I think Fry's essay "Art and Life" makes the better case, and is the central—though early—formulation of Fry's formalism.

3. See the discussion in Chapter II.

4. "Criticism and Commerce," *Burlington Magazine*, Vol. 4, No. 11 (February 1904), 108–111.

5. The pamphlet is reprinted in a 1999 collection of Fry's pieces, *Art and the*

*Market: Roger Fry on Commerce in Art*, edited by Goodwin Craufurd (Ann Arbor: University of Michigan Press, 1999), 111–123. It was given first as a lecture on the occasion of an exhibition of advertising posters, sponsored by the Arts League of Service at Oxford.

6. Helen Anrep, two decades younger than Fry, was unhappily married to Boris Anrep at the time she met Fry. Boris, a native of Russia, was a mosaicist about whose art Fry had written an article in 1923; Fry had included some of his work in the Post-Impressionists show. There are also mosaics by him in the National Gallery and Westminster Cathedral.

7. Fry's writings on the subject that has come to be known as cultural economics are collected in *Art and the Market*. The relative newness of this subject as a focus for scholarly work may account for some of the harsher opinions it elicited. Here is a review of *Art and the Market* from 2002 that can serve as an example: "The book, rather misleadingly entitled *Art and the Market* (since there is a lot about art but not much on the market), consists of Fry's writings with an excellent 65 page Introduction by Crauford Goodwin. Having thoroughly enjoyed reading that, I found Fry's writings almost impossible to concentrate on. They peregrinate through a number of issues with the languor so well evoked in the portraits of Keynes (one of which is by Roger Fry . . . ) that evokes leisurely conversations between intelligent gentlemen in their clubs." *Art and the Market: Roger Fry on Commerce in Art*, edited by Goodwin Craufurd (Ann Arbor: University of Michigan Press, 1999), reviewed by Ruth Towse in *Economic Journal*, Vol. 112, No. 477 (February 2002), 151–153.

8. *Burlington Magazine*, July 1926, 11.

9. In honor of the sun god, Aten, Pharaoh Amenhotep IV (d. 1336 BCE), changed his name to Akhenaten ("Effective for Aten"). He turned away from traditional polytheistic religion to a radical monotheism, focused on Aten. During his reign he showed a keen interest in realistic representation in the arts. The discovery in 1907 of his tomb, by the British archeologist Flinders Petrie and others, led to a great revival of Egyptian archeology, about which Fry would have kept informed.

10. Fry probably had in mind the way some modern French artists resisted the conventions of the Academy—obviously made up of opificers in Fry's view—and heroicized the example of Cézanne, among others. Of course, Fry's own Post-Impressionists exhibition was part of this history of the avant-garde.

11. "Art and Commerce," in *Art and the Market*, 117.

12. Woolf, *Roger Fry: A Biography*, 292.

# BIBLIOGRAPHY

Anon. "Criticism and Commerce." *Burlington Magazine*, Vol. 4, No. 11 (February 1904), 108–110.

Anon. "J. P. Morgan's Testimony. The Justification of Wall Street." http://memory.loc.gov/service/gdc/scd0001/2006/20060517001te/20060517001te.pdf.

Anon. "Sir Charles John Holmes." *Burlington Magazine*, Vol. 39, No. 220 (July 1921), 49.

Ardizzone, Heidi. *An Illuminated Life: Bella da Costa Greene's Journey from Prejudice to Privilege*. New York: Norton, 2007.

Arscott, Caroline. "Walter Sickert and Roger Fry: 'Alight Here for Whiteley's'." *Journal of the Warburg and Courtauld Institutes*, Vol. 71 (2008), 295–314.

Auchincloss, Louis. *J. P. Morgan: The Financier as Collector*. New York: Harry Abrams, 1990.

Bailey, Colin B. "Henry Clay Frick, Roger Eliot Fry and Rembrandt's *Polish Rider*," *Frick Members' Magazine*, Spring/Summer 2002, 10–12.

Behrman, S. N. "The Days of Duveen." *New Yorker*, September 29, 1951, 33–61.

Bell, Clive. *Art*. New York: Frederick A. Stokes, 1914.

———. *Old Friends: Personal Recollections*. New York: Harcourt Brace, 1956.

Bell, Quentin. *Virginia Woolf: A Biography*. New York: Harcourt Brace Jovanovich, 1972.

Broughton, Panthea Reid. "Impudence and Iconoclasm: The Early GRANTA and an Unknown Roger Fry Essay." *English Literature in Transition, 1880–1920*, Vol. 30, No. 1 (1987) 68–79.

Bullen, J. B., ed. *Post-Impressionists in England*. London and New York: Routledge, 1988.

Burt, Nathaniel. *Palaces for the People: A Social History of the American Art Museum*. Boston: Little Brown and Co., 1977.

Byman, Jeremy. *J. P. Morgan: Banker to a Growing Nation*. Greensboro, NC: Morgan Reynolds Publishers, 2001.

Chernow, Ron. *The House of Morgan: An American Banking Dynasty and the Rise of Modern Finance*. New York: Grove Press, 1990.

Cohen, Rachel. "Priceless: When Art Became Commerce." *New Yorker*, October 8, 2012, 64–71.

Cuno, James, ed. *Whose Muse? Art Museums and the Public Trust*. Cambridge, MA: Harvard University Press, 2004.

Department of Greek and Roman Art. "The Cesnola Collection at The Metropolitan Museum of Art." In *Heilbrunn Timeline of Art History*. New York: Metropolitan Museum of Art, 2000–. www.metmuseum.org/toah/hd/cesn/hd_cesn.htm (October 2004).

Dickinson, Goldsworthy Lowes. *The Autobiography of G. Lowes Dickinson*. London: Duckworth, 1973.

Elam, Caroline. "'A More and More Important Work': Roger Fry and *The Burlington Magazine*." *Burlington Magazine*, Vol. 145, No. 1200, Centenary Issue (March 2003), 142–152.

———. *Roger Fry and the Re-Evaluation of Piero della Francesco*. New York: Council of the Frick Collection, 2004.

Fletcher, Pamela, and Anne Helmreich. "The Periodical and the Art Market: Investigating the Dealer-Critic System in Victorian England." *Victorian Periodicals Review*, Vol. 41, No. 4 (Winter 2008), 323–351.

Fox, Daniel M. *Engines of Culture: Philanthropy and Art Museums*. New Brunswick, NJ: Transaction Publishers, 1995.

Fried, Michael. "Roger Fry's Formalism." The Tanner Lecture, 2001. Available online at http://tannerlectures.utah.edu/_documents/a-to-z/f/fried_2001.pdf.

Fry, Roger. *Art and the Market: Roger Fry on Commerce in Art*. Craufurd D. Goodwin, ed. Ann Arbor: University of Michigan Press, 1998.

———. "The Berensonian Method," *Burlington Magazine*, Vol. 52, No. 298 (January 1928), 47–48.

———. *Cézanne: A Study of His Development*. New York: Noonday Press, 1958. A reprint of the 1927 original edition.

———. *Letters of Roger Fry*, volumes I and II, Denys Sutton, ed. London: Chatto & Windus, 1972.

———. "The New Movement in Art in Its Relation to Life: A Lecture Given at the Fabian Society Summer School." *Burlington Magazine*, Vol. 31, No. 175 (October 1917), 162–163, 166–168.

———. "The Painters of North Italy," *Burlington Magazine*, Vol. 12, No. 60 (March 1908), 347–349.

———. *Transformations: Critical and Speculative Essays on Art*. London: Chatto & Windus, 1926; New York: Doubleday Anchor, 1956, reprint.

———. *Vision and Design*. London: Chatto & Windus, 1920; New York: Meridian Books, 1957, reprint.

Graham, Jenny. "A Note on the Early Reputation of Roger Fry," *Burlington Magazine*, Vol. 143, No. 1181 (August 2001), 493–499.

Green, Christopher, ed. *Art Made Modern: Fry's Vision of Art*. London: Merrell Holberton, 1999.

Gross, Michael. *Rogues Gallery: The Secret Story of the Lust, Lies, Greed and Betrayals That Made the Metropolitan Museum of Art*. New York: Broadway Books, 2009.

Hadley, Rollin Van N., ed. *The Letters of Bernard Berenson and Isabella Stewart Gardner: 1887–1924*. Boston: Northeastern University Press, 1987.

Hamnett, Nina. *Laughing Torso*. New York: Ray Long and Richard Smith, 1932.

Hannah, Leslie. "J. P. Morgan in London and New York before 1914." *Business History Review*, Vol. 85 (Spring 2011), 113–150.

Harding, Jason. "Goldsworthy Lowes Dickinson and the King's College Mandarins." *Cambridge Quarterly*, Vol. 41, No. 1 (2012), 26–42.

Harrison, Charles. *English Art and Modernism, 1900–1939*. Bloomington: Indiana University Press, 1981.

Haycock, David Boyd. *A Crisis of Brilliance: Five Young British Artists and the Great War*. London: Old Street Publishing, 2009.

Holmes, Charles. "Roger Fry and the *Burlington Magazine*." *Burlington Magazine*, Vol. 65, No. 379 (October 1934), 145–146.

Hooper-Greenhill, Eilean. *Museums and the Interpretation of Visual Culture*. London and New York: Routledge, 2000.

Horne, Herbert P. *Sandro Botticelli*. London: Chiswick Press, 1908. Available on line at http://archive.org/details/alessandrofilipe0Ohorn

James, Henry. *The American Scene*. New York: Library of America, 1993; original edition, 1907.

Laing, Donald A. *Roger Fry: An Annotated Bibliography of the Published Writings*. New York: Garland, 1979.

Levey, Michael. "The Earliest Years of the *Burlington Magazine*: A Brief Retrospect." *Burlington Magazine*, Vol. 128, No. 1000 (July 1986), 474–477.

Macginnis, Hayden B. J. "Reflections on Formalism: The Post-Impressionists and the Early Italians." *Art History*, Vol. 19, No. 2 (June 1996), 191–207.

———. "The Role of Perceptual Learning in Connoisseurship: Morelli, Berenson, and Beyond." *Art History*, Vol. 13, No. 1 (March 1990), 104–117.

Marks, Arthur S. "A Sign and a Shop Sign: The Ω and Roger Fry's Omega Workshops." *British Art Journal*, Vol. XIII, No. 1 (2009), 18–36.

Melius, Jeremy. "Art Connoisseurship, Painting, and Personhood." *Art History*, Vol. 34, No. 2 (April 2011), 288–309.

Morphet, Richard. "Roger Fry: The Nature of His Painting." *Burlington Magazine*, Vol. 122, No. 928 (July 1980), 481–489.

Nathanson, Carol A. "The American Reaction to London's First Grafton Show." *Archives of American Art Journal*, Vol. 25, No. 3 (1985), 2–10.

Nicolson, Benedict. "Post-Impressionism and Roger Fry." *Burlington Magazine*, Vol. 93, No. 574 (January 1951), 10–15.

Pope-Hennessy, John. "Roger Fry and the Metropolitan Museum of Art." In *Oxford China Italy: Essays in Honour of Sir Harold Acton*, 229–240. London: Thames & Hudson, 1984.

Preziosi, Donald, ed., *The Art of Art History: A Critical Anthology*. Oxford and New York: Oxford University Press, 1998.

Procter, Daniel, ed. *The Autobiography of G. Lowes Dickinson and Other Unpublished Writings*. London: Duckworth, 1973.

Reed, Christopher, ed. *A Roger Fry Reader*. Chicago: University of Chicago Press, 1996.

Rubin, Adrianne. *Roger Fry's "Difficult and Uncertain Science": The Interpretation of Aesthetic Perception*. Pieterlen, Switzerland: Peter Lang, 2013.

Saarinen, Aline B. *The Proud Possessors*. New York: Random House, 1958.

Samuels, Ernest. *Bernard Berenson: The Making of a Legend*. Cambridge, MA: The Belknap Press, 1987.

Satterlee, Herbert L. *J. Pierpont Morgan: An Intimate Portrait*. New York: Macmillan, 1939.

Simpson, Colin. *Artful Partners: Bernard Berenson and Joseph Duveen*. New York: Macmillan, 1986.

Spalding, Frances. *Roger Fry: Art and Life*. Norwich: Black Dog Press, 1999. A reprint of the 1980 edition.

———. "Roger Fry and His Critics in a Post-Modernist Age." *Burlington Magazine*, Vol. 128, No. 1000 (July 1986), 489–492.

Strouse, Jean. *Morgan: American Financier*. New York: HarperCollins, 1999.

———. "The Unknown J. P. Morgan: A Biographer Uncovers the Private Life of the Famous Banker." *New Yorker*, March 29, 1999, 66–79.

Taylor, David G. "The Aesthetic Theories of Roger Fry Reconsidered." *Journal of Aesthetics and Art Criticism*, Vol. 36, No. 1 (Autumn 1977), 63–72.

Tomkins, Calvin. *Merchants and Masterpieces: The Story of the Metropolitan Museum of Art*. New York: Henry Holt, 1970; revised edition, 1989.

Trask, Jeffrey. *Things American: Art Museums and Civic Culture in the Progressive Era*. Philadelphia: University of Pennsylvania Press, 2012.

Woolf, Virginia. *Roger Fry: A Biography*. London: Hogarth Press, 1940.

# INDEX

Illustrations are indicated by *italics*; extended discussions are <u>underlined</u>.

Fry, Roger (*continued*)
life of: and America (trips to), 78, 100–104; and Berenson, Bernard, 58, 127, 191; and *Burlington Magazine*, 69–71, 132; at Cambridge, 42; change in title, 121–122; on Chantrey Bequest, 72–73; "cleaning scandal," 116–118; commitment as practicing artist, 52; discusses salary with Morgan, 97; elaborate dinner in Washington, 92–96; and experimental gallery, 114; financial need, 105, 137; first goes to Paris, 50; first meets Morgan, 3; invited to New York, 77; living in father's house, 49; and Metropolitan Museum of Art, 90, 91–92, 134; moves into Durbins, 138, 178; 1907 tour with Morgan, 122–127; Omega Workshop, 3, 188; public lecture series, 68; Quaker faith of, 42, 71, 76, 105, 133, 208; skepticism of, 3; and Slade Professor (1933), 72, 134, 194; terms of salary, 103, 107, 121; trip to Poland, 100
as painter: 3, 53, 177–178
writings by: "Art and Commerce" (1926), 206–212; "Art and Life," 183; "Art and Religion," 54–56, 68; "Art and Socialism," 192–193; *Art and the Market* (2002) 232n7; "Art in a Socialism" (1916), 202–206; "The Artist and Psychoanalysis" (1924), 198; for *Athenaeum*, 53; "The Author and the Artist" (1926), 209–210; on Berenson, Bernard, 63–66; coins "opificers" and "opifacts," 208–209; "Criticism and Commerce" (1904), 198–202; *Discourses of Sir Joshua Reynolds*, 83, 88, 100; for *Burlington Magazine*, 69–71; "An Essay in Aesthetics" (1909), 198; *Giovanni Bellini* (1899), 60–62, 195; hallmarks of, 179; "The Idea of a Gallery," 109–112, 124; journal reviews, 50; "Poster Designs and the Art of Mr. McKnight Kauffer" (1925), 209; *Last Lectures* (1936), 206; *The Last Phase of Impres-*sionism, 172–173; monograph on Cézanne, 185–187, 191; monograph on Giotto, 66–68, 195; on "trade advertising," 210; *Transformations* (1926), 206; *Vision and Design* (1920), 67, 183; "What Men Do When They Go Down, III-Art (1889)," 47–49. *See also* Renoir
Fry, Sir Edward, 42, 49, 51

Gaddi, Taddei, 131
Gainsborough, Thomas, 27, 36
Gardner, Isabella Stewart, 28, 32, 57, 63, 97, 123, 133, 165, 166, 200
Garfield, James A., 119
Garland, James A., 34–35
Gauguin, Paul, 169
*Gazette des Beaux Arts*, 70
General Electric Company, 24
George Peabody & Co., 13
Gertler, Mark, 168
Getty, J. Paul, 145
Ghirlandaio, Domenico, *Portrait of an Old Man and a Boy*, 95, 123
Gilded Age, 155
Giotto, 55, 83, 111, 173; fresco of *Raising of Lazarus*, 127
Goodwin, James, 16
Gordon Square, 169
Göttingen University, 13
Gould, Jay, 18
Grafton Gallery (London), 170, 194
Gramsci, Antonio, 212
*Granta* (journal), 47
Grant, Duncan, 169, 187
Greene, Belle da Costa, 31–32, 33, 36, 39, 90, 132–133, 138; Berenson, Bernard, 34; social world of, 34
Greener, Richard Theodore, 31
Guaranty Trust, 159

Hals, Franz, 144
Hammersmith, 50
Hampstead, 127, 131
Hannah, Leslie, 23–25
Harvard University, 14, 31, 37, 150
Havemeyer Collection, 196

Shaw, George Bernard, 53, 230n16; Fry solicits funds from, 188–190
Shepheards Hotel (Cairo), 162
Sickert, Walter, 52
Siena, 126
*Sight-Seeing in Berlin and Holland Among the Pictures* (John G. Johnson), 119
skepticism, 7
Slade Lectureship (Oxford), 135
Slade Professor of Fine Art, 54, 72, 87, 108, 212; Fry appointed as (1933), 194
Slade School of Fine Art, 167–169
South Kensington Museum (Victoria and Albert Museum), 27, 38, 84, 103
Spencer, Stanley, 168
Standard Oil Company, 156
Steichen, Edward, portrait of JPM, 2
Stogdon, John, 62, 63
Storey, George, 107
Strachey, Lytton, 169
Sturges, Amelia "Memie," (JPM's wife), 15; lying-in hospital, 16; Mediterranean honeymoon, 16
Stuyvesant, Rutherfurd, 35, 39; acquires Dino collection, 146
Symonds, John Addington, 52

Taft, William Howard, 149, 155–156
Tarnowski, Count Ladislas, 99
Tate Gallery, 73
Titian, 61
Tommaso, 63
Tonks, Henry, 168, 178
Tracy, Frances Louisa (JPM's wife), 17
Trevelyan, Robert "Trevy," 49, 56, 60, 72, 75
Tutankhamen, tomb of, 152

Uffizi Gallery, 52, 88
Umbrian art, 126
United States Steel Corporation, 24, 154, 155
Untermyer, Samuel, 155–156, 161–162
US Government Revenue Act, 27

Valentiner, William, 141–145, 142, 164; describes Morgan, 143
Vallotton, Félix, 170
Vanderbilt, William K., 165
Van Der Weyden, Rogier, 119
Van Dyck, Anthony, 99
Van Eyck, Jan, 119
Van Gogh, Vincent, 169, 170
Veblen, Thorstein, *The Theory of the Leisure Class* (1899), 203
Vermeer, Johannes, 144; *A Lady Writing*, 122
Verroccio, Andrea del, 143
Victoria and Albert Museum. *See* South Kensington Museum
Villa I Tatti, 58
Vinci, Leonardo da, 111, 145
Vlaminck, Maurice de, 170
Vollard, Ambroise, 175
von Bode, Wilhelm, 141, 195
Vuillard, Edouard, 51

Wadsworth Atheneum, 21, 164
Walters, Henry, 77, 94, 152
Wedd, Nathaniel, 47
Werner, Alfred, 51
Whistler, James Abbott McNeill, 52, 121
Whitehouse, Frederic Cope, 52
Widener Collection, 92, 196
Wilde, Oscar, 86
Wilkinson, Charles, 150
Williams, F. Ballard, 113
Winlock, Herbert E., 150
Wilson, Woodrow, 155, 162
Witz, Konrad, 98
Woolf, Leonard, 189
Woolf, Virginia, 43, 53, 169, 171, 178, 187, 213; biography of Fry, 218n20; description of Fry, 46, 170; on Fry as lecturer, 46; on Helen Fry, 75–77;

Yale University, 139, 150, 152
*Yellow Book*, 86

Lightning Source UK Ltd.
Milton Keynes UK
UKHW011951051022
409984UK00005B/543